FACES OF HOLINESS

FACES OF HOLINESS

MODERN SAINTS IN PHOTOS AND WORDS

ANN BALL

Our Sunday Visitor Publishing Division
Our Sunday Visitor, Inc.
Huntington, Indiana 46750

International Standard Book Number: 0-87973-950-9
Library of Congress Catalog Card Number: 98-65863

Cover design by Tyler Ottinger
950

Dedication

This book is lovingly dedicated to our Holy Father, Pope John Paul II, who has, for the entire time of his pontificate, shown great courage in carrying out the wishes of the fathers at our last council in giving to the Catholic world holy and exemplary models from all countries and all walks of life and by so doing has greatly encouraged us all in the knowledge that we, too, should strive for sanctity.

Declaration Of Obedience

In loyal and loving obedience to the decrees of several Roman Pontiffs, in particular those of Pope Urban VIII, I declare that I in no way intend to prejudge Holy Mother Church in the matter of saints, sanctity, miracles, and so forth. Final authority in such matters rests with the See of Rome, to whose judgment I willingly submit.

The Author

Contents

Introduction

Ours is an age of saints. John Paul II has raised to the altars more men and women than any other pope in history: nearly a thousand blesseds and saints. Millions of pilgrims have flocked to St. Peter's in Rome or churches around the world to hear him officially declare that holiness is still flourishing in the Church.

In a century as brutal as our own, saints remind us of the power of God's grace. Saintly men and women are signs that the Church's life is robust. They are role models for the faithful, confirming that sanctity can thrive everywhere — from the mountains of Vietnam, to the deserts of Africa, the towns of France, and the highlands of Papua New Guinea. Ann Ball's fascinating book recounts the ordinary but exhilarating lives of holy heroes. Her stories of simplicity and courage, of devotion and honor, tell believers how the Church is truly "holy."

Indeed, the author is a kindred spirit to John Paul. She, too, wishes to convince us that the primary calling of every Christian is "to be holy in all conduct" (1 Peter 1:25). Like the Holy Father, she finds new exemplars of holiness among those who lived their baptism faithfully in their professional, social, and family lives. The author tells the stories of Peter ToRot, the married catechist from Papua New Guinea who suffered martyrdom at the hands of the Japanese in the Second World War; of Anuarite Nengapeta, a nun from Zaire who was murdered in 1964 while resisting rape; of Miguel Pro, who shouted above his executioners, "Long live Christ the King!"; and of Gianna Berretta Molla, an Italian pediatrician who died rather than endanger the life of her unborn daughter. They are rich and poor, educated and ignorant, men and women, lay and religious, old and young. What unites them all is simple — they lived the Gospel with a deep faith, unrelenting hope, and ardent charity.

Holiness, as Ann Ball points out again and again, has many faces. It has the battered face of Isidore Bakanja, beaten to death for refusing to take off his scapular; the suffering face of the mystic Rafka de Himlaya; the handsome face of the saintly student Pier Giorgio Frassati; the wise face of Mother Thecla, who founded the Daughters of St. Paul; and the sturdy face of the housekeeper, Sister Marie Léonie Paradis, who cooked and scrubbed for priests and seminarians. If Catholics once associated officially recognized holiness almost exclusively with consecrated individuals and clergy, this is no longer the case. Icons of holiness are now found among all members of the people of God.

At the end of the last century, the recently proclaimed Doctor of the Church, Saint Thérèse of the Child Jesus, prepared for the twentieth century's harvest of holiness. The "little way" encouraged Christians to seek sanctity on the path of trust and self-abandonment to divine mercy. And this path is for everyone. It has been trod in the slums of New York by Dorothy Day, in the Carmel of the Andes by Sister Teresa of Jesus Fernandez, in the streets of urban Italy by the physician Joseph Moscati, and in the prison camps of Korea by Father Emil Kapaun.

Martyrs: Witnesses to Fidelity

The blood of the martyrs has stained the twentieth century. Not since the early Church have so many laid down their lives for Christ. Even so, the century which has given rise to the Gulag and the swastika has also brought forth exceptional holiness. Totalitarian systems have given birth to a new "white-robed army" which has reaped a harvest of freedom and religious revival. In Spain, Vietnam, Korea, Germany, Poland, and elsewhere thousands were slaughtered, and some hundreds have been beatified. Through Ann Ball's accounts of martyrdom we are reminded that "the Church has once again become the Church of martyrs" (*Tertio Millennio Adveniente*, 37).

The pope has insisted that the heroic witness of the martyrs must not be forgotten. Again and again he urges local churches throughout the world to safeguard the precious memories of their martyrs. Other Christians, too, proudly recall their own martyrs for the Faith. By shedding their blood for the love of Christ, these men and women manifest that communion in grace which is fully realized in heaven. For John Paul, the communion among Christians "even if it is still incomplete, is truly and solidly grounded in the full communion of the saints — those who, at the end of a life faithful to grace, are in communion with Christ in glory. These saints," the pope goes on to say, "come from all the Churches and Ecclesial Communities which gave them entrance into the communion of salvation" (*Ut Unum Sint*, 84).

Besides the ecumenical bridge forged by all Christian martyrs, John Paul sees in them an embodiment of true Christian living. Because of their total willingness to trust in God's law, they attest to its holiness and absoluteness. In his encyclical *Veritatis Splendor* the Holy Father writes: "By their eloquent and attractive example of a life completely transfigured by the splendor of moral truth, the martyrs and, in general, all the Church's saints light up every period of history by reawakening its moral sense" (No.

93). In her tales of Isidore Bakanja, Ann Ball forcefully reminds us that genuine love of God entails obedience to his commandments, even in the more dire circumstances. The saints confirm the inviolability of the moral order and the utter holiness of God.

Being Named a 'Saint'

Many of the men and women presented in this book are officially recognized by the Church as "blessed" or "saint." But the author has not limited her selection to this elite group. Rather, she includes a large number of people who are not yet publicly venerated. Although the holiness of Agnes McLaren, Carlos Rodriguez, and Santos Franco Sanchez has not yet been formally acknowledged, their lives are being studied, admired, and emulated.

In the very early Church all the baptized were called "saints." But soon the title "saint" was particularly attributed to those who were martyred for bearing witness to the Gospel. Martyrdom was the definitive seal of total conformity to Christ. During the age of persecutions, the veneration shown to martyrs was extended to those who had been tortured or imprisoned for the Faith. By the fourth century, the title "saint" was also given to those in whom the image of God brilliantly shone forth: to virgins, ascetics, and great bishops. The Church commemorated their heavenly birthdays with feast days, invoked their intercession, and exalted them as models of Christian life.

While martyrs could be venerated as certainly being with God, how was the Church to know with surety that others with a reputation for holiness died in friendship with God? In the fifth century, St. Augustine answered that a miracle can be taken as proof of the sanctity of the one in whose name it was wrought.

From Augustine onwards a local Church and its bishop were responsible for publicly acknowledging the cult of individual Christians and making way for them in various local calendars of the saints. Around the turn of the first millennium, the Holy See began to control the proliferation of local cults and, thereby, also to strengthen its authority. At the same time the popes also sought to formalize canonization as a juridical process for "making saints." Because the Church claimed divine guidance for this discernment, the procedures surrounding this determination were carefully spelled out. To be enrolled in the official "canon," or list of the saints, meant that one could be publicly venerated and proposed for imitation.

Over the centuries the procedures became increasingly canonical and bureaucratic. After the local investigation was finished, the "cause" went to Rome. In effect, candidates for the altar were put on trial. Their lives were probed for heroic virtue, their writings for proven orthodoxy, and the miracles claimed through their intercession for authenticity. Here the postulator for the candidate and the "devil's advocate" squared off. Before the pope agreed to beatify a candidate, besides heroic virtue, two miracles — usually physical healings — had to be shown to have been worked through the candidate's intercession. Two further miracles were needed for canonization.

Updating the Process

During the papacy of John Paul II, the Congregation for Cause of Saints, which is charged with "making saints," has been working overtime. According to the Holy Father, personal holiness is the path of authentic Church renewal. Contemporary men and women need models of sanctity to imitate.

Because the procedures for beatification and canonization were cumbersome, adversarial, and lengthy, John Paul decided to simplify them, making them both less expensive and more collegial. In 1983 he streamlined the whole process in the apostolic constitution *Divines Perfectionism Magister*. No longer modeled after a courtroom, the procedure would, in Kenneth Woodward's description, "employ the academic model of researching and writing a doctoral dissertation." To this end the pope introduced four major changes.

First, he let bishops have a much greater responsibility at the front end of the process. Second, in an effort to speed up the proceedings, the Holy Father cut back on the number of miracles required for both beatification and canonization: from two to one for each stage. Third, in order to foster the causes of contemporary men and women, he reduced the time lapse between death and canonization to ten years.

Lastly, John Paul changed the place of public proclamations of holiness. Formerly held exclusively in Rome — in St. Peter's Basilica at the Vatican — he now frequently takes the ceremony on the road. The highlight of a pastoral visit to a country is often the honoring of one of its own citizens. He has beatified martyrs in Korea; Teresa of the Andes in Chile; Mary MacKillop in Australia; Marie Léonie Paradis in Canada; Peter ToRot in Papua New Guinea; Edith Stein in Germany; and Juan Diego in Mexico.

From Servant of God to Saint

As outlined in John Paul's 1983 apostolic constitution, the current process for beatification and canonization has three principal stages.

The first stage begins at the local level. It is up to the local bishop, in dialogue with the bishops of the surrounding region, to conduct a preliminary investigation of the candidate. He conducts a long and detailed examination of the person's life, writings, and heroic virtue. Upon successful completion of this study, the individual is declared a "servant of God."

The paperwork then goes to Rome. This second state is the most difficult. If successfully concluded, the Congregation for the Causes of Saints recommends that the pope declare the servant of God "blessed." This means that the candidate has demonstrated the necessary "heroic virtue" and that this reputation for holiness has been confirmed by a miracle. Its authenticity is determined by a special team of doctors appointed by the Vatican.

Miracles proved to be obtained through the candidate's intercession is an essential part of the process, with one notable exception. Those who are beatified or canonized as martyrs require no miracle. No further testimony is needed than the fact that an individual freely gave his or her life for the Faith.

The third stage is canonization itself: The enrolling of the blessed in the canon of saints proposed by the Church as worthy of veneration and imitation by Christians everywhere. Originally beatification was intended to distinguish local saints from those of interest to the universal Church. This distinction is now irrelevant. Confining veneration of the blessed to the local church is impossible in the global village. When proof can be obtained of a second miracle for a blessed, canonization follows, even though the saint has limited appeal.

When the Church officially recognizes her saints, she is not adding names to her heavenly hall of fame. Rather, she is inviting us to honor them and to petition their help. To take these steps, we need the stories of Ann Ball. Her book presents thrilling stories of heroic men and women, often from backgrounds as ordinary as our own. Her tales tell of God's graciousness. In ways beyond our wildest dreams he transforms schoolboys and catechists, mystics and physicians, housekeepers and mothers into his friends. The saints are vessels of love who shine like a pillar of fire, leading the pilgrim Church into the dawn of the third millennium. With the freshness of her examples and the vigor of her style, Ann Ball convinces us of what Leon Bloy once wrote: "Here is but one sadness . . . and that is for us not to be saints."

J. Michael Miller, C.S.B.
President, University of St. Thomas

Dr. Agnes McLaren

1837-1913

Medicine Woman

Chapter I

An old saying holds that "God moves in a mysterious way His wonders to perform." Mysterious yet wondrous is the dictate of Divine Providence that led Dr. Agnes McLaren, a convert and lay woman, to provide the inspiration and impetus for modern professional medical mission work by religious women. Her dream of sister-doctors in the missions has become a reality which has grown and spread worldwide.

Agnes was born July 4, 1837, in Edinburgh, Scotland, the daughter of a well-to-do Presbyterian businessman who was also a member of the Scottish parliament. Agnes's mother was the second of Mr. McLaren's wives, and she died when Agnes was only three. His third wife, Priscilla, was a Quaker who was excommunicated from her faith for her mixed marriage. Priscilla took the five stepchildren from Mr. McLaren's previous marriages to her heart, and they loved her as well. The births of three other children completed the family.

Agnes was brought up in a strict religious atmosphere where strong moral principles were constantly preached. Charity to others and devotion to duty were two main tenets of the family beliefs. The children studied the Bible and read the lives of the saints. This family background was a strong influence on Agnes in her later years.

From her earliest days, Agnes proved to be a good student, interested in learning. History and literature were her favorite subjects. As a young woman, Agnes dressed simply and expended all of her energy on her studies and in the practice of charity.

People jokingly referred to her as the "Sister," because she spent her generous allowance for the poor. She had a natural aptitude for teaching, and a great love for children. She loved to tell the little ones stories of national heroes, martyrs, and saints. All facets of the study of religion interested her.

Agnes's father was interested in many of the political and religious movements of his time, and the McLaren home became a meeting place for politicians and social workers. Agnes became interested in politics as well as in social-service work, and she became a member of the first committee formed in Great Britain to bring about women's suffrage.

When her father died in 1886, Agnes inherited an ample fortune and was able to continue her cherished studies and to travel. During these years, she began to feel guilty that she was not doing more for others. She told some of her friends, "I feel myself a traitor, when my life does not include some work for the welfare of my fellow creatures."

At the age of thirty-nine, she resolved to serve others by the practice of medicine, and bent all her efforts to obtain an education as a doctor. She said, "Is not medicine one of the best means of helping suffering humanity? Yes, Christ is the supreme physician. During His mortal life, the sight of suffering humanity stirred up His pity, He cured them by miracles; those who work to cure them by science and devotion are sure to please Him, since they follow in His steps." In spite of her prejudices against Catholicism, she visited two of the most distinguished Catholic churchmen of the day: Cardinal John Henry Newman and Cardinal Henry Edward Manning. Cardinal Manning gave her a letter of introduction to the celebrated medical school in Montpellier, France. She was admitted, and after a number of years of study, she passed her examinations, earning the coveted doctorate of medicine and becoming the first woman to graduate from this school.

During her medical studies, Agnes boarded with a group of Franciscan Hospital sisters. Sister Françoise later wrote, "She was an accomplished young lady and one whom I never saw commit the least imperfection during the time that she passed in the house. Only once did I see her show some sign of displeasure, but even on that occasion it was more than excusable, for someone had forgotten to deliver a message to her concerning one of her patients. On Fridays, she fasted, and her mortification in food at other times was not wanting. On one occasion the lentil soup was burned. All of the other boarders sent it back without having touched it. Miss Agnes

Dr. Agnes McLaren, Scottish physician and Catholic convert.

alone ate hers to the last spoonful. Miss Agnes was not very affectionate in her speech, but it was a real happiness for her to send small gifts to her friends. She would stay up late at night to finish little presents for those whom she loved; at other times, these gifts were made for someone who had offended her. A certain Miss C., living in the same house, caused her much annoyance by tales that were entirely false. . . . From that day on, she lavished on Miss C. kindliness and friendliness. If anyone questioned her about her action, she said, 'In the Gospel is written: Do good to those who do you evil.' The Gospel was her rule of conduct and she followed it to the letter."

In order to practice medicine in England and Scotland, Agnes needed a state degree. She obtained this by successfully passing the examination of the Royal College of Physicians at Dublin, the only school in the United Kingdom which legally admitted women to the practice of medicine. Later, she was made a member of honor of this college, and in 1882 was raised to "*Socius*," an additional honor accompanied by certain privileges.

While studying in Montpellier, Agnes often attended services at the Catholic Church, and yet remained Protestant. She felt that as a Catholic she would be forced to give up her freedom of thought and judgment. She had a number of other misconceptions about the Church.

When she was passing through Lyons on her way to England one Christmas, she stayed with the Sisters of Providence. Here she met Father Perra, who attempted to dispel some of her prejudices. The following year, he was surprised to receive a letter from Agnes asking permission to make a retreat under his direction. The retreat of a Protestant under the direction of a Catholic priest was unusual, to say the least. There was no confession or Communion. Instead, Father Perra gave her conferences, mainly on Christian virtues. Agnes told Father Perra that she wanted to become more closely united with God, so that in becoming more holy, she might be able to do more good. Father Perra avoided points which would have antagonized her, but extracted from her a promise to say three Hail Marys each day after pointing out the references to the Blessed Virgin in the Book of Common Prayer.

Every year for nearly twenty years, when she made her annual trip to Scotland to visit her friends and relatives, she stopped at Lyons and made a retreat under Father Perra's direction. At the age of sixty-one, she submitted to a movement of grace and on November 30, 1898, received conditional baptism. On December 8, she made her First Communion. She was confirmed at the convent of the Sisters of Bethany, an order whose work among penitents she greatly admired. In 1900, she became a member of the Third Order of Saint Dominic.

During the next few years, Agnes decided to make war on what she called the "legal regulating of vice." She had a high idea of the mission of the Christian woman, not only in her own family but in society at large. She began to lobby against legislation which she felt encouraged immorality. In order to accomplish this, she prayed, wrote, and traveled to speak in a number of countries. Although her work was commended by two papal blessings, she was not very successful in her political efforts. She continued to promote morality, however, by encouraging early Christian education in the home as a fundamental factor of the integrity of public morals.

About this same time, Agnes had the idea to organize groups of women from all over the world who would qualify as women doctors in order to practice their art for the benefit of souls as well as bodies. She envisioned the group as lay women, thinking they might more easily overcome the objections of governments that were hostile to religious orders.

Determined to make the first effort for her dream of female medical missionaries, at the age of seventy-two, Agnes McLaren traveled to India. She founded a fully equipped hospital and several dispensaries in Rawalpindi. A number of Catholic bishops were impressed with Agnes's idea, and asked to have her charitable work in their own countries. In order to carry out her vision, Agnes appealed for generous souls, only to meet with bitter disappointment.

At last, she addressed a kind of questionnaire to the superiors general of several religious orders. She was advised to check with the Holy See, so she began writing requests to various church officials. These letters were brief, clear, and sincere.

From a 1950s-era pamphlet that included Dr. McLaren's biography and a prayer.

In one she wrote, "I am glad to have the opportunity of seeing your Excellency before Ascension as it was at this time that Our Lord gave the Commandment: 'Preach the gospel to every creature,' and the only way to reach many women in India is to send them medical women."

None of the religious orders she had approached were ready to have their sisters study to be medical missionaries. Although she had interested a number of bishops, she had not obtained the needed permission to allow religious women to practice medicine. Although some religious had received dispensations to study medicine, as a general rule this was prohibited. Dr. McLaren was a woman ahead of her time; she planted the seeds of her idea in Rome, but did not live to see it flower.

After five trips to Rome in three years, in 1912, Agnes retired to Antibes because of failing health. Here she bought a little house with a chapel, which she decorated and opened to the people of the neighborhood. She obtained permission to have the Blessed Sacrament reserved, and cared for the chapel herself. In order to have the services of a chaplain, she invited priests in need of rest to come for a visit.

Agnes planned to make a final trip to Rome to gain approval for her plan to recruit religious medical missionaries, but in early 1913 she came down with a severe case of influenza and pleurisy. On April 7, she asked for the last sacraments.

Agnes had asked for a sister to nurse her, and this sister left a clear record of her last days. The sister reported that her patient was quiet, obedient, gentle, and prayed continually, offering her sufferings for the pope, who was himself ill at the time. She spoke of death calmly.

On the evening before her death, Agnes told her that "Tomorrow will be a great day for me. I shall see God, my creator and my father. I look forward to the resurrection!"

Agnes died peacefully on April 17, 1913, without any agony.

In 1911, the Franciscan Missionaries of Mary took over Saint Catherine's Hospital, which Dr. McLaren had founded in Rawalpindi. In 1920, Dr. Anna Dengel, who had been inspired by Agnes McLaren to study medical mission work, took charge of Saint Catherine's Hospital and worked there for three-and-a-half years. Realizing the great field open to medical missionary women in India, Dr. Dengel went to England and America in 1924 to raise money for this purpose. This led to the founding of the Society of Catholic Medical Missionaries. In 1925, Dr. Dengel founded the first community of Medical Mission Sisters in Washington, D.C. The community was established to provide doctors and trained medical personnel for the missions.

The official answer to Dr. McLaren's plea came in 1936, when Rome issued an Instruction which not only confirmed the work of the Society of Catholic Medical Missionaries, but also urged other communities to educate sisters as doctors for the missions.

Mother M. Angeline Teresa McCrory

1893-1984

Mother to the Aged

"Dearest Lord, may I see Thee today and every day in the person of the aged and sick, and while caring for them, minister unto Thee."

Mother M. Angeline Teresa McCrory founded the first modern American congregation for the aging and infirm, which has always had a special American insight and lively spirit. Its special genius is in challenging men and women to live their later years in dignity and independence. Its basis is in seeing Christ in each person they serve. Years ahead of her time, Mother Angeline led her Carmelite Sisters for the Aged and Infirm as trail-blazing pioneers in the field of modern geriatrics. Today, Mother Angeline's followers expend themselves in extending Christ's compassion to make the latter years of elderly people's lives meaningful and happy.

Mother Angeline began her work in the middle of the Great Depression. "At the time I was called a revolutionary, but I went ahead with my plans for creating a new hotel-like residence for the aged where they would have full freedom and privacy and would be encouraged to retain their independence. It [provided] living quarters for aged couples, and recreational facilities, as well as medical care."

During the depression, many elderly Americans faced especially difficult human and financial crises. Mother Angeline's personal charism and spirit combined the wonderful heritage of service she learned from the Little Sisters of the Poor and the contemplative spirit of the Carmelites. From the beginning of her ministry she taught her sisters a vision which precluded the depersonalizing and regimentalized institutionalization of the elderly in favor of a respect for personal dignity with an emphasis on interested concern for each resident as an individual. She aimed to make each of her foundations a "true home" for the residents.

Brigid McCrory was born January 21, 1893, the second of five children

Bridget McCrory at age eight.

of Thomas and Brigid McCrory of Mountjoy, Northern Ireland. She was baptized Brigid Teresa McCrory at the parish church on the following day.

At the age of four, she was enrolled in the little parish school in Mountjoy adjacent to the church. Here she was taught to write her name as *Bridget*, which she continued from then on. The young family worked as farmers, and barely eked out a living while suffering from the anti-Catholic prejudice of the times. In 1901, when Bridget was eight, the family emigrated to Scotland, where her father obtained work at a steel works outside Glasgow.

Bridget excelled at school, and at her confirmation in 1901, when she was ten, she won a medal for her recitation of the Prologue to Saint John's Gospel, a piece which she could quote from memory for the rest of her life. She picked Teresa of Ávila as her confirmation patroness. This great Carmelite saint seems to have placed a thread on the young Irish girl which drew her inexorably and eventually to Carmel.

Vivacious and full of fun, the young girl with the large brown eyes and clear complexion was a natural leader in the childhood games played with her siblings and friends. As the family fortunes improved, they moved from their little worker's row-house in Motherwell to a home in a better suburb. The backyard was separated from the parish church only by a fence, and the McCrory children had easy access. Although she was a lively child, Bridget could also be serious, and when she wasn't at home she could usually be found at the church making a devout visit to the Blessed Sacrament or helping the pastor arrange the flowers she loved for the altar.

The family home had two stories, and one morning while her mother was doing housework on the second floor she was shocked to see Bridget looking in at her, eye-to-eye, from the window. The three McCrory children had borrowed stilts from a neighbor, and Bridget wanted her mother to see them at play.

In 1906, at the age of thirteen, Bridget entered a convent high school, where her favorite subject was French. She excelled in all of her studies and graduated in 1912. By this time, Bridget had grown to be a charming young lady, tall and slim with chestnut brown hair and sparkling brown eyes. Her constant smile and spontaneous wit belied the serious side of her nature, for she was quietly contemplating a religious vocation.

During her high school days, in 1911, tragedy struck the family. Thomas, at the young age of forty, was fatally wounded in an industrial accident when he was covered with molten metal. Only her father's face was unburned, and he died after twenty-nine agonizing days in the hospital. Bridget never forgot the extraordinary expression of faith and acceptance of God's will with which her mother accepted the news from the co-workers who brought word of the accident.

In February 1912, Bridget entered the Little Sisters of the Poor, a congregation engaged in the care of the destitute aged. Years later, when asked what attracted her to service in the care of the elderly, she said that first of all it was "my close association and deep affection for my eighty-two-year-old grandfather." In addition, she replied, "As a child, I remember that I always thought of the aged as lonely, hungry, and cold, and my heart went out in sympathy to them." Although she admired other charitable works, "it was my strong love for old age and its infirmities that influenced me. It has always been my belief that old people . . . have great need for love and individual care."

The evening before she left home, her parish priest and friend Father Cronin took her to his library and told her to chose any book she wished to take with her as a remembrance from him. She chose the *Life of Saint Teresa of Ávila*.

Bridget made her novitiate with the Little Sisters of the Poor in LaTour, France. She took the name Sister Angeline of Saint Agathe. After profession in 1915, she was sent to the United States. She spent nine years in Brooklyn, New York, then after a year's work in Pittsburgh she was named, at the age of thirty-three, the superior of the Bronx home. Until her death, she always recounted the many graces she had received while she was with the Little Sisters and said, "I have always loved my former Congregation and value the spiritual formation that was mine and the reverence and respect for the aging that I learned in the Congregation."

During an annual retreat in 1927, Mother Angeline felt the call to adapt the

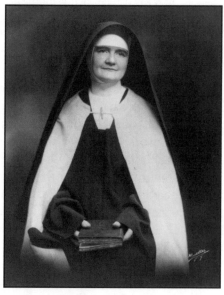

Mother Angeline Teresa at the silver anniversary of her profession.

care of the aged to the special needs of Americans, and to extend this care to all classes of people.

"My heart went out to these elderly folk of the middle class who asked to pay a little for their own room . . . and also the group whose savings had been depleted but who were accustomed to a middle class standard of living. I was even more troubled by the sight of old couples facing the threat of separation, except during visiting hours, if they accepted the established type of institutional life."

Unable to effect these changes in her present situation, she sought the advice of Cardinal Hayes of New York, who encouraged and supported her ideas. With his blessing, she and six other sisters withdrew from the Congregation of the Little Sisters of the Poor and were granted permission from Rome to begin a new community which would put into effect her ideals. Thus, through the inspiration she received in a congregation dedicated to the aged poor, Mother Angeline was able to develop her apostolate to reach other aged people in need of care.

From the beginning, the Carmelite Fathers in New York took a deep interest in the little group. In 1931, the sisters became affiliated with the order.

Mother Angeline was blessed with a warm and wonderful sense of humor. In addition, she inherited the Irish way of "telling a good tale." She described one of their first resident's arrival like this: "Our first applicant was a frail old gentleman of eighty. From his pocket he drew out two hundred single dollar bills. They were soiled and worn; by the looks of them they must have been in circulation as long as himself. Placing them carefully on the table before me he said, 'Mother, I want you to take this money and keep me for the rest of my life and bury me.' The old gentleman seemed to have about six months of life in him, and it seemed a good offer at the time. I accepted and gave him a home. Twenty years later he was still with us. And true to my promise, I buried him at the ripe old age of a hundred. He got his money's worth."

In spite of the bleak background of the Great Depression against which the work was begun, they were supported generously by Cardinal Hayes and Catholic Charities of New York. From the very beginning, Mother was able to attract young women to her ideals, and the order grew and prospered. At the time of her death, there were over three hundred professed sisters who cared for the elderly in thirty residences for the aged and infirm. At the opening of each new foundation, Mother Angeline, radiant with joy, would tell the sisters, "We have a new Tabernacle for Our Lord." Full of faith and courageous in her decisions, Mother believed Saint Teresa's axiom, "With God, all things are possible." She had a unique ability to inspire others with enthusiasm for the work. When a sister once hesitated to accept a responsible assignment, telling Mother Angeleline, "I can't do it," the foundress replied, "I know you can't. Neither can I, but did you ever stop to think that Jesus and you can?"

Accolades were heaped on Mother Angeline during her long life. She explained the success to the sisters by saying, "Our apostolate is not only to staff and operate up-to-date homes for the aged. As religious, it is to bring Christ to every old person under our care. Bringing Christ means giving them His compassion, His interest, His loving care, His warmth — morning, noon and night. It means inspiring the lay-people who work with us to give the same type of loving care.

"Old age is a lonely period. At no time in a person's life is kindness so much needed and appreciated. Efficiency is wonderful, but it should never replace kindness. All professional skill should stem from the kindness and compassion of Christ. As long as it does, God will bless our Congregation spiritually and materially.

"Ours is a very special vocation, and we will be blessed eternally for any little thing we did to bring happiness to the old people."

With her practical sense, Mother Angeline taught the sisters how to carry out the work of compassion:

> Loving care means planning little parties and surprises to break the monotony; being concerned when an old person is sick and confused. It means bidding an old person the time of the day, and saying a few kind words to them. In short, doing all those little thoughtful things you would want someone to do for your own mother or father. . . . A priest very kindly told us that our vocation was the greatest in the Church. . . . That we, in caring for the aged, were taking care of the lonely, dying Christ. All of us can reflect well on this thought.

The following prayer, found among Mother Angeline's papers, mirrors her charism: "Dearest Lord, may I see Thee today and every day in the person of the aged and sick, and while caring for them, minister to Thee. Though Thou hidest Thyself behind the unattractive guise of the irritable, the exacting, the unreasonable, may I still recognize Thee and say, Jesus, my Patient, how sweet it is to serve Thee."

Mother Angeline at the golden anniversary of her profession.

Mother Angeline delighted in spending hours before the Blessed Sacrament. She reminded the sisters of the importance of prayer: "We all know that labor done for God is high and holy, but it must not habitually replace the spiritual exercises of the Rule. We must, as Carmelites, lead a contemplative and active life, giving the required time to prayer which is more important than our work."

Mother Angeline guided her young congregation for many years and through trying times. Her efforts were blessed abundantly. Although she governed the community from its foundation in 1929 to 1978, when she knew her health was declining, she always told the sisters that from the very beginning she placed Our Blessed Mother as head of the congregation. She never attributed her success to herself, but always to the "wonderful sisters" God sent her. She was renowned for her reverence for the priesthood, and she encouraged many priests in their noble vocation, sharing both spiritual and material blessings with them.

As is common with the beginning of all religious orders, there were a number of sorrows and heartaches which Mother Angeline had to weather. Her life of interior sufferings embraced misunderstandings, contradictions, betrayals, disloyalties, and desertions. She also endured spiritual sufferings in her deep prayer life, and constantly battled against herself in order to put God first and His work above herself. She also had many physical sufferings. In her later years, she suffered from arteriosclerotic heart disease and her speech was slurred, but as long as it was physically possible, she was generous of herself. These, plus the crippling effects of old age with its problems of locomotion and speech, Mother accepted with equanimity, patience, and loving trust.

Toward the end of her life, her physical deterioration led to complete dependence on the loving care of the sisters. Mother Angeline was an example of perfect resignation to God's will. Her speech had become impaired, but when she was able to speak (with difficulty) she said, "I'll do anything you want me to do." She also often said, "Thank God I have my own sisters with me."

Mother Angeline's ninety-first birthday fell on January 21, 1984. Since she was not well, there were no special festivities planned. Just as the night nurse was leaving that morning, Mother coughed and prayed, "Infant Jesus, where are you?" About ten, a priest friend came to celebrate Mass in her room, and she received the Precious Blood. Later she was being fed by one of the sisters when she had a coughing spell and couldn't get her breath. She was helped back to bed, the sisters were called, and a priest came to anoint her. Three priests and eight of the sisters were with her when her soul passed to the loving hands of the Father, while the other sisters prayed the rosary in the chapel.

From Sunday, January 22, to Wednesday, January 25, Mother Angeline's body, clothed in her beloved Carmelite habit, lay in the chapel of the motherhouse while an almost continuous succession of mourners stopped to pray by the charismatic foundress. Many touched their rosaries or other articles to her body as they passed, a silent witness to their conviction of her sanctity. A number of Masses were offered in the little chapel before the Mass of Christian Burial on Wednesday, after which she was interred in the Queen of Carmel Cemetery on the grounds of Saint Teresa's Motherhouse at Ávila on Hudson, Germantown, New York.

Today, the Carmelite Sisters for the Aged and Infirm carry on Mother Angeline Teresa's charism of loving service, bringing Christ's healing ministry and love to the residents and staff of the health-care facilities under their supervision.

Carla Ronci

1936-1970

A Living Tabernacle

Chapter 3

"The thought that has touched me the most is this: God is in me. I am a living tabernacle. It does not have to be difficult to live in union with God. That means to live an interior life . . . I am happy to exist. I am content with everything that surrounds me because in everything I detect a gift of God. All the peace which fills and pervades my heart comes from possessing Jesus." So wrote the young Carla Ronci, a member of the secular institute Mater Misericordiae of Macerata.

While remaining in the world, Carla Ronci followed the vocation to sanctity, to which all are called. Once, while on a retreat with the Passionist nuns, one of the sisters was talking about the difficulties in the apostolate, and Carla told her, "Sister, when all of you are tempted, think of us who are fighting in the world." During her life, Carla fought so well, in spite of the difficulty of remaining in the world, that after her early death in 1970, her cause for canonization was introduced in 1980, and approved by Pope John Paul II in 1982.

Carla was born April 11, 1936, in Rimini, the first of three children of Mario and Yolanda Ronci. She was baptized in the hospital two days later, receiving the name Carla Sandrina. She was a docile child, well-behaved and easily moved to tears at the sight of any suffering, from that of a crying baby to the sight of a poor person. She attended the Ursuline school, where she was noted for her love of music, movies, dancing, and all forms of entertainment. She loved to sing, and was an excellent swimmer. Carla was affectionate and vivacious. At school she was remembered as a model pupil, although she was more fond of song and dance than of her studies.

Carla's family was not particularly strong in their religion, and the only source of religious instruction in the town was the catechism given by the Ursulines. Nonetheless, she was admitted to First Communion and

A youthful Carla.

Carla on outings with the young girls (Benjamins) of Catholic Action.

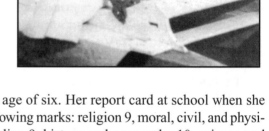

confirmation in 1942 at the age of six. Her report card at school when she was seven displayed the following marks: religion 9, moral, civil, and physical education 9, work 9, Italian 9, history and geography 10, science and hygiene 9, drawing and handwriting 9, singing 9, attendance 11.

After she finished elementary school, Carla stayed for a time with a lady studying sewing. Also she often went out with her mother with a little cart selling seeds and nuts. In 1950, after attending a mission preached by the Passionists, the fourteen-year-old Carla experienced what she called her "conversion." The topic of the mission had been the Way of the Cross, and Carla began to realize that her life was more given to pleasure than to anything else. She began to think about what sacrifice she could make. She resolved to give up dancing for a week. After the first week, she felt that this was not very much, so she increased the time limit and wound up by not going to dances for that whole year. Slowly, she came to realize that God wants all people to become holy, and in one way or another she began to give more time to prayer and to penance. Carla herself said:

> I am so bad, but the Lord has not abandoned me. In 1950, I saw all the Ursuline Sisters go to Mass no matter how cold it was, nor how much snow. I saw them always serene, recollected, always poor. I

began to reflect, "Why are they doing all this? Why are they so happy and serene in the midst of privations?" One night, leaning at a window looking out, I saw a face with a smile such as I have never seen. In my heart I heard a voice and an invitation. I felt a horror of myself. Looking at my inner self, I saw my fourteen years given to enjoyment and my future suspended over an abyss. I doubted. I wondered. I closed my eyes in order to see my interior the better, and again I proposed, but limited it. Tomorrow, yes tomorrow I will do like them. I will give the church a part of myself so that God will stop tormenting me with His voice — so that God will no longer castigate me with his justice. I will give a part of myself to see if it is that which gives the Ursulines so much joy and serenity. The promises and the uncertainty kept coming back while I slept, but the vision of that face never left me. In the morning, as soon as I could, I ran to church and found it empty. A red lamp on the altar and four sisters in black in the benches. And in that silence, the prayer of the priest. How impressive! I understood and I did not understand. The world lay before me in all its reality. I took a place in the back of the church. I do not know if I prayed. I thought much and in my thoughts I saw again that face I had seen the evening before — Jesus ! It was the first time that I cried without knowing why. . . . I hurried home and hid myself in order to quiet my interior confusion and try to make my plans. I was not generous . . . I was like an unskillful dressmaker who, by means of her imagination, is trying to make a dress out of a very small piece of cloth.

Carla began to feel that she had a vocation to the religious life and wanted to join the Ursulines, but her parents would not hear of it. So she turned to Catholic Action, a popular movement in Italy to combat irreligion by action of the part of Catholics in guiding the young people, visiting the sick, and in general to bring religion to all they met. "After some time I found such peace and strength and divine light that I developed a great enthusiasm for the good and I began to long to give and to do for others. In others I began to see Jesus. I felt that I could meet Jesus in the poor, the suffering and little. How happy I was when at the end of my

Carla Ronci on her beloved motor scooter.

first year of my apostolate in Catholic Action I was given ten little children!"

Carla's apostolate with Catholic Action began with the teaching and care of the "Benjamins," the youngest children. Later, she was placed in charge of the teenagers. She first won the love of her charges, and after that she could lead them to God with her words and actions. Carla understood these teenagers quite well. She wrote, "How lovely it is to live in the midst of adolescents. It is difficult to understand them and one needs to be patient and to follow them, but it is beautiful." Carla allowed herself to be guided by her heart, and thus, it was difficult to say "no." She arranged outings, parties, amateur theatricals, and other entertainments for her charges. She taught them that love and laughter are perfectly at home in the will of God. Eventually, she was working with Catholic Action in five parishes.

Much of Carla's spirituality is displayed through her diary, which she began to write in 1955.

Carla had an intense longing, a hunger and thirst for God and the need to make Him known and loved by souls. She had not given up her hopes for a religious life and at last she obtained her mother's consent to enter the Ursulines, although her father still had objections. In 1958, she entered the novitiate at Scanzo. Carla remained in the novitiate only a few months. After a visit from one of the superiors, the local superior was told to send her home, as she did not have a vocation for their order and God had other plans for her. Carla returned home and took her place in the house again. When a friend visited her, Carla told her that she was content with her return because "In the will of God is our peace."

Her confessor told her not to be sad at having to live in the world. He reminded her, "You can become a saint with the help of God."

In the fall of 1958, Carla opened a little workshop in sewing and dressmaking. She employed several young people to work with her. In addition, she helped her parents manage a small fruit and vegetable store.

After vainly searching for an institute which she might enter, at the age of twenty-four she heard of the Handmaids of the Mother of Mercy. She made her first vows with this group in 1962. This is a secular institute whose members remain in the world. Here she was able to have a spiritual life based on the institute's precepts, as well as being able to remain with her family. As part of her spiritual exercises, on the eighteenth of each month she made a retreat. Each Tuesday, she observed an hour of meditation, and daily she kept adoration as a "living lamp" before the Blessed Sacrament.

"I feel something beautiful and deep within me; I would say, like a call to what is divine, which invites me to better myself so as to give a hand to our priest. I believe that the vocation to the priesthood is something marvelous and that he who lives it totally cannot feel he is so alone; only overflowing with life and love to be communicated to others." Carla realized that for the Church to be holy, it was necessary to have good and holy priests. In prayer, she offered herself as a victim of love for priests. Carla's love for the priesthood remained with her always. If she heard of a priest in trouble, she would go to the telephone and ask her friends for prayers and sacrifices for him in this crisis. If she heard of a priest who was leaving the priesthood, she would send him a letter, recalling him to his vocation, and asking others to pray for him. In priests, she saw and venerated Jesus. She asked others, "Pray for priests. The world goes from bad to worse because we do not have holy priests."

Carla dedicated herself without reserve to every form of apostolate and charity. She lived the gift of the counsels. After her death, her parish priest wrote a testimony in which he said, "Thank you, Lord, for having given Carla to me, a luminous example of holiness, guardian of my priesthood, untiring collaborator and generous in the parish apostolate."

In the summer of 1969, Carla caught a severe cold. A number of remedies were tried but she got worse. In January of 1970, she entered the hospital of Saint Ursula in Bologna, where she stayed until April. In her diary, she describes her suffering and her thoughts about her condition, which was growing ever worse. In April, she entered the clinic Villa Maria in Rimini, where she died peacefully on April 2, only a few days before her birthday. Shortly before her death, she said, "Jesus smiles at me." Carla's confessor, Don Succi, was so convinced of her sanctity that he gave the funeral Mass wearing white vestments. Part of the text he used in his sermon was, "Where God has sown thee, be fruitful." In his remarks, he points out one of

Carla in the late 1960s.

the greatest lessons of Carla's life: that sanctity does not lie hidden only in the cloister, but can exist in the world, and indeed it is the will of God for it to do so.

Carlos M. Rodriguez

1918-1963

Joyful Lay Apostle

"We read in the Old Testament that Elias [Elijah], who expected the manifestation of 'He Who Is,' did not find Him in the storm, nor in thunder, nor lightning, but rather in the 'blowing of a soft breeze, upon which he covered his head.' . . . You must understand that it is in that simple soft breeze, and not in the spectacular, that our Lord is to be found." So wrote Carlos Rodriguez, a Puerto Rican layman who joyously lived the life of the "Alleluia" he loved.

The Church needs saintly models, especially of lay men and women who have not done anything extraordinary in this world, but who, like the Servant of God Carlos "Charlie" Rodriguez, have done the ordinary things with a great love for God and His Church.

The last two years of his life, Charlie fought a loosing battle with intestinal cancer. At his death, his entire estate consisted of a small piece of property which his family planned to sell to help pay for his hopelessly high medical bills. Some doctors, hearing of this plan, came to the family and said, "Tear up our bills. We owe Charlie far more than he owes us."

Carlos Manuel-Santiago Rodriguez was born November 22, 1918, in Caguas, Puerto Rico, a large town in a valley surrounded by beautiful mountains. The second of five children in a close and loving Catholic family, he was baptized on May 4, 1919, in the parish church. His given name was Carlos Manuel Cecilio. The name Cecilio was given to the child because he was born on the feast of Saint Cecelia. Carlos's father, Manuel, owned a small-goods store next to the family home. When Charlie was six,

Carlos (at left) with his family.

Carlos "Charlie" Rodriguez

a fire destroyed the store and house, and the family lost all they had.

From the time he was a small child, Charlie was inclined towards the things of God. With his sisters Haydee and Titay, he played at saying Mass, using a large trunk as his altar and making the girls into altar girls. His grandmother happily became the congregation, telling the girls that the miniature priest was very fervent but that the antics of the servers sometimes distracted her. Later, as an adolescent, Charlie saved his pennies and bought his sisters a missal, for which he paid the high sum of thirty-five cents. In those days, the Mass was celebrated in Latin. Charlie bought a missal with an English translation because one with a Spanish translation was more expensive. So that his sisters could understand, he explained the meaning of the liturgy. He also taught them to bring home and live what they celebrated in church.

The fire in which his family lost most of their worldly goods and which caused them to seek help from a maternal aunt is credited with helping Charlie to find his special love for spiritual things. He learned early the lesson that our worldly goods are unstable and untrustworthy. "The Lord shall provide . . . we'll see," he used to say.

Even as a child, Charlie was devoted to the Virgin, and delighted in celebrating her feasts with great detail. Family celebrations were carried out in the dining room, and for Marian feasts Charlie would help to arrange the table with a blue-and-white tablecloth, and paper napkins that he provided with symbols relating to the different feasts of the Virgin. He kept a small altar, inherited from his grandmother, with an image of Our Lady in his room, where for much of his life he kept a daily votive candle burning. Charlie saw Our Lady foremost as the *Theotokos*, the Mother of the Word Incarnate. His devotion to her led to his Christocentric piety. He understood her message at Cana: "Do as He tells you."

Charlie had an inquiring nature and a prodigious memory. He took a few months of formal instruction on the piano, and then completed studying and practicing on his own until he became a proficient player. As a youngster, he took part in a theatrical production and later organized a puppet show. In both cases, he easily mastered the memorization of the dialog.

He loved music and was happy when he inherited some seventy-eight r.p.m. records from one of his uncles. The classics and Gregorian chant were among his favorites.

Once, when Charlie was thirteen, a neighbor's vicious dog broke loose and ran into the Rodriguez's house. Charlie was holding a one-year-old cousin by the hand and the dog rushed toward the child. Without hesitation, Charlie heroically attempted to defend the child as best he could.

Until this time, Charlie's health had appeared normal. Today, it is thought that the stress of this incident may have possibly triggered the first attack of the ulcerative colitis with which he was to be afflicted for the rest of his life. Charlie continuously suffered from what he called "an upset stomach." In fact, the disorder is an inflammatory disease of the bowels, and there were many embarrassing and humiliating situations which he suffered as a result, without ever losing his good-natured disposition.

Charlie attended Catholic grade school, where he proved to be a brilliant pupil. He completed the eighth grade with honors, winning the first prize for the class. In addition, he was given a special prize for religion, presented by the donor. After graduating from grammar school, he began to attend the local public high school, but because of recurrent sickness, he took six years to complete the four-year course.

Charlie did all that he could to make people happy, often using creative ploys. When his sister Haydee spent a year studying abroad, knowing that she would be homesick, he wrote her a little newsletter which he called "*La Chismosa*" ("The Gossip Column") to keep her up to date with family and local news. When his brother Pepe also left for a year of study in the United States, Charlie created a newsletter for him, too, which he titled "*La Cotorra Muda*" ("The Mute Parrot").

The celebration of Easter and the Resurrection was the high point of his life. Returning home with his family, he would take the candle lighted from the Paschal candle at church and in total darkness would light a candle at home while the family sang "Light of Christ." He often told his family, "Next year we will celebrate it even better, until we finally make perfect this celebration at the Parousia."

During World War II, Charlie was rejected by the draft board for medical reasons and became a secretary at a nearby Army base, working in the Commissariat of Camp O'Reilly at Gurabo. After the war, at the age of twenty-eight, he studied for a year at the University of Puerto Rico, where he maintained excellent grades in spite of many days absence due to his poor health. After this year, he abandoned his formal studies for good, but continued his prodigious reading at home. He had become convinced of the need for a lay apostolate dedicated to students, who tragically often tend to lose their faith during their later school years. He spent the rest of his life in this mission.

Charlie returned to the university to continue his battle for young minds, not as a student but as a moderator for a student discussion club. He directed three discussion clubs each week in three different towns. He taught CCD classes for public high school students every Sunday morning, and since most of his students could not afford expensive books, he mimeographed reading material for them. Charlie also published a weekly four-page liturgical bulletin, which he mailed at his own expense to anyone interested in receiving it. He wrote to a priest friend, "My main interest in this work is none other than to attract souls to the 'primary and indispensable source of a genuine Christian spirit,' the Sacred Liturgy, according to the words of Pope Pius X." Charlie also assisted Father Alvaro de Boer, O.P., in writing the constitution for a new religious order, the Sisters of Jesus Mediator.

Charlie worked full-time as a clerk in the Estacion Experimental Agricola, Departmento de Economia, University of Puerto Rico. His co-workers and supervisors at the Agricultural Experiment Station recall him as being very conscientious in his work, humble, and quiet. Charlie usually spent most of his lunch hour typing and mimeographing. His modest salary was spent on stencils, stamps, paper, and envelopes, and for the purchase of spiritual books. Much of the remainder was given to the poor.

In spite of his poor health, he carried out a prodigious activity, including attendance at daily Mass, a ceaseless person-to-person apostolate, and comforting visits to the sick. He set aside hours for prayer and reading of spiritual materials daily. Among the students and professors of the Centro Universitario Catolico of the University of Puerto Rico, Charlie managed to promote a love for the special wisdom with which to balance the knowledge of the Faith with the demands of the lay state. This was the intent of his little mimeographed publication *Cultura Cristiana*. His efforts to promote a better and fuller participation in the liturgical acts of the Church came from his true understanding and appreciation for the treasures of the Church. Self-taught and extremely well-read, Charlie was a kerygmatic precursor of the liturgical and Christocentric renewal. From his study of the pontifical encyclicals of the forties and their biblical basis, Charlie understood, lived, and taught the role of the laity in the apostolic, evangelizing, and sanctifying work of the Church. Charlie was already putting into practice things that were later called for by Vatican Council II. In his understanding that the call of Jesus was for everyone, Charlie was also a pre-council precursor of the ecumenical movement. By his enthusiasm and joyfulness, he convinced many that the Christian life made sense.

Small of stature and of a shy disposition, Charlie seemed to shine when he began his talks with the groups of students at the university's Catholic Center. The members left feeling renewed and with a clearer understanding of the day's topics. One student recalls that Charlie received a great joy in sharing with the students. When the mother of one of the students thanked

Charlie, saying, "May God reward you," he laughingly quipped, "Or put it on my credit." Another student recalls that after a discussion on the Divine Office, she realized that the call to a Christ-centered liturgy was "virile," as opposed to the tendency of the time to stuff people with such pious sentimentality that it drove them away.

Among the students, Charlie realized an urgent need to raise the level of religious instruction. When he corrected their errors, it was always in a fraternal spirit, never ridiculing them and almost always with a sense of humor. To illustrate the pastoral importance of the vernacular language at Mass, he told the story of the student who had misunderstood what the priest said in Latin when he spoke of *sanguis* (referring to Communion under both species). The student asked for the "sandwich" that the priest had promised. He also told a humorous story about the student who asked him about the use of cruets in the Mass, which the student thought contained oil and vinegar.

Sometimes, Charlie arranged what he called "Days of Christian Living" with a group of students. They would get together at some place outside the city, each bringing food to share with the others. Charlie would give two or three talks and the group would pray the Divine Office for the Laity. They would sing, pray the rosary, and enjoy wholesome recreation and games. If time permitted, they ended the day with a Mass. Sometimes, "brothers" of different denominations would be invited to join in, in an ecumenical spirit.

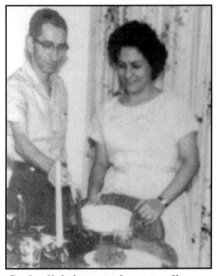

Carlos lighting an advent candle.

In his prodigious reading Charlie studied the lives of the saints. The saints were his friends, and he was fond of quoting them. He was especially fond of phrases and ideas that could convey an effective message, and many of his favorites he took from the words of the saints.

Charlie was hospitalized in the fall of 1962 but was released in time to make his Advent preparations. He began working again at the Centro, and celebrated Christmas, but his health worsened. In the spring of 1963, he was hospitalized again. The stress of the hospital environment and the lack of privacy bothered him, but he told his doctor, "Poor patients, what they have to endure," as if he was not suffering in the same way. At this time, doctors did not consult with their patients about the methods of treatment as as they do nowadays. On March 12, the doctors began exploratory surgery. Cancer of the rectum was diagnosed. The operation continued for seven hours, during which Charlie was given a colostomy. The movement of his left arm was damaged, possibly due to the trauma of hyperextension during the long surgery. He awoke deprived of the dignity and privacy, which he had treasured during the long years of his infirmity. "They didn't tell me . . . ," he siad, and Charlie's eyes filled with tears.

This was Charlie's last, and very personal, Lent. Physiotherapy on his arm was fruitful only for the personnel who attended him, not for Charlie. His appetite, which had never been good, deteriorated. His abdominal pain and diarrhea became worse; the colostomy irritated his skin. After consulting with him and his family, he was transferred from the public hospital to a small private dispensary belonging to a doctor friend who was a great admirer of him and his life.

Here he rarely complained. Rather, he often begged pardon of his caregivers for causing them trouble — "so much inconvenience" — especially when they had to change his colostomy bag. Visitors became used to sharing long hours in silence, interrupted only by brief, edifying conversations. By Holy Week, Charlie's cancer had spread. The pain increased and for a while he was given opiates. On Good Friday his sister Titay stayed with him, reciting the solemn ceremonies of the day, while Charlie endured his own cross in silence, uncomplaining. His friends brought him a candle lit from the Paschal candle, but Charlie still had a lot to suffer before his own Easter. Three weeks later he was transferred to his home in Caguas, where he was cared for by his mother and his sister Titay.

Charlie was too ill to attend the ordination of his brother Pepe, but a week later he made a heroic act in order to attend his brother's first solemn Mass, watching from the sacristy in a wheelchair. This was Charlie's last appearance in public.

Within days, he had to be admitted to the hospital again. His brother Pepe was given permission by his superior to stay with him. When a feeding tube had to be inserted into his stomach, in a weak voice the patient whispered, "If it is possible, don't do it, but if you have to, do what you think is best. How much longer. . . ." The tube was necessary because his veins had collapsed. Charlie greeted his visitors, but preferred them to wait outside in the corridor afterwards. "I'm grateful for their visit, but I can't wait on visitors the way I should." For his last month, he had periods of lucidness between dreams and fainting spells, and he suffered through a period of his own personal "dark night of the soul." For the last week of his life, he received daily Communion but he remained in spiritual darkness. One day, he asked for his mother and told her goodbye, then began asking his brother insistently, "Pepe, what is that word that has a special meaning for me?" Again and again he repeated his question. At last he found the word — *Dios*. God. Plain and simple, the word *God*, which had such profound meaning in his life. Immediately, he became peaceful, even in the midst of his suffering.

A few days before, he had told his brother, "The thirteenth is a good day." On the morning of July 12, they brought him Communion as usual, but before receiving it, Charlie said, "Summon me, Angel, and I will answer." Later that morning he began to pray, and his brother heard him repeating the phrase "be my salvation" and the word "alleluia." Charlie turned towards the crucifix and seemed to alternate between praying and singing, sometimes calling for his mother and his sister, peacefully calm and smiling. At eleven at night his family gathered in the room and his brother said the rite for a departing soul, and afterwards prayed Charlie's favorite canticle, the Exultet of the Easter vigil. Shortly after midnight, Pepe intoned the Exultet for the last time. Charlie gave three great sighs and stopped breathing.

From the moment of his death, Charlie's family and friends had experienced a great sense of peace. His entire family had gathered and was present for his final moments, except for his sister Haydee, who was in a convent. She had sent a beautiful letter to him shortly before his death in which she had thanked him for his life and told him goodbye, saying, "We shall meet again in our homeland in heaven, singing the 'Alleluia' which you taught me to sing." Pepe's Benedictine community helped to arrange the funeral, and his brother celebrated the funeral Mass.

There is an old saying which holds that "it rains when a saint dies." The sun shone brightly that Saturday in July when Carlos Rodriguez was carried for the last time to the parish church. Its heat beat down on the little Puerto Rican church where the hope of the Resurrection was preached for one who lived the joy of Easter. The funeral of Carlos Rodriguez closed with a sudden rainstorm that almost halted the burial.

Three Blessed Carmelites of Guadalajara

Sister Mary Pilar of Saint Francis Borgia, 1877-1936
Sister Mary Angel of Saint Joseph, 1905-1936
Sister Teresa of the Child Jesus, 1909-1936

Spanish Martyrs

Chapter
5

"Receive as Viaticum," the priest said in a trembling voice as he gave the Sacred Host to each of the eighteen Carmelite nuns of the Monastery of Saint Joseph. The priest consumed the remaining sacred particles. Then, dressed in secular clothes and in small groups, he and the sisters slipped silently and furtively from the monastery into the streets, hoping to find shelter with friends.

It was the night of July 22, 1936. That day, the city of Guadalajara had fallen into the hands of the Spanish Reds. Just as in many other cities of Spain in the awful days of the Spanish Civil War, Guadalajara had been turned into a veritable inferno of fire, bloodshed, and pillage. Before leaving, the nuns had hung a small scapular in the oratory, begging Our Lady and Saint Joseph to preserve their monastery and to faithfully guard it in their absence. For some, including the faithful chaplain, their final Communion was indeed Viaticum; for others, their hearts became a resting place for Our Lord driven from the tabernacle, as they were unable to receive Holy Communion again for over two years.

Almost immediately after the nuns escaped, the Reds came and took possession of the monastery. They decided to use the house for their own purposes rather than burn it, as was their original intent. For long hours that seemed never-ending, the nuns slipped silently through the streets of

Guadalajara, seeking refuge with friends who risked their own lives to shelter the women. Some of the nuns were elderly, having been in the cloister forty or fifty years; some were in poor health. Three of the Carmelites were discovered and killed, dying as martyrs for the Catholic faith. Their bodies were thrown into a common grave with a number of others. Five years later, the bodies were discovered, identified, and brought back in a solemn funeral procession to be reverently placed in a crypt in the Monastery.

One of the sick sisters, Sister Agnes, is looked upon by the Carmelites as the fourth martyr of the community. The previous Holy Week, she had made an offering of herself to God as a victim for the conversion of sinners and the salvation of Spain. At the time of the dispersal of the convent, Sister Agnes was in a dying condition. Forced to leave the house where she and some other religious and members of the Rightists had taken shelter, she attempted to travel with the others. It was impossible for her to go far, and the others tried to have her taken for medical aid. What eventually happened to her is unknown. God alone knows the final details of her martyrdom.

The three Carmelites.

The other members of the community traveled a long Way of the Cross with many bitter sufferings and separations before their eventual reunion. The three acclaimed martyrs of the community are but three of a vast number of heroic souls who died for their Faith during the Spanish Civil War. Throughout the country, there was a fierce persecution of religious; entire communities, priests, and seminarians died in the bloodbath. Spanish Catholicism was watered with the blood of her martyrs.

Marciana Valtierra Tordesillas, in religion Sister Mary Angel of Saint Joseph, was born March 6, 1905, at Getafe, near Madrid. She was the youngest child of a large and pious Catholic family. Her mother died when she was only three, and she became the consolation of her bereaved father. As a child she was devoted to the Infant of Prague and often recited the "little crown" in His honor. From the time of her First Communion at the age of eight, she was determined to become a religious. Marciana was an extremely tender-hearted and sympathetic person who could not bear to see others in poverty or suffering without trying to bring them some measure of relief. She became the angel of her home, caring tenderly for her aging father and an invalid aunt. Therefore, she did not enter the community of Carmelites until she had reached the age of twenty-four.

Naturally unselfish and thoughtful, Sister Mary Angel's great desire in the cloister was to serve others unnoticed. At recreation, her childlike simplicity overflowed; she loved to make the other sisters laugh. In spite of this unaffected happiness, she felt deeply the sorrows of the Church and the loss of souls. In 1934, she pronounced her solemn vows of religious profession. A letter she wrote at this time tells what was to be the program of her life: "Love is nourished with sacrifice. Let us love Jesus Christ a great deal, suffering much for His love, because He suffered more for us." After the bitter struggle broke out, and on hearing the reports of the deaths in the country, Sister Angel told her sisters, "Oh, if we could have the happiness of being martyrs!"

After her death, the nuns found a note written in one of Sister Mary Angel's books: "O my God, receive my life amid the suffering of martyrdom and in testimony of my love for You, as You have received the offering of so many souls who have loved You and have died for love of You." God did indeed receive her offering as she was the first of the martyrs to die, shot down in the street.

Jamie Martínez Garcia, in religion Sister Mary Pilar of Saint Francis Borgia, was born at Tarazona, in the province of Zaragoza, on December 30, 1877. Jamie loved life and had a kind and genial disposition. Her cheerful character made her popular with all. She dressed well, and seemed to have an innate talent for needlework and embroidery. When Jamie's elder sister Severina entered the Carmel of Zaragoza, the fifteen-year-old Jamie was asked if she, also, wanted to become a nun. Her reply was a curt "No." However, in the next five years her soul matured and she followed her sister, now Sister Mary Araceli of the Blessed Sacrament, to Carmel.

In the cloister, this gentle, modest nun prayed constantly for those in the world. The all-absorbing devotion of her soul was to the Sacred Heart of Jesus, and she was consumed with the desire to make Him known and loved. Long years of prayer, sacrifice, and suffering prepared Sister Mary Pilar for the supreme moment of her life. On July 23, while in hiding with several of the nuns, Sister Pilar spoke gently to the prioress, her natural sister: "Do not be afraid, Mother. I have begged our Lord to take me and to spare you and the community." When she was taken, just as her Savior did, she prayed for forgiveness for her persecutors.

Eusebia Garcia y Garcia was born March 5, 1909, at Mochales in the Province of Guadalajara. At the age of nine, she told her confessor that she wished to make a vow of chastity, and seemed already to have made up her mind to consecrate herself to God in religion. Her confessor, not wishing to dampen her enthusiasm, permitted her to make a private vow of chastity, but only for a year at a time. Shortly thereafter she read *The Story of a Soul*, the autobiography of Thérèse of Lisieux, who had died only twenty years before. Her reading inspired in her heart a wish to enter Carmel, which she did at the age of sixteen. In religion, Eusebia took the name Teresa of the Child Jesus, in honor of the Little Flower, who had been beatified two years before.

The experience of separation from her warm Catholic family, especially her baby brother who hugged his "*Chacha*" tightly and didn't want to let her go, seemed like death to Eusebia. She offered this separation as her first holocaust to the Lord. Sister Teresa was musically inclined, and was happy to be called upon to play during the solemn novena celebrating the canonization of her beloved Saint Thérèse during her first month in the cloister. After her entrance, Sister Teresa set herself to emulate the life and virtues of her holy patroness. With a strong and ardent nature, it was not always easy for her to be meek and patient, and to overcome her strong natural likes and dislikes. She once told her sisters, "I do not like those lives of the Saints in which nothing is said of their faults, as though they were born saints. They do not glorify the mercy of God. If you ever write a death notice for me, please be sure to tell all my faults. I want God's mercy to be known."

Like her heavenly patroness, Sister Teresa had a burning desire for souls. Often she begged the superiors to be allowed to remain in prayer after Matins at night. It was hard for the superiors to resist her eagerness to win grace for a soul recommended to her prayers. Often she fell asleep during these prolonged vigils, but Our Lord looked at her desires and granted her petitions. The parish priest who had baptized Eusebia attended her clothing ceremony. As the radiant young girl entered the chapel for the moving ceremony, he exclaimed, "We have another little Saint Thérèse. All that is lacking is the halo, but this child will have to earn it." Earn it she did, a mere eleven years later, affirming the kingship of her Jesus as she died.

The remainder of the night of July 22, 1936, sisters Pilar, Angel, and Teresa spent, along with their prioress and another sister, in the basement of the Hibernia hotel. At five the next morning, they recited the prayers from their breviary. The fifth sister had a heart ailment, and had a minor attack. After this, they were moved to the top floor of the hotel, where they could look out over the city and see the smoke from many fires. Every hour the terror increased as the news came of the deaths of so many, including relatives

Teresa, Pilar, and Angel

and friends. Only five priests in the entire city escaped the slaughter. The houses were constantly searched, and the small group decided to split up. The prioress and the ailing sister moved on to a boarding house on the same street where two other Carmelites were already staying and where there was room for two more. Sisters Pilar, Angel, and Teresa planned to make their way to the nearby home of some friends of Sister Teresa. Shortly after three o'clock in the afternoon, the five left the hotel.

A little after four, the nuns, who had rejoined their sisters at the boarding house, heard a volley of shots nearby. Together, the four prayed the Salve Regina for the victims of the shots. Although the sisters did not know it at the time, the victims were their own sisters in religion from whom they had so recently separated.

On leaving the hotel, the other three made their way up Teniente Figueroa street. Near the Palace hotel was a parked Jeep where a group of Red Army members, male and female, were eating lunch. It is not known how they were recognized, but one of the soldiers, a young woman, suddenly shouted, "Shoot them! They are nuns!" Another of the soldiers, a male, objected, whereupon the young woman began deriding him and calling him a coward.

The frightened sisters fled into Francis Cuesta street and took shelter in the vestibule of number five. One of the Communists followed them and ordered them to return to the street, which they did, becoming defenseless targets for the persecutors.

Sister Mary Angel fell near the doorway at the first volley of shots. A bullet had pierced her heart and it is believed that she died instantly.

Sister Mary Pilar staggered a few feet across the street. As she fell, she was heard to exclaim, "My God, my God, ¡Viva Cristo Rey!" Hearing those words, the infuriated murderers shot again, leaving her covered with wounds. One of them reached down and slashed at her with a knife.

A number of people came up, including some Guardia de Asalto police in the employ of the Republic who did not approve of the excesses of the Reds. One of the guards rebuked the assassins for their savagery and then attempted to obtain help from a nearby pharmacy for the poor sister. The owner, however, in fear for his own life, advised the Guards to take her to the Red Cross. They stopped a passing car, but the driver showed them a dagger and threatened to kill her if he was forced to take her in. A second car stopped and the badly wounded nun was placed in it and taken to the Red Cross. Passing through the Plaza de Marlasca on the way, they encountered a band of Reds who had come from Madrid for the capture of Guadalajara. On discovering that the car contained a nun, they attempted to prevent the Guards from carrying her into the dispensary. Miss Maria Carrasco, a volunteer at the Red Cross, tenderly assisted the grievously wounded nun, and attempted to relieve her burning thirst by placing ice chips on her lips. Sister Pilar was riddled with bullets, her vertebral column was fractured, and one kidney was exposed by knife wounds. She was still conscious, though almost drained of blood, and suffering in a horrible agony. She gasped, "Water, water . . . Oh, how I suffer! What have I done to them that they should treat me thus?" Then, according to testimony, she pronounced the words of her divine spouse in His own agony, "My God, forgive them; they know not what they do." Sister Pilar was wrapped in an enormous roll of gauze and cotton, which soon turned crimson with her blood. A health commissioner standing near was deeply moved and told her not to be afraid, that she would be taken care of. All who saw her were filled with compassion, even those who were known to have Communist leanings.

Sister Pilar was placed on a stretcher and carried to a hospital. Here a Daughter of Charity cared for her, with tender reverence. This same nurse later gave Sister Pilar's community the report of her heroic death. This sister held a crucifix to Sister Pilar's lips. In her agony, the dying nun kissed it, and repeated ejaculations. At last, her nurse bent close to hear her final words. Again, Sister Pilar repeated, "My God, pardon them, because they do not know what they are doing."

Sister Teresa was not hit by any bullet. In the general confusion she took refuge in the doorway of number one. Frightened and bewildered, she did not know what to do. Just as she was going to attempt to leave her place of concealment, she was approached by one of the soldiers named Palero, who pretended concern for her safety. He and four or five companions led her along Saint John of God street, through the Davalos piazza, across the Saint Anthony bridge, and down the street to a spot near a cemetery.

Witnesses overheard their grim intentions; the young, attractive Sister Teresa was not simply to be killed. Fearlessly, she rebuked her tormentors, among whom she had recognized some who had shot her companions. They grew furious and determined to conquer her. They surrounded her with loaded guns. They demanded that she pledge allegiance to the president of the Republic, and praise Communism. Instead, she shouted to each of their demands, "¡Viva Cristo Rey! Long live Christ the King!" Finally she was ordered to go ahead a few steps. She spread her arms wide, in the form of a cross, and ran to the glory of martyrdom. They shot her in the back. She died there, and was later carried into that same cemetery, where she was buried in a common grave with her two sisters and a number of others who were killed that day.

The mission of a Carmelite is to live only for God. Living only for God, how could they hesitate to die for Him? Nonetheless, the nuns and the faithful friends were filled with sorrow when they heard of the death of their dearly loved companions.

It was these same faithful friends of the convent, those who so often had been the recipients of the nuns' prayers in their own time of sorrow and trial, who carefully collected all the reports given by the eyewitnesses of the events of that tragic afternoon. To them we owe the testimony used in the process of beatification.

The bodies of the three nuns were hastily buried in a common grave together with all those who had fallen that day. The sorrowful community members did not even know where they had been placed. Five years later, they were discovered and identified. The remains of the three martyrs were brought back in a solemn funeral procession and reverently placed in a crypt in the monastery.

The heroic virtue of these three Spanish Carmelites was proclaimed by Pope John Paul II at their beatification in 1987. These Carmelites of Guadalajara are only three of a vast number of heroic souls who perished during the Spanish Civil War, most of whom will never be known.

Saint Clelia Barbieri
1847 - 1870

A Heavenly Voice

On July 13, 1871, the first anniversary of the death of their foundress, the Sisters Minims of Our Lady of Sorrows were united in evening prayer in the chapel when "suddenly there was the sound of a high-pitched, harmonious and heavenly voice that accompanied the singing in the choir; at times it sang solo, at others it harmonized with the choir, moving across from right to left; sometimes it passed close by the ears of one or other of the sisters." This wondrous event occurred a second time, and the sisters thought about giving up their night's rest and remaining in prayer all night long. In the absence of the Blessed Sacrament, they decided to go to the nearby parish church to adore the Blessed Sacrament in the tabernacle. "But how great was our surprise when we realized that the voice had followed us and accompanied us as we began our prayers!"

On her deathbed, twenty-three-year-old Clelia Barbieri had promised her companions that although she was leaving them physically, she would never abandon them and would remain with them spiritually. True to her promise, her voice has joined in the prayers and hymns of her fellow nuns since her death. Even today, in all the communities of her spiritual daughters, the Sisters of the Minime dell'Addolorata, the "voice" has joined in the services, always using the language local to the house with perfect pronunciation. The "voice" has been heard by young novices who had not heard of the phenomenon and by outsiders. The "voice" never speaks alone but joins in with the voices of the other nuns, almost as if she were present as a member of the community. To many who have heard it, there is a feeling of a presence among the group. Not all of the sisters hear the "voice" and those who do are not always the most "saintly," according to written and verbal testimony.

Clelia Barbieri was born February 13, 1847, at Le Budrie, a small village in the suburbs of Bologna, Italy. Her parents were poor hemp workers. A younger sister, Ernestina, was born in 1850.

Clelia's father died in the cholera epidemic that swept Italy in 1855, when Clelia was only eight years old. His death swept the family into ab-

Saint Clelia Barbieri

ject poverty. Although Clelia's paternal grandfather lived and worked with the family, in those days there were few social services, so even at such a young age, Clelia was forced to sit and spin the hemp yarn along with her mother. Although Clelia remained a bright and happy little girl, the hardship and deprivation of her early life undermined her fragile constitution and paved the way for the "consumption" (tuberculosis) that afflicted so many of the poor, undernourished people of the time.

Although poor, Clelia's family was of exemplary character, and she was brought up in an atmosphere of sound morality and with a natural sense of devotion. Clelia herself developed an innate sense of piety at an early age. She was diligent at school and at home taught the catechism lessons she had learned to her younger sister.

According to the custom of the times, Clelia was confirmed at the age of nine before making her First Communion when she was eleven. From the time of her confirmation, Clelia began to pray with great devotion, to read Christian doctrine, and to listen attentively to the parish priest's sermons; she seemed to be trying to understand all that she heard and read within her own being. The evening before her First Communion, at the suggestion of the priest, she knelt before her mother with great humility and asked her forgiveness for any wrong she had ever done. She vowed to obey her mother and asked for her blessing. She spent a sleepless night, repeating over and over again, "A God for me, a God for a poor creature like me." After receiving the Body of Christ, Clelia lay prostrate before the statue of Our Lady in a profound state of contrition and returned with an intimate and joyful gentleness that showed its mark on her entire life.

At fourteen, Clelia became active in her parish community as a member of a group called "The Workers of the Christian Catechism." Eventually, she became the spiritual inspiration of her parish. The other parishioners, especially her own contemporaries and the younger adolescents, admired the wholesomeness of her virtues and her ready smile. The parish priest, Don Gaetano Guidi, sent the young girls to her and she guided them in learning Christian doctrine and preparing for the sacraments.

Clelia developed an intense life of meditation and prayer, spending hours in the church in front of the Tabernacle. Her favorite topic for meditation was the Passion of Christ. Her prayer life did not distract her from the sufferings of her neighbors, and the love and charity of Christ led her to begin visiting her neighbor's homes to aid and comfort the sick.

Clelia was slim with delicate features and a noble, yet simple bearing. Her blond hair was usually worn plaited, with a part down the center. Her grace and charm and her natural kindness attracted people to her. By the time she was seventeen, she had already received two offers of marriage. Her uncle brought suit on behalf of his sister's son, but Clelia put him off politely telling him that as she was not planning to marry he should talk to her sister. Another suitor, the son of the parish carpenter, eventually married her cousin. Desiring to be wholly the Lord's, she had refused his offer of marriage.

As a very young child, Clelia had mentioned to her mother her wish to "leave the world." In childlike innocence at the time of her confirmation she had asked how one became a saint. Now, she began to think of gathering a small group of young girls around her to share her aspirations and apostolic zeal. In prayer, she asked God to give her a friend to share her ideals and goals. Theodora Baraldi, a girl six years older than Clelia, became the friend she had prayed for. In 1868, the two girls made a pact to devote themselves to Christian virtue, converse with God, live in fraternity, and attempt to attract others to practice this way of life.

Don Guidi realized that the two friends had formed an intention that was not simply a burst of religious infatuation or a passing phase, and he began to nurture their vocation by giving them spiritual readings. A third young girl, Orsola Donati, who was two years younger than Clelia, soon joined them. They began meeting on Sunday afternoons and then at more regular intervals. During the summer months, the girls took walks along the river banks and discussed their plans. They wanted to live a life in common without any special formalities and without the necessity of a dowry so the poorest of girls could join them.

We know from the records that Clelia had moments of discouragement, and it was perhaps worry that aggravated her always poor constitution, so that at the age of twenty in 1867 she became so ill that the priest came to give her the last rites. Her family was shocked to discover that Clelia was wearing a penitential chain with sharp points on it wound three times around her body.

Just as the priest was about to give her Extreme Unction, Clelia recovered and, looking at her family near her bedside, she asked, "Why are you weeping? Don't be afraid; the Lord will not take me away this time; He is still expecting more from me."

The arrival of a fourth young woman, Violante Garagnani, convinced Clelia that the time to begin their foundation had come. The village schoolmaster's wife had died, and he gave up his small house annexed to the village school. Don Guidi rented it from the owner and, using the limited resources of his parish, he fitted it out for the four young women who so desired to please Our Lord and serve their neighbors. They planned to live a semi-monastic lifestyle consecrated to prayer, contemplation, and good works. Clelia's mother and the parents of the other three girls gave their consent.

The political climate of Italy at this time was extremely anticlerical. Acts had been passed in 1850 and 1856 suppressing religious orders, making it impossible for them to own real estate, and providing for immediate house arrest without trial for any person suspected of being opposed to the new regime. A number of people, including Clelia's uncle, criticized Don Guidi's plan for the Budrie "retreat" and felt it constituted a challenge to the state and a deception. One opponent went so far as to request an injunction against the formation of the retreat under the Suppression of Religious Orders and Guilds Act.

A document dated November 29, 1867, charged Don Guidi with renting to "house some nuns," and requested the prefect of Bologna to take action. The priest had to endure a humiliating bureaucratic investigation to explain that the humble institution was completely lawful; it was not monastic in character and the girls had not taken any vows. Instead, this was a group of young ladies who intended to live a life of work and charity together. After a final discussion with the civil authorities, permission was obtained and the girls moved into the house on May 1, 1868. That evening, their first meal was a single egg, shared between the four, with a small helping of polenta and only well-water to drink.

Simple gifts from the good hearts of the local people soon began to arrive; the first was a present of four pieces of bread brought by a young child. Later, Clelia said, "I like the idea that our house resembles the crib where the shepherds bring their gifts." The house was furnished with leftovers from the girls' homes and a few pieces of furniture brought by the parish priest. The small community immediately began to live a life of poverty and sacrifice. They each wore a gray dress, with a kerchief knotted at the neck, and sandals. Food was meager and unpretentious and earned with the fruit of their own labor. In the morning, they arose for meditation and during the day there was spiritual reading and special prayers which most often accompanied their labor of sewing, spinning, and weaving. Their work was carried out during the day and partially at night. They slept on simple hard straw mattresses. Within only a few months, they welcomed a fifth arrival, Luigia Nanni.

The young ladies continued to encourage the parishioners and the little house became the meeting place for girls who wanted to learn the catechism and prepare to receive the sacraments. Often the girls from the retreat took the catechumens to the sacraments.

From the first, Clelia was considered and respected as the leader of the small community. When they entered the house, they committed themselves to the protection and patronage of Our Lady of Sorrows and of Saint Francis of Paola, the founder of the Order of Minims. Later, the congregation was to take the name Suore Minime dell'Addolorata (Little Minims of Our Lady of Sorrows). Clelia realized the need for a more formal rule of life and, together with Orsola Donati, she went to Bologna where they attended a course of spiritual exercises given by Don Carlo Mingardi, a well-known educator of youth. After a long discussion with him, Clelia returned to the Budrie Retreat and wrote such an appropriate rule that very little of it had to be changed as time passed and the institute grew. The rule was based on four features: 1) the sense of community, 2) the spirit of contemplation, 3) the service of charity, and 4) simplicity and joy.

Saint Clelia Barbieri

On her return from Bologna, Clelia was burning to get to work, but she realized that the group would need material means to carry out their plans. She took an active part in the tiring work of weaving and sometimes assisted in reaping corn in the fields to acquire food for the community. One day, she confided in her companions that she had "seen" the person who would help them. She then instituted the practice of the thirteen Fridays in honor of Saint Francis of Paola, begging him as their example of poverty, to help them meet the needs of their work.

On the final Friday, a stranger arrived to speak with Don Guidi, saying he had been sent by a Vincenzo Pedrazzi from Anzola. The letter from Mr. Pedrazzi, a total stranger to the priest, stated that he wished to learn more about the Retreat. He had heard a little about it from a man who had sold him some yarn. Don Guidi replied by describing the way of life led by his seven protegees. The unknown benefactor sent an initial gift of three baskets of grain. A wealthy man who had reformed his life, Pedrazzi continued to send help to the institute in order to alleviate their worry about their supply of daily food. Clelia thanked their benefactor in a letter which he kept with him for the rest of his life.

A number of mystical lights were given to Clelia at this time which are recorded in the testimony of her sisters. These include times when Clelia's face would become transfigured as if she were in ecstasy, conversations she would seem to be having with someone who was not seen but whose presence was felt, and levitation. Her complete and utter trust was also a visible mark of grace.

One morning Anna Forni, the cook, had nothing in the house to eat and went to Clelia with a small bottle of oil. "What shall we do?" she asked. "This is all we have in the house to eat!"

Clelia directed her to put the oil in the lamp in front of the statue of Saint Francis of Paola, light it, and to have faith.

Reluctantly, Anna followed Clelia's orders. A few hours later, there was a knock at the door and, although it was not her turn for duty as portress, the cook went to the door. There stood a man with a large basket full of flour, bread, wine, and other edibles. The sisters had done some work for this man, so Anna asked if this were the payment for their work.

The man replied that they would be paid later, but that the basket was simply something he had felt particularly urged to do for the house that day.

After thanking the man, Anna ran quickly to show the gifts to Clelia, who only smiled calmly and told Anna that next time she should obey faster.

A fragment of her only extant letter shows Clelia's boundless devotion to Jesus: "My dear Spouse, Jesus: I want to write to You so that I shall ever remember it. Great are the graces which God gave me on January 31, 1869, while I was in church hearing Mass; I felt a great inspiration to mortify my will in all things, to please our Lord ever more; and I felt the desire to do so, and yet I do not have sufficient strength. O great Lord God, You see that my will is to love You and to try to avoid offending You. O Lord, open Your heart and throw out the flames of love. Enkindle my heart with these flames and burn me with love."

Toward the end of 1869, Clelia's tuberculosis worsened. Her uncle, the town doctor, confirmed it and left her room in tears; the faith of the young girl had overwhelmed him. Seven months of suffering followed before Clelia entered the final stages of the disease in full possession of her faculties. Clelia asked to have the image of Saint Francis of Paola in her room, and to have it transferred to the chapel after her death. An illuminated image of Our Lady of Mount Carmel remained at the foot of her deathbed. On her last day, July 13, 1870, Clelia spoke to reassure her companions: "Be brave because I am going to paradise; but I shall always remain with you, too; I shall never abandon you!"

Her death crowned her life. Immediately, seven young girls asked for admission to the community. The Budrie Retreat became a place of spiritual attraction for a host of young people, and conversions multiplied. Due to the anticlerical sentiment of the times, Don Guidi was twice arrested and a civil inquiry was held regarding their institute. The inquiry completely cleared them. Shortly after this, the archbishop allowed Mass to be celebrated in a small chapel in the retreat, and his successor allowed Holy Communion to be given to the young girls living there. Pope Pius IX gave his blessing to the unassuming work he saw being undertaken.

As with any new community, the first years had their ups and downs. Less than ten years of Clelia's death, a generous benefactor provided a new house for the community at the exact spot she had predicted before her death. After intercessory prayers to their foundress, a dry well drilled on the property filled with water which still flows today. New foundations in other cities were made. The constitutions of the Minims were solemnly approved in 1905. The sisters work today as educators and nurses, and for the spiritual education of the young.

The cause for the beatification of Clelia Barbieri was opened in 1920 and she was beatified October 27, 1968, by Pope Paul VI. She was canonized April 9, 1989, by Pope John Paul II.

Saint Clelia

Blessed Cristobal Magallanes and Companions
Martyred 1915-1937
Twenty-five Mexican Martyrs

Twenty-five Mexican martyrs were beatified by Pope John Paul II on November 22, 1992. Twenty-two of these were diocesan priests; three were laymen. They were killed in hatred of the Faith during the turbulent years from 1915 to 1937.

Father David Galvan
Martyred January 30, 1915, at Guadalajara, Jalisco

David Galvan entered the seminary of Guadalajara at the age of fourteen, and completed the preparatory course with good grades. He left the seminary and went to work for three years, and he began to live a dissipated lifestyle. During one episode, he got drunk and was taken to jail for hitting his girlfriend.

However, David seemed to feel God calling him, and he changed radically. He put away his affection for worldly things and supported difficult and adverse circumstances with patience and tranquility. After a year of stringent probation, he was allowed to return to the seminary. He was ordained in 1909, and became a teacher at the diocesan seminary.

During the *carranzista* revolution, he was arrested for being a priest, but was eventually released. There were often skirmishes in the area, and in mid-January of 1915, during one of these, Father Galvan spent more than six hours in the line of fire, helping the fallen soldiers spiritually.

On January 30, there was another confrontation in downtown Guadalajara between the villistas and the

Father David Galvan

Father Luis Batiz

David Roldan

carranzistas. The streets of the city were covered with wounded and dead. When Father Galvan prepared to go to their aid, one of his friends told him he might be killed. He answered, "And if I am killed? What greater glory is there than to die saving a soul?"

He went to look for another priest to help him. The first one he asked excused himself, saying he wasn't a pastor. Father Galvan said, "I am not going because of obligation, but because of charity." Father Jose Araiza offered to go with him, and they left to assist the fallen. On the way into town, they were arrested by soldiers and taken before Lieutenant Colonel Vera at the Civil Hospital, who ordered their execution. Father Galvan was shot, but Father Araiza was ransomed and released.

Father Luis Batiz, David Roldan, Salvador Lara, Manuel Moralez
Martyred August 15, 1926, at Chalchihuites, Zacatecas

The four martyrs of Zacatecas were killed under the pretense that they were trying to rouse the town against the government. The National League for the Defense of Religious Liberty (LNDLR) was founded in Chalchihuites with the aim of defending, by peaceful and legal means, the rights of the Catholic Church against the attacks of sectarianism on the part of the Mexican government. July 29, there was a meeting attended by about six hundred people. At the meeting, the president of the league, Manuel Morales, said, "The League will be peaceful, without mixing in political affairs. Our project is to plead with the government to order the repeal of the constitutional articles that oppress religious liberty." When these martyrs were apprehended, the townspeople were told that they would be taken to the capital of the state to render their declarations. Instead, without formal or legal judicial means, they were shot a little distance from town.

Father Luis was the spiritual director of the seminary at Durango, and the parish priest of Chalchihuites. A zealous pastor, he created a workshop for Catholic workers and established a school for the children. At night, he taught catechism to both children and adults. In 1925, on the last day of the public cult, he cautioned his parishioners that the closing of the churches was not done by the government, saying that Catholics could not take up arms but rather must conduct themselves in a Christian manner. After the meeting of the National League, he was accused of plotting an uprising and a group of soldiers arrested him in the private home where he was staying.

David Roldan was born in Chalchihuites in 1907. His father died when he was only a year old. He entered the seminary, but had to leave because of family finances. An orderly and responsible young man, he often helped Father Batiz with his pastoral duties. A mineworker, he was held in high esteem by his supervisors and his co-workers. David was a member of A.C.J.M. (the youth of Catholic Action) and was vice president of the National League. He worked hard gathering signatures on a petition to overturn the oppressive antireligious laws.

Salvador Lara was also attending the seminary in Durango, and also because of his family's poor finances had to drop out and go to work. He helped Father Batiz with his parish work, was president of Catholic Action, and secretary of the League. When Father Batiz was arrested, he called a meeting to see how to free the priest by legal means. A group of soldiers broke into the meeting at Salvador's home and called out the names of the officers of the League. They were taken to the municipal offices where Father Batiz was being held. The soldiers told Salvador's mother they were taking the young men to Zacatecas to present their declarations.

Salvador Lara

Manuel Morales, the president of the National League, was also a former seminarian who had to leave to help support his family. He married and had three children. An exemplary husband and father, he was the secretary of the circle of Catholic Workers and a member of Catholic Action. He was arrested with Lara and Roldan.

About noon on August 15, the four were put in two cars which left on the road to Zacatecas. In the mountains near Puerto Santa Teresa, the cars pulled over and the prisoners were taken out. They were offered freedom if they recognized Calles's antireligious laws. All four refused. Father Batiz and Manuel were led forward. Father Batiz asked the soldiers to free Manuel Morales because he had children to support, but Manuel told them, "I am dying for God, and God will care for my children." Then he raised his hat, and the soldiers fired, killing both. The two youths were brought forward then and, facing their executioners, each cried out, "Long live Christ the King and the Virgin of Guadalupe!" Salvador's cry was so loud that it unnerved the executioners, and he had to be given the coup de grace. His youth and heroism impressed one of the soldiers who said, "What a pity we had to kill this man so grand and strong."

Manuel Moralez

Father Jenaro Sanchez
Martyred January 18, 1927, at Tecolotlán, Jalisco

Father Sanchez was pastor of the church at Tecolotlán, Jalisco. During the persecution, he continued exercising his ministry as well as he could, with apostolic zeal and good organization. He was not afraid of anyone or

anything. He told a friend, "I think in this persecution many will be killed and I believe I will be one of the first."

On January 17, Father Sanchez was in the countryside with some villagers when a group of soldiers began following them. He was arrested and taken back to Tecolotlán. Near midnight, he was led out to a place called La Loma, where there was a large mesquite tree. A man living nearby testified as to what happened next.

The soldiers put a rope around the priest's neck. He said, "Good, my countrymen, you are going to hang me. But I pardon you, and my Father God also pardons you and long live Christ the King!"

After the execution, one of the soldiers went to the

Father Jenaro Sanchez

house and told the man who later testified, "We are putting you in charge of the man who is hanging there. If anyone cuts him down, we will hang you, too!"

After the soldiers left, the man went to look at the body of the priest and realized it had been shot and stabbed with a bayonet. The body remained where it was for some time before anyone recognized who it was, because it was so badly disfigured. When identified as the parish priest, it was taken to the cemetery and buried.

Father Mateo Correa
Martyred February 6, 1927, at Durango, Durango

After attending the seminary of Zacatecas on a scholarship, Father Mateo Correa was assigned as parish priest of Concepción de Oro. Here he became a close friend of the Pro-Juarez family. He baptized Humberto Pro, and gave First Communion to Miguel Pro, both of whom were later killed in hatred of the Faith. Father Correa was sent to Colotlan and after 1910, because of the persecution, he stayed in hiding for a time at León until things calmed down. In 1926 he was assigned to Valparaiso.

Father Mateo Correa

One day, the elderly Father Correa, obediently continuing the ministry to the people in his area, was taking Viaticum to a sick person when he was surprised by a group of soldiers.

He consumed the host to avoid its desecration, and was taken to the military commander where he was accused of being in league with the Catholic *libertadores* (a group of men who advocated force in order to achieve religious freedom; also called the *Cristeros*). He was taken first to Zacatecas and then on to Durango. The priest was sent to hear the confessions of some of the Cristeros who were in jail, awaiting execution. Father Correa prepared the young men for death, encouraging them to face the firing squad bravely. When the commander, General Ortiz, demanded to know what they had told the priest in their confession, the brave confessor refused. The irritated general then told Father Correo that he also would be shot. "You can do that," Father Correo said, "But don't you know, general, that a priest must guard the secret of confession? I am ready to die." Father Correo was taken out of the city and shot on February 6, 1927.

Father Julio Alvarez
Martyred March 30, 1927, at San Julian, Jalisco

Father Alvarez served at Mechoacanejo, Jalisco, all of his priestly life. A zealous pastor, he inculcated in his parishioners a great love for the Eucharist and for Our Lady. Indefatigable in his ministry, he continuously visited all the ranchos in the area. A man of profound prayer, his parishioners would often find him reciting his breviary in front of the Blessed Sacrament. He encouraged his parishioners to help with the cleaning and decorating of the church, giving them each offices. He had a special love for the poor, going so far as to give his own clothes away to them. After the suspension of the public cult, he exercised his ministry in secret, often performing baptisms in the mountains and valleys near the town.

Father Julio Alvarez

On March 26, Father Alvarez was going to a rancho to say Mass when he was surprised by a party of soldiers. They led him, tied to the saddle of a horse, through several cities to León where General Amaro sentenced him to be shot.

On March 30, about five in the morning, Captain Grajeda called out the priest. Father Alvarez asked if they were going to kill him and the Captain explained that they had orders to do so. "Good," responded the priest. "I know that you have to kill me because you are ordered to do so, but only let me say a few words." The Captain acquiesced and the priest continued, "I am going to die innocent because I have done nothing wrong. My crime is to be a minister of God. I pardon you." He then crossed his arms and the soldiers received the order to fire. His body was thrown onto a trash heap near the parish church of Mechocanejo.

Father David Uribe
Martyred April 12, 1927, at Cuernavaca, Morelos

The willing and able pastor of Iguala, Guerrero, Father David tried to integrate Christian spirituality in all phases of his parishioners' lives. He

said, "You should always try to help your parishioners see how they can intelligently unite their social life with the Christian life."

Because of the persecution, he was driven into hiding and forced to leave his people from time to time. At one time he went to Mexico City, but constantly thought of returning to his people. In one letter he wrote, "I was anointed with the oil of the saints and made a priest. Why should I not be anointed with my blood in defense of souls?"

Returning to Iguala, he was recognized, arrested, and taken by train to Cuernavaca. On the eve of his death while he was in prison, he wrote, "I declare that I am innocent of the things of which I am accused. I am in the hands of God and the Virgin of Guadalupe. I pardon all my enemies and I beg pardon from any that I have offended."

Father David Uribe

On April 11, 1927, he was removed from his cell and was apparently being taken to Mexico City. On the morning of April 12, near San Jose Vidal, he was shot in the back of the head and his body was abandoned.

Father Sabas Reyes
Martyred April 13, 1927, at Tototlán, Jalisco

Sabas Reyes Salazar finished his early education and seminary in Guadalajara and was ordained in the Diocese of Taumalipus in 1911. He ministered in parishes in Guadalupe. When the persecution began, he was

sent to Tototlán.

In January 1927, government troops took over the parish church, converting it into a stable for the horses after breaking the images and setting fires in the sanctuary. Father Sabas exhorted his parishioners to prayer and when they asked if he would leave because of fear, he responded, "We must have faith. Aren't we Christians? . . . I have been offered the chance to leave and help in other places, but here is where God put me, and here I wait to see what God disposes."

On April 11, he had just completed a baptism in a private home when federal soldiers arrived and demanded, "Where is the priest?" Serenely, Father Sabas

Father Sabas Reyes

answered, "Here I am."

They tortured him horribly in an attempt to make him tell the hiding place of two other priests. His hands and feet were burned, he was starved, placed in the sun, and given nothing to drink. He was beaten until a number of his bones were broken and his skull was fractured. He suffered the torture with heroic patience. On April 13, 1927, at nine at night, he was taken to the cemetery and shot. Three or four times the rifles spoke; each time, Father Reyes rose and cried out, "Viva Cristo Rey." One of the soldiers said, "It took much to kill this priest, and he was killed unjustly."

Father Roman Adame
Martyred April 12, 1927, at Yahualican, Jalisco

Ordained in 1890, from 1913 until his death Father Adame was the parish priest of Nochistlán, Zacatecas. Here, he founded the Daughters of Mary of Nocturnal Adoration. In his parish ministry, he was especially known for his great charity to the sick. He built chapels in the villages in the surrounding areas. When the persecution began, he continued his ministry in secret. On April 18, 1927, he went to the rancho Veladores to give the Lenten sacraments, where he expressed his sentiments by saying, "What happiness to be a martyr, to give my life for my people."

Father Roman Adame

One of the men of the rancho denounced the priest to Colonel Quinones, who arrested Father Adame at dawn of April 19.

He was first taken to Mexticacan, and then forced to walk barefoot to Yahualica. One of the soldiers offered his horse when he realized the elderly (age sixty-eight) priest couldn't walk anymore. The soldiers of the regiment made fun of this soldier for his compassionate gesture.

The Colonel had taken over the priest's residence in Yahualica and during the day Father Adame was kept tied to the columns in front. At night he was thrown in a cell. For three days he was given no food or water. Some countrymen offered to pay a ransom for the priest and the Colonel asked for six thousand dollars.

In spite of the fact that they paid the money, on April 21 he was taken to the cemetery to be killed. A grave had already been dug. Antonio Carillo, one of the soldiers from the firing squad, refused to shoot him. The person who testified to seeing the execution could not hear everything clearly. The soldier in charge gave a strong blow in the face to Carillo, and he was shot as well as the priest. The priest raised his hand and pulled back as if to signify that he had completed his duty as the impact of the bullets knocked him directly into the grave.

Father Cristobal Magallanes and Father Agustin Caloca
Martyred May 25, 1927, at Colotitlán, Jalisco

As a priest, Father Magallanes had carefully studied Pope Leo XIII's ideas in the encyclical *Rerum Novarum*, and he attempted to put them into practice. He established catechetical centers and schools in his villages, built a dam for water, and set up small land developments for the poor. He began a small magazine called *El Rosario* (*The Rosary*) to teach his people.

On May 21, 1927, fighting broke out between the federal forces under General Goni and the Cristeros. Father Magallanes was on his way to a rancho to celebrate Mass when he was captured and taken back to Totatiche, where he was the parish priest. He was jailed next to his curate, Father Caloca, and taken to the Colotitlan municipal palace.

Father Agustin Caloca had been in the seminary in Guadalajara when it was closed, but he had continued his studies under Father Magallanes and was ordained in 1923. He was assigned as curate at Totalice, and was also the prefect of the seminary.

Father Cristobal Magallanes

In May of 1927, when the government troops were approaching, he ordered the seminarians to disperse. He was attempting to go into hiding when he was captured.

The government troops accused Father Magallanes of promoting the Cristero movement in the region. In defense, he asked them to bring the copy of *El Rosario* where he had written: "Religion is not propagated nor conserved by means of arms. Neither Jesus Christ, nor his apostles, nor the Church has to employ violence to accomplish their ends. The weapons of the church are to convince and to persuade by means of the Word." While awaiting execution, Father Magallanes told Father Caloca, "Cheer up, God loves the martyrs . . . one moment and we are in Heaven." Father Caloca, understanding the words, added, "We have lived for God and in Him we die."

Before he was shot, Father Magallanes distributed his few possessions among the soldiers who were ordered to shoot him and gave them sacramental absolution. He asked permission to speak and said, "I am innocent and I die innocent. I forgive with all my heart those responsible for my death, and I ask God that the shedding of my blood serves toward the peace of our divided Mexico."

Father Agustin Caloca

About midday on May 25, 1927, the priests were

shot by a firing squad in front of an adobe wall behind the municipal building. In 1933 when Father Caloca's remains were translated to Totalice, his heart was found to be entire and incorrupt with a piece of a bullet in it.

Father Jose Isabel Flores
Martyred June 21, 1927, at Zapotlanejo, Jalisco

Born in Zacatecas in 1866, Father Flores was one of the outstanding alumni of the seminary of Guadalajara. From 1900, he served as the parish priest of Zapotlanejo, Jalisco, with his residence in Matatlán.

An exemplary priest, he had a great love for the poor, and his ministry was characterized by his kindness and responsibility. He valiantly refused to abandon his parishioners during the worst of the persecution, although he was prudent in exercising his ministry.

The municipal president of town, Jose Orozco, had a great hatred of priests and offered a reward for the capture of any priest in the area. Father Flores was denounced by a man named Nemesio Bermejo, an ex-seminarian who lived with him, in order to gain the reward. Father Flores was arrested and offered his freedom if he would accept the Calles laws, but he refused.

Father Jose Isabel Flores

He was taken to the priest's residence in Zapotlanejo, which had been converted into a jail, where he was held for three days and nights without food or water. Orozco played music outside the prison and told the priest, "You have only to sign Calles's law and I will set you free." The priest responded, "I am going to hear more beautiful music in heaven." When his sister visited him, Father Flores told her, "God knows I am here; this is His Will for me."

On June 21, 1927, he was taken between one and two in the morning to the municipal cemetery, where they began to torture him. He was lassoed by the collar and hung from a tree limb; they lifted him up and down three or four times but the priest didn't say anything. Finally he told his tormentors, "This is not the way you are going to kill me my children; I will tell you how to do it. But before, I want to say that if any of you received from me the sacraments, don't cripple your hands." One of those present said, "I am not going to do this; the priest is my *padrino* (godfather). He baptized me." The commander indignantly said, "Well, we will kill you too," at which the man responded, "Then I will die with my padrino." The man was immediately shot. The priest then divided his few possessions among the soldiers. They intended to shoot him, but the guns would not fire, so the commander, Anastasio Valdivia, slit his throat. He was buried immediately in the place where he was killed.

Father Jose Maria Robles
Martyred June 26, 1927, at Tecolotlán, Jalisco

Jose Maria Robles entered the seminary of Guadalajara at the age of twelve, and while still a seminarian he began working in the Diocese of

Tehuantepec at the invitation of the bishop. He was ordained in 1913. Especially devoted to the Heart of Jesus, he founded the congregation of sisters known as the Hermanas del Corazón de Jesus Sacramentado. He was named pastor of Tecolotlán, and during the persecution he exercised his ministry in secret. When many suggested that he leave, he responded, "The shepherd can never abandon his sheep." From January 14, 1927, he celebrated the sacraments in certain houses in secret.

During the last five months of his life, he gave admirable proof of his virtues by his study, his prayer, and his Christian mortification. Holy Mass and adoration before the Blessed Sacrament were hallmarks of

Father Jose Maria Robles

his life. He tried valiantly to maintain a spiritual Christian life in his parish.

On June 25, 1927, Colonel Calderón ordered a search of the houses of the town. Father Robles was getting ready to celebrate Mass. He himself opened the door and tranquilly went with the soldiers, who took him to the headquarters of the *agraristas*. Legal defenses were made for his liberty and an *amparo* (a stay of execution) was obtained. However, about ten that night, he was taken from the jail and murdered close to a nearby rancho. The soldiers took him with his horse near an oak tree, and he knew that his hour had come. He prayed briefly, blessing his parish, pardoning and blessing his murderers. Then he kissed the rope and put it around his neck, and the executioners completed their duty.

Father Miguel de la Mora
Martyred August 7, 1927, at Cardona, Colima

From 1912 until his death, Father de la Mora served as chaplain of the Cabildo of the Cathedral of Colima. When the persecutions began, he was found and taken prisoner but allowed to leave under bail. When the churches were closed and the public cult suspended in 1926, his friends insisted that he flee with them to the family ranch at El Rincón del Tigre. Father de la Mora refused, asking them "How can you ask me to leave

Father Miguel de la Mora

Colima without a priest?"

General Flores constantly applied psychological pressure to get him to establish a church in opposition to the Catholics, so at last he told his brother he was going to the ranch because he was afraid he would not be able to hold up against the bullying orders of the general.

On the way to the ranch, Father and a group of friends stopped at Cardona for breakfast. A woman asked if he was a priest, and asked him to marry her daughter. Some *agraristas* overheard the conversation, and Father de la Mora and his companions, including his brother, were captured and taken to military headquarters at Colima.

General Flores was furious and informed the prisoners that he was going to shoot the priest and his brother. On hearing the sentence, Father Miguel took out his rosary and began to recite it. He was taken to the stable and placed between the manure piles. About noon, the soldiers received the order to shoot, and he was killed in front of the horrified eyes of his brother Regino. A soldier gave him the coup de grace. Regino was freed due to the fact that he had a family to support.

Father Rodrigo Aguilar
Martyred October 28, 1927, at Ejutla, Jalisco

In 1927, Father Aguilar was the acting priest in Unión de Tula, Jalisco. At the beginning of the persecution, he said, "The soldiers may take our life, but never our faith."

The priest was full of faith and charity, and was a talented poet. From January 1927 he practiced his ministry in secret. He was hiding at a rancho when he was betrayed and captured by *federales* under General Izaguirre in October.

At one o'clock in the morning of October 28, on the orders of the general, he was taken to the main square of Ejutla to be hanged from a mango tree. Taking the rope in his hands, he blessed and forgave his executioners, giving his rosary to one of them. One of the soldiers arrogantly asked, "Who lives?" and told the priest that he wouldn't kill him if he would cry out "Long live the supreme government." Instead, in a firm voice, the priest responded, "Christ the King and Our Lady of Guadalupe."

Father Rodrigo Aguilar

Furiously the rope was pulled to hang him in mid-air. Then he was lowered and again asked, "Who lives?" A second time, without hesitation, the priest responded "Christ the King and our Lady of Guadalupe." A third time, with vile provocation, he was asked the same question. His answer, with his tongue agonizing in the death throes, remained the same. He was suspended again and died.

Father Margarito Flores
Martyred November 12, 1927, at Tuliman, Guerrero

After his ordination in 1924, Father Flores was a professor at the seminary and the vicar of Chilapa, Guerrero.

From a poor family, he was always pious and serious, but happy in his ministry. Because of the persecution, he was sent to Mexico City, where he attended the academy of San Carlos. He was captured in June of 1927, but freed through the influence of the Calvillo family, who obtained his release from General Roberto Cruz. (Cruz was also involved in the execution of Blessed Miguel Pro, S.J.) He returned to his diocese at Chilapa.

On hearing of the saintly death of Father Uribe, Father Flores also ardently desired martyrdom, and in October, one day before he returned to Chilapa, he made a holy hour and celebrated a Mass in which he offered his life for the salvation of Mexico.

Father Margarito Flores

He arrived at the diocesan headquarters and put himself at the disposal of the bishop. The vicar general explained his anguish that he could not find a priest willing to go to the parish of Atenango del Rio because the municipal governors had promised to kill any priest who would dare to go there. Father Flores immediately volunteered for the dangerous mission.

On November 10, accompanied by a guide, he left to enter the area in a roundabout way. For the sake of prudence, they did not intend to go to the priest's residence. In spite of their caution, he was identified by government agents, arrested, and taken to Captain Manzo at Tuliman. He was forced to walk in the blazing sun half-naked, barefoot, and tied to the saddle of a horse.

On November 12, Captain Manzo ordered his execution. Although a ransom was offered, the captain refused to take it. Serenely, Father Flores shared his last meal with the soldiers who held him captive, and about eleven in the morning he was taken to the place of his execution behind the church.

Before the executioners formed up to shoot him, they allowed him to make the sign of the cross over them near the door of the church. As they took him to the place of execution he was praying. When he finished with this, he stepped in front of the soldiers and told them he was ready. They couldn't believe their eyes. They shot him and threw his cadaver in a grave in the cemetery immediately. At the exhuming of his remains several months later, his blood flowed as if it were fresh. Later, in 1945, his remains were transferred to Taxco to the church of his childhood.

Father Pedro Esqueda
Martyred November 22, 1927, at San Juan de los Lagos, Jalisco

From his ordination in 1916 until his death, Father Esqueda Ramirez exercised his ministry at San Juan de los Lagos, Jalisco. The center of his life was the Holy Eucharist; this was also his apostolate, and he organized the association Cruzada Eucaristica. He especially loved to attend to the catechism and formation of the children making First Communion.

During the suspension of public cult, he exercised his ministry in various places without leaving San Juan. To answer the suggestion that he leave, he responded, *"Dios me trajo, Dios sabra* [God put me here; He knows]." November 17, 1927, in the middle of the night he was in the little room he kept as his oratory where he guarded the Blessed Sacrament, and he invited the family of the house to join him in his meditation. He told them, "I am going to make myself ready to die."

On the morning of November 18, Lieutenant Colonel Santoyo and a group of federales surrounded the

Father Pedro Esqueda

house. They entered forcibly and found the place under the floorboards where the priest and the sacred vessels were hidden. They took Father Esqueda prisoner, beating him as they left. He was taken to jail and held incommunicado for four days. Each day, he was tortured brutally. Father Esqueda suffered these torments in silence, maintaining a tranquil soul and supporting the torture with resignation.

November 22, 1927, sometimes on foot and sometimes on horseback, but always bound, he was taken to the place of execution, where Colonel Santoyo ordered him to climb into a mesquite tree. Father Esqueda attempted to do this several times but couldn't because his arm was broken from the torture. Near midday, after more torture, Santoyo shot him.

Father Jesus Mendez
Martyred February 5, 1928, at Valtierilla, Michoacan

As parish priest of Valtierilla, Father Mendez was devoted to the Eucharist, and he fostered a Eucharistic spirit in his parish. Dedicated to his people, he was assiduous in the confessional, immediate in his attention to the sick, and personally attended meetings of the parochial associations.

In 1928 when the federales entered the town, his brother advised him to leave, but he replied, "What happiness to be a martyr. Those of us that die as martyrs are given life in Our Lord."

Father Jesus Mendez

Father had just given Communion to his sister and another lady at the office of an attorney when they heard shots and fighting outside. He attempted to leave by a back window, taking the chalice under a *tilma* (cloak). He was spotted by soldiers who thought he was carrying arms. On seeing it was only the chalice, they told him they weren't after his jewels, but asked him if he was a priest. He serenely admitted he was. They took him into custody as he hurriedly consumed the hosts. Spying his sister watching, he told her, "Be comforted, this is the Will of God." Turning to the soldiers, he said, "Now you may do to me what you wish; I am ready." The soldiers took him to the town plaza and put him in front of a tree. Three times Captain Munoz attempted to kill him. The first time, he attempted to shoot him, and his pistol malfunctioned. The second time, he ordered the soldiers to fire and but no shot hit, possibly because no one wanted to kill him. At last, they removed his medals and cross, and the third volley wounded him. One of the soldiers gave him the coup de grace. The soldiers put his body on the railroad tracks, but the wives of the town officials rescued the body and were permitted to hold a wake and to bury the humble and valiant priest.

Father Toribio Romo Gonzalez
Martyred February 25, 1928, at Tequila, Jalisco

Toribio Romo Gonzalez was born in Jalostotitlán on April 16, 1900, and began attending the seminary at San Juan de Lagos at the age of thirteen. In 1920, he transferred to the seminary in Guadalajara, where he was a good student, a member of Catholic Action, and was distinguished in social work. He was ordained in 1922. He worked in the apostolate with the workmen and propagated Eucharistic devotion. For a time, he worked with Father Justino Orona in Cuquio, Jalisco.

Father Romo was assigned to the parish of Tequila, Jalisco, in 1927. He

set up his living quarters and an oratory in an abandoned factory. Because of the persecution and the ever-present danger, the young priest prayed constantly that God would allow him to have courage and remain without fear. He told his sister, "I am cowardly, but if one day God wants me to be killed, I hope He will give me a rapid death with only the time necessary to pray for my enemies."

On February 23, 1928, he seemed to be very preoccupied and after Mass the next day he told his sister that if anyone came to look for him to tell them he was occupied or a little ill: "I want to put everything in order." He worked all day and night, and when his sister chided him for working too hard, saying he could finish the next day, he insisted on continuing. He fin-

Father Toribio Romo Gonzalez

ished his work about four in the morning of Sunday the twenty-fifth. His eyes were nearly closed with sleep, but the oratory was ready for Mass. He told his sister that he was going to rest a little before celebrating. At five in the morning some federale and agrarista troops entered town and forced the mailman to show them where the place of the hidden Mass was. They surprised Father Romo and shot him in his bed. The second volley killed him as he fell into the arms of his sister Maria. The soldiers stripped the priest of his clothing and threw his naked body in front of the city hall in Tequila.

Fathers Justino Orona and Atilano Cruz Alvarado
Martyred July 1, 1928, at Cuquio, Jalisco

Father Orona was the son of an extremely poor family, and after his preliminary studies, he worked for a while in order to help his family. He entered the seminary at Guadalajara in 1894, and he suffered many heartaches while he studied, thinking always of the poverty of his family. He was a good student, held in high esteem by his superiors and his peers, and was ordained in 1904.

As parish priest at Cuquio, he edified everyone by his exemplary conduct, exercising his ministry in spite of anticlericalism and religious indifference in the area. In his parish, he began a religious congregation to care for poor and orphaned young girls. When the persecution increased, he was advised to leave, but he responded, "I am here with my people, live or die." He wrote to a friend, "We must follow the road of our native land with happiness, serving God on earth and giving ourselves for the good of the people. Those of us who walk the road of sorrows with fidelity can leave for Heaven with security."

Father Justino Orona

On June 28, 1928, he went to the Rancho Las Cruces, the home of the Jimenez-Loza family, along with his brother Josemaria and Torribio Ayala. Ayala was a self-effacing Christian who was himself hanged shortly after the assassination of Father Orona for his "crime" of assisting the priest. The following day, Father Orona's vicar, Father Atilano Cruz, joined them. They wanted to plan how to carry on their ministry during the dangers of the persecution.

Father Atilano Cruz Alvarado was a young priest, only twenty-six years old, who had been ordained in 1927. On his arrival at the rancho, he and the pastor

Father Atilano Cruz Alvarado

recited the rosary together and then stayed up late, making plans for their pastoral ministry. When Father Orona asked Father Cruz if he were not afraid of the government, Father Cruz replied that he would greet them with the words, "Long Live Christ the King."

At dawn on the first of July, some federales under Captain Vega along with the municipal president of Cuquio broke into the house where the two priests were sleeping. Father Cruz opened the door of his room and greeted them with the words "Viva Cristo Rey" in a strong clear voice. Father Orona was killed immediately; Father Cruz was mortally wounded. The bodies of both were thrown on the patio of the house and afterward were taken to the main plaza of town and left there. The faithful took the bodies and buried them in the cemetery of Cuquio.

Father Tranquilino Ubiarco
Martyred October 5, 1928, at Tepatitlán, Jalisco

Under Mexican President Carranza, the seminaries were closed, so Tranquilino continued his education in private homes. He was ordained in

1923, and sent to the parish of Tepatitlán. A zealous pastor, he established a Christian newspaper to teach the faithful and began a soup kitchen for the poor and the refugees from the persecution. This area was a common place for battles between the Cristeros and the government forces, so his ministry was carried out in hiding.

In March 1928, he told a group of young girls that he had asked for the grace of giving his life for Christ.

On October 4, he spent the night in a private home where early in the morning he was going to celebrate Mass and perform a wedding. The next morning after Mass, he was arrested and thrown in a cell with some other men. He heard their confessions and led them in saying the rosary.

Father Tranquilino Ubirarco

Two hours later, Colonel Lacarra ordered that he parade around the sidewalk and enter town. Before he left, he asked the soldiers which one was commissioned to kill him. When all remained silent, he said, "All of this is God's will; the man who is made to kill me is not responsible." One of the soldiers then said he was the one chosen, but he couldn't do it.

Later, Father asked with what instrument he would be killed. They told him he would be hanged, and with total tranquillity he blessed them. They hanged him from a branch of a eucalyptus tree at the entrance of town. The soldier in charge of the execution refused to carry out the order, so he, himself, was shot on the same day.

Father Pedro de Jesus Maldonado
Martyred February 11, 1937, at Chihuahua, Chihuahua

Pedro de Jesus Maldonado Lucero entered the seminary of Chihuahua at the age of seventeen. In 1914, because of the political conflict, classes were suspended and he dedicated himself to learning music. Eventually, he was able to finish his studies and was ordained in El Paso, Texas, in 1918.

In 1924, he was named pastor of Santa Isabel, Chihuahua. In his priestly ministry, he was especially dedicated to the catechism of the children, he increased night adoration, and he established many Marian associations in his parish.

During the intense persecution in the years from 1926 to 1929, he continued his ministry in his parish, cementing the faith of his parishioners and inculcating in them a love and respect for the Holy Father and his legitimate priests.

Father Pedro de Jesus Maldonado

In 1931, the persecution recurred in Chihuahua and the churches were closed again. Father Maldonado was detained in 1932 but released; in 1934 he was arrested again. He was imprisoned, mistreated, threatened, and sent back across the border to El Paso. Here he stayed in safety for some time, but his heart was with his parish and he begged his bishop to be allowed to return, as his sheep were without their shepherd. At last the bishop gave his permission and Father Maldonado returned to exercise his ministry in the townships and villages of his parish.

There was a fire in the public school, and the authorities blamed the priest. On February 10, 1937, a group of armed and drunken men arrested him at his house and made him walk barefoot to Santa Isabel. He recited his rosary along the way. He was taken to the city hall, where the municipal chiefs beat him up, hitting him on the head with the butt of a rifle so hard that it caused his left eye to pop out and knocked him unconscious. At a holy hour shortly before his death, he had prayed for the grace of receiving final Communion before his death. He had the sacred host with him in a reliquary, and when his murderers found it, one of them, Jesus Salcido, forced him to eat it, saying, "Eat this, this is your last communion!" They beat him again and again with their rifle butts until he was unconscious, bathed in his innocent blood. They then took him to the Civil Hospital of Chihuahua, where he died on February 11.

First Knights to Be Beatified

Six of these Mexican martyrs were members of the Knights of Colombus, and are the first members of that organization to be beatified.

As tensions and persecutions in Mexico mounted, so did the membership in the Knights, and by 1923 there were forty-three councils with nearly six thousand Knights, many of who were in the forefront of the Catholic Action movement. The Mexican government outlawed the Knights and banned distribution of their publications. While many in the U.S. attempted to ignore the problems south of the border, and while coverage in the secular press was often at variance with the reality of the religious persecution and blamed all problems solely on socioeconomic motives, the Knights vigorously campaigned to rally U.S. support for Catholics in Mexico. The Supreme Council personally lobbied President Calvin Coolidge to help the Mexican Catholics, and the Knight's publication, *Columbia*, ran dozens of articles accompanied by graphic photos regarding the persecution. A million dollars was raised by the Knights to support refugees and exiles and to publish pamphlets about the persecution. In his 1926 encyclical on the persecution, *Iniquis Afflictisque*, Pope Pius XI praised the Mexican Knights for founding a program to continue Catholic education and the National League for the Defense of Religious Liberty.

The six beatified Knights and their respective councils are: Father Luis Batiz, 2367; Father Mateo Correa, 2140; Father Jose Maria Robles, 1979; Father Miguel de la Mora, 2140; Father Rodrigo Aguilar, 2330; Father Pedro de Jesus Maldonado, 2419. The layman Salvador Lara is believed to have also been a Knight, although no records can be found to confirm his membership.

Dorothy Day
1897-1980

Catholic Worker

Dorothy Day is well-known as the co-founder of the Catholic Worker Movement, as well as for her strong stands for social justice and against violence. Even those who counted themselves among her political opponents recognized the great works of mercy and social service she began in the Catholic Worker houses of hospitality. She is known as a controversial radical who is often dismissed as just another social worker. Few Americans have seen a clear picture of Dorothy Day — the picture of a contemplative, a mystic, a faithful Catholic, and a saint.

Dorothy herself realized that her ideas would be easily mistaken. "We feed the hungry, yes. We try to shelter the homeless and give them clothes, but there is strong faith at work; we pray. If an outsider who comes to visit us doesn't pay attention to our praying and what that means, then he'll miss the whole point."

The works of mercy were at the heart of what Dorothy did. These were not simply obligations for her. She said, "We are here to celebrate Him through these works of mercy."

What disturbed many about Dorothy was that she was not critical of what the Church taught, but only of its failure to live out its teaching. For Dorothy, faith and action intertwined. "I loved the Church of Christ made visible," she wrote, "not for itself, because it was so often a scandal to me . . . (but because) the Church is the Cross on which Christ was crucified; one should not separate Christ from His Cross."

Dorothy suggested that Christ's revolution was a revolution of the heart. Her strong sense of community was built on the nourishment of the Eucharist. "When we receive the Bread of Life each day, the grace we receive remains a dead weight in the soul unless we cooperate with the grace. When we cooperate with grace, we 'work with' Christ, in ministering to our brothers. Most cradle Catholics have gone through, or need to go through, a second conversion which binds them with a more mature love and obedience to the Church."

Dorothy Day was born in Brooklyn on November 8, 1897, the oldest of

© Marquette University Archives

Dorothy and her older brothers.

four children of John Day, a journalist, and his wife, Grace. Nominally, John was a Congregationalist and Grace was Episcopalian, and although Dorothy was baptized in her mother's faith, religion was not a strong part of their family life.

The family moved several times in Dorothy's early years until, when she was eight, they settled into a tenement flat over a tavern on Chicago's South Side. They had lost their home, and John had lost his job, in the 1906 San Francisco earthquake.

The apartment was so poor that after school, Dorothy entered another building until her friends walked on past, because she was ashamed of the place her family lived.

At a friend's house one day, looking for one of her chums, she found the girl's mother praying on her knees at the side of her bed. Serenely, Mrs. Barrett told Dorothy where her daughter was and returned to her prayers. This small incident so impressed Dorothy that she began to overcome the anti-Catholic prejudice that she had often heard her father express at home. Later, Dorothy counted Mrs. Barrett's lack of dismay and embarrassment on being "caught praying" as one of the significant factors in her conversion to the Catholic Church.

Dorothy's father finally got a job as sports editor of the *Inter Ocean* and the family moved into a large and comfortable house on the north side of Chicago.

From her earliest years, long before she converted to Catholicism at age thirty, Dorothy longed for the Source of love. At fifteen, her letters reveal that she was struggling with the meaning of the Acts of the Apostles. Her longing grew side by side with a consciousness of the suffering and needs of the poor, and the scriptural mandates to help them. She could not understand why Christians did not live the message of the gospels.

A letter from this time to a school friend mentions that among other books, Dorothy was reading the Bible (a practice she continued for the rest of her life):

I'm still in the Acts. I never went over it so thoroughly before and now I find much more in it. Isn't it queer how the same verses will strike you at different times? "We must through much tribulation enter into the Kingdom of God." How true that is! Only after a hard bitter struggle with sin and only after we have overcome it, do we experience blessed joy and peace. The tears come to my eyes when I think how often I have gone through the bitter struggles and then succumbed to sin while peace was in sight. And after I fell how far away it fled. Poor weak creatures we are, yet God is our Father and God is love, ever present, ready to enfold us and comfort us and hold us up. I have so much work to do to overcome my sins. I am working always, always on guard, praying without ceasing to overcome all physical sensations and be purely spiritual.

From her father, Dorothy inherited a great love of reading, as well as her journalistic bent. Books were her companions throughout life. Literature influenced and awakened Dorothy's religious sensibilities. It raised her consciousness of, and sensitivity to, the needs of the poor. A brilliant student, as an adolescent Dorothy read the works of Dostoevsky and Tolstoy. These great novels addressed the issues of good and evil, heroic service and sanctity, and had a profound effect on her. Some of her favorite maxims in later life are quotes from Dostoevsky: "Love in practice is a harsh and dreadful thing compared to love in dreams," and "The world will be saved by beauty," are ones she repeated often.

A quiet, intense young woman, Dorothy was such a good student that at sixteen she earned a scholarship to the University of Illinois at Urbana. Away from home, she resolved not to ask her father for financial help and determined to support herself by her own labor. For two years she supported herself by washing, ironing, and caring for children while attending

Dorothy, center, participating in a protest during her college years.

Dorothy and Tamar, about 1932.

college, taking only those classes that interested her. She began to adopt a radical view. Impressed by the Marxist slogan, "Workers of the word unite! You have nothing to loose but your chains," she began to think that charity wasn't enough; what was needed was work to get rid of the social evils themselves. She questioned the lack of saints who would "not just minister to slaves but [who would] do away with slavery." At eighteen, she quit school and moved to New York City to "get into real life."

Dorothy wanted to be a journalist, but being young and without a degree, she had difficulty finding a job. At last, she got a job on the socialist paper *The Call* at pay of five dollars a week. She moved from reading about radical-change movements to direct participation in them. Along the way she developed her lifelong connection with the poor and suffering.

Also along the way, this thoughtful young woman, who had written so beautifully of her daily struggle with sin when she was fifteen, allowed sin to win a battle or two. She had an unhappy love affair that ended with an abortion, a short common-law marriage with an anarchist, and she published an autobiographical novel called *The Eleventh Virgin*. Her words and writings from this time period indicate that although she slipped, her struggle was a constant one.

Nothing horrified Dorothy more about her past than the memory of the fact that she had killed her own unborn child in the womb. At one time, the painful memory caused her to attempt to track down and destroy as many copies of *The Eleventh Virgin* as she could find. Strong words from a priest in confession at this time remained with Dorothy all her life. He told her, "You can't have much faith in God if you're taking the life he has given you and using it that way. God is the one who forgives us, if we ask him; and it sounds like you don't even want forgiveness — just to get rid of the books."

In 1926, Dorothy was living on Staten Island with her common-law husband, Forster Battreham, when she became pregnant. To her, this seemed like a miracle and a revelation of the mercy and forgiveness of God. She was overwhelmed with the desire to give her child the religious faith that she, herself, was so constantly seeking, and determined to have her baptized in the Catholic Church. Her husband, an atheist, was passionately against all religion, especially the Catholic Church. When a sister began visiting to give Dorothy instructions in the Faith, Forster would leave angrily. Painfully, Dorothy wrote, "I knew that I was going to have my child baptized a Catholic, cost what it may. I knew I was not going to have her floundering as I had done, doubting and hesitating, undisciplined and amoral."

Tamar was born in July 1927. After a final and harsh break with Forster, Dorothy herself was baptized in December of that year. Of her conversion, she said "It was something I had to do. I was tired of following the devices and desires of my own heart, of doing what I wanted to do, what my desires told me to do, which always seemed to lead me astray."

Conversion and baptism alone did not bring her peace. She loved Forster and his defection hurt her; he left, and doubt remained. Only at her confirmation the following year did the uncertainty she felt finally leave her.

As a single parent, Dorothy struggled to earn a living as a freelance writer. She struggled, too, with the quandary of bringing together her radical convictions about an unjust social order and her religious faith. It seemed as if all the radicals who felt the way she did about the social order were atheists. On the other hand, almost all Catholics seemed to ignore any thought of working for the same social justice it preached.

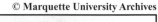
© Marquette University Archives

Dorothy occasionally wrote for two Catholic magazines that were concerned with social issues: *Commonweal* and *America*. Once, covering a communist–inspired "hunger march" from New York to Washington, D.C., she watched from the sidelines as jobless men and women were finally allowed, by court order, into the capital to bring their petitions for jobs, health care, and unemployment. She was struck by the feeling of her insignificant work since becoming Catholic. She realized she was "self-centered and lacking in a sense of community." She

Dorothy in about 1935.

was overwhelmed with the feeling that Christ must love these people, even if they didn't love Him. It was December 8, 1932, and Dorothy went to the unfinished shrine of the Immaculate Conception to pray in the crypt. "There I offered up a special prayer, a prayer which came with tears and anguish, that some way would open up for me to use what talents I possessed for my fellow workers, for the poor."

Her prayers for God's direction of her talents were answered the next day in New York City when she met Peter Maurin, who introduced her to the ideas that led to the founding of the Catholic Worker Movement in 1932. A French immigrant, Peter had been a Christian Brother in Paris. His faith was colored by his peasant roots. After leaving the Christian Brothers, Peter had spent some years in Canada and the United States doing menial work. Dorothy credited Peter with teaching her everything she knew. He introduced her to the great Catholic saints and writers of history, to the great traditions of Catholicism, and put flesh on Catholic social teaching for her. At the same time he presented his program of houses of hospitality, round-table discussions with scholars and workers for the clarification of thought, and agronomic communities or universities. It is clear, however, that as they worked together over the years, Dorothy and Peter influenced each other. From the beginning, Maurin was the theorist and Dorothy the activist in their partnership. His personalism gave a philosophical grounding to Dorothy's incarnational approach to life.

Catholic authors from the personalist movement centered in France provided much of the intellectual base for the Catholic Worker movement and its practical response in service to the gospels. They also influenced Dorothy's spirituality.

These authors emphasized the need to bring religious values to the moral and social issues of the day, the concept of personal responsibility, and the dignity of the human person both as an individual and as a member of society. They critiqued the bourgeois world of consumerism, acquisitiveness, and comfort-seeking and called for heroic sanctity. Dorothy integrated the personalist philosophy with the practice of the works of mercy: "Not only is there no chance of knowing Christ without partaking of that Food that He has left us (the Eucharist), but also we can't know each other unless we sit down to eat together. We learn to know each other in the breaking of the bread. When the stranger comes to us to be fed, we know because Christ told us so, that inasmuch as we have fed one of His hungry ones we have fed Him. That is why the most fundamental point in the Catholic Worker program is emphasizing our personal responsibility to perform Works of Mercy."

Dorothy Day and Peter Maurin believed that the works of mercy should be performed personally and at a personal sacrifice. This personal sacrifice involved voluntary poverty and a life of simplicity as opposed to consumerism.

All the writers that influenced Dorothy Day called for the spirit of heroism, identified simultaneously with sanctity and with a radical return to gospel living. They taught that the laity must follow the universal call to holiness and are called to be leaven for the common good in the world.

Peter urged Dorothy to use her journalistic talents and start a newspaper. When she questioned how to finance such a venture, he simply told her, "Pray. God sends you what you need when you need it."

Soon houses of hospitality followed. Almost immediately after the first issue of *The Catholic Worker* was published in 1933, it became part of a lay movement that even today is represented by houses of hospitality and other communities scattered across the United States and some other countries. The Catholic Worker movement has become well-known for offering an example of radical Christian living that centers on hospitality but which also protests violence and social injustice. Until her death, Dorothy, as well as other members of the movement, had often protested and gone to jail for acts of civil disobedience in support of their views. Dorothy's was a daily living of the way of the cross. "It is the living from day-to-day, taking no thought for the morrow, seeing Christ in all who come to us and trying literally to follow the gospel that resulted in this work."

Dorothy's vision and practical living out of the works of mercy themselves was unique. She stressed that since for the Catholic Worker the works of mercy included not only feeding the hungry, sheltering the homeless, visiting the sick and those in prison, and burying the dead, but also enlightening the ignorant, "We put the publication of the paper, our going out into the street and carrying picket signs and posters, giving out leaflets, and even, on occasion, going to jail as part of the works of mercy."

In the words of one who knew her well, Daniel Berrigan, S.J., Dorothy Day "urged our consciences off the beaten track; she made the impossible probable, and then actual. She did this, first of all, by living as though the truth were true."

In 1955, Dorothy became a Benedictine lay oblate. For years she had been drawn to the Benedictine charism, which places great value upon identification with Christ, on community, on hospitality, and on a harmony between work and prayer. As Dorothy understood it, this Benedictine-inspired program involved a life of voluntary poverty, as well as a synthesis of prayer, intellectual productivity, and manual labor. It was in such a setting that beauty and joy could flourish. Benedict's Rule emphasized the love of Christ as expressed in hospitality, based on the twenty-fifth chapter of Matthew: "I was a stranger and you welcomed Me."

All beauty spoke to Dorothy of God. This concept enabled her to see beauty hidden even in the lives of the poor. Once a donor gave Dorothy a diamond ring, which Dorothy put into her pocket. A little later that day, a rather demented lady, one of the more irritating regulars at the house, came in, and Dorothy gave her the ring. One of the staff asked Dorothy if it wouldn't have been better to sell the ring in order to pay the woman's rent for a year. Dorothy reminded the staff member that the woman had dignity and could herself choose to sell the ring and use the money for her rent. She also could enjoy wearing a diamond ring on her hand like the woman who gave it away. Dorothy asked, "Do you suppose that God created diamonds only for the rich?"

Dorothy and her grandchildren in the late 1950s.

The Benedictine emphasis on hospitality, a hallmark of the Catholic Worker movement, was, for Dorothy, closely related to the doctrine of the Body of Christ. Dorothy understood that the Christ dwelling within her loved the Christ within another, either actually present through grace or potentially through God's desire that all be members of Christ's Body. She recognized with Saint Paul that if one person suffered, all share in this suffering; if one person rejoiced, then all share in that joy.

Throughout her lifetime, Dorothy had to respond to charges that the Catholic Worker hospitality only maintained the present order and that they were only a partial, temporal aid to a few. Critics did not believe that this work would really change things. She wrote, in response to this charge, "We consider the spiritual and corporal Works of Mercy and the following of Christ to be the best revolutionary technique and a means for changing the social order rather than perpetuating it. Did not the thousands of monasteries, with their hospitality, change the entire social pattern of their day?"

Dorothy Day brought a unique gift to the Catholic Worker in her charism of pacifism. A pacifist prior to the foundation of the Catholic Worker, she wrote often of the opposition of "the work of love" to "the work of violence or war." In 1937 she wrote, "I do not believe that love can be expressed by tear gas or police clubs, by airplane bombardments and wholesale slaughter." Her pacifism was related to the Lord's teaching in the Sermon on the Mount.

Dorothy Day believed that prayer was the first duty of all those working for social justice, and that only that which was done for Christ, and with Christ, was of value. She loved the rosary and prayed it often. She felt that when people loved enough, they "repeat our love as we repeat our Hail Marys on the rosary." Dorothy had long lists of people for whom she prayed daily. When illness confined her to her room, she continued to receive daily Communion, and to pray constantly.

Dorothy looked to the saints as models for greatness in their capacity to love. Always returning to Matthew 25, she emphasized that in the end we will be judged on love — love in practice. She spoke and lived the maxim: "Love is the measure by which we shall be judged."

Many of the saints influenced Dorothy. She synthesized their thoughts into her own actions. The Little Flower, for example, talked of a "little way." Dorothy said, "Paperwork, cleaning the house, dealing with the innumerable visitors who come all through the day, answering the phone, keeping patience and acting intelligently, which is to find some meaning in all that happens — these things, too, are the works of peace, and often seem like a very little way."

At the age of eighty, Dorothy was ailing with the burdens imposed by a gradually weakening heart: coronary insufficiency and congestive disease, with occasional episodes of shortage of breath. She was also inflicted with swollen ankles, tiredness, loss of appetite, and a certain "moodiness" she was the first to acknowledge. Still, she worked in the soup kitchen. Pale and weak, she mentioned to a visiting friend that she felt lucky to be alive, although she had been looking forward with increasing eagerness to her departure to meet her Maker. Until that day came, she said she hoped she would be able to "be of some use, still, to our guests. I pray to God that He will give me a chance to pray to Him the way I like to pray. If I pray by making soup and serving soup, I feel I'm praying by doing. If I pray by saying words, I can sometimes feel frustrated. Where's the action that follows the words or precedes them? I may be old and near the end, but in my mind I'm the same old Dorothy, trying to show the good Lord I'm working for Him, to the best of my ability. The spirit wishes, even if the feet fail some days!"

At Maryhouse, the custom was that the one watching the house in the evening would dispense medicines to those who took them. One evening in 1980, a priest was "on duty" and went to give Dorothy the required heart medicine. After taking it, she looked at him and in a tired voice said, "Father, it takes so long to die." A week later, on November 29, her human heart gave out.

Father Emil Kapaun

1916-1951

Chaplain and Prisoner of War

Chapter 9

Four emaciated soldiers, dressed in the baggy blue uniforms of prisoners of war, walked together into Freedom Village. The village had been constructed to receive the repatriated U.S. soldiers held as prisoners of war (P.O.W.) in the Korean conflict. One of them, Captain Ralph Nardella, carried a three-foot crucifix, which had been carved in their P.O.W. camp, and which had been used in religious services there.

The crucifix, carved from firewood, was made in memory of the Catholic chaplain, Father Emil Kapaun. The grateful family of soldiers interred with Father Kapaun wanted to make a memorial to his memory that would continue to inspire them with hope, as he had done, and that could be a focus for the religious services led by Captain Nardella until their liberation.

When Father Kapaun realized that his death was imminent, he asked Nardella to continue religious services for the men, especially saying the rosary and prayers from the missal. Nardella promised, and kept his pledge. The other prisoners, of all faiths and beliefs, came together as a family in their admiration and respect for their heroic chaplain.

Major Gerald Fink, a Jewish Marine fighter pilot, did the carving on the crucifix. It took him two-and-a-half months to complete. Before doing the actual work, he had to make his own tools for the project. The knife was made from the steel arch support of a discarded boot and the chisel from a drain-pipe bracket. The twenty-six-inch corpus is carved from scrub oak and the forty-inch cross is of cherry wood. The crown of thorns was made from scraps of radio wire that resembles barbed wire. The soldiers titled the crucifix "Christ in Barbed Wire." Most of the carving was done during the day, without the permission of the communist guards.

After the crucifix was completed, Nardella used it, suspended from the ceiling, during the religious services. Some of the Chinese captors showed it respect; others, who had no Christian contacts, just stared at it. When the Big Switch operation to return the P.O.W.'s began, the Communists were unwilling to allow it to be taken from the camp. Nardella had to argue and

Emil at age six at the family home in Pilsen, Kansas.

haggle with them, and it was referred to "higher headquarters" before its removal was allowed. Today, the crucifix hangs in the lobby of Kapaun Mount Carmel High School, in Wichita, Kansas.

What was it about the mild, unassuming priest that inspired such dedication on the part of these men? To them, Father Kapaun had "spoken, acted, and looked like Christ." His four months of ministering on the front lines of battle before his capture, and two hundred two days of brutal captivity before his death at age thirty-five in a North Korean P.O.W. camp, were marked by incredible selflessness. His patriotism and spiritual leadership never faltered. Father Kapaun worked hard and then risked his life to meet the spiritual and physical needs of his fellow prisoners of war.

As one of the soldiers later testified, "I knew Father Kapaun; he saved my life, he made me fight to stay alive when dying was so simple; it was easier to die than live in those days; death was a welcome relief. We owe our present happiness to that heroic man who gave his all, who sacrificed himself for his fellow man, who worked himself to death.

"This man who was held in such high esteem — respected, admired and loved — was a real threat to our Communist captors. . . . They didn't know quite how to handle the priest because he could not be scared, threatened, cajoled or humiliated. On the contrary, they feared this man whom they couldn't break; they trembled at the control and influence he had with all the men. It worried them that this man could be so powerful with just his mild manner and soft speech where they resorted to screaming, threatening with all forms of sadistic torture known to these barbarians, and still couldn't influence us like this man of God."

Another prisoner noticed that Father Kapaun's helmet liner with its white cross on the front was lying on the garbage heap. When he asked the priest about it, Father said, "Mac, if I wear it, it will only antagonize the Chinese, so I won't; but the fact that it is lying on this garbage heap causes every man to see it and it reminds them of their God. You know, Mac, I often wonder just how many silent prayers are offered at this old heap. God moves in strange ways."

After Father Kapaun's death, the soldier got the liner and broke it, tearing off the part with the cross and hiding it. He was able to bring it home and sent it as a precious relic to Nardella, who passed it along with the other few salvaged possessions of Father Kapaun.

Emil Kapaun was born April 20, 1916, in a small farm house near Pilsen, Kansas. The first of two sons of a hardworking Bohemian farm couple, he was baptized in the parish church a few weeks after his birth.

As a child, Emil was taught to say his daily prayers in both English and Bohemian. Religious pictures, prayer books, holy cards, and mission magazines were prevalent in the Kapaun household, and even before he could read young Emil showed his later love for reading and study by looking at the pictures and asking for their explanation.

Emil loved the outdoors and enjoyed fishing. At the age of six he caught a large channel catfish; excitedly, he raced home to get his parents to come and see his catch. Unfortunately, the young fisherman had left his pole and catch near the bank; on the arrival of the excited child and his proud parents, no fish was to be seen. It had flopped back into the water, taking line and pole with it.

At the age of eight, Emil began learning to serve at the altar. He practiced each gesture kneeling before a tree in the backyard. Later he built an altar in the front room where he played at "being a priest."

As a farm boy, Emil could always find work to be done, and his parents recall that unlike most boys he didn't constantly find ways to avoid work. He developed skill in building and repairing farm implements. This skill would later be of great help in the P.O.W. camp.

Emil was quiet and retiring, with an arresting grin and a drawling, down-to-earth sense of humor. He attended grammar school at the Pilsen School, District 115, which was staffed by Sisters Adorers of the Precious Blood of Wichita, Kansas. A bright student, he finished all eight of the elementary grades in six years, with a record of good attendance and high scholastic achievement. He went to school an hour early in order to serve Mass for the parish priest, and often brought wild flowers he had gathered for the altar. He had a particularly deep devotion to the Blessed Mother.

In the fall of 1928, he began attending the Pilsen High School, which offered a two-year course. One of his high school teachers remembers that Emil was always interested in a magazine about the foreign mis-

Emil at his First Holy Communion.

sions. He read the magazine eagerly, and each month sent to its publishers a spiritual bouquet of prayers and sacrifices he had said and done for the missions. This sister was one of the first to recognize his vocation to the priesthood and suggested he apply to the Columban fathers, as Emil was worried that his parents would not be able to afford to send him to seminary. Emil wrote his appeal, and the Columban fathers agreed to accept him, although with no financial assistance. On receipt of their letter, one of the other sisters suggested that he talk with the parish priest, who immediately offered to pay Emil's way to the seminary and who thought Emil should become a parish priest. After talking the matter over, Emil and his parents agreed to the pastor's plan. The teenager seemed content as long as he could become a priest, but he always kept his interest in the foreign missions.

In September 1930, Emil went to Conception, Missouri, a boarding high school and college with a strictly classical course. In academic matters, Emil remained quiet and retiring, and always finished near the top of his class. Although he was not a particularly good athlete, he played football, and there was a certain toughness and pertinacity to him that always seemed to get him in the middle of things, no matter how hopeless the struggle. Schoolmates and professors alike describe him as "quiet, friendly, pleasing, likeable, dependable."

Emil as an eighteen-year-old seminarian.

At Conception, Emil worked in the sacristy and he customarily made a visit to the Blessed Sacrament before and after his work. He was active in dramatics, in the Blessed Virgin Sodality, and in the Polyphonic Choir. His favorite sport was handball, and he loved to walk, often hiking out to the grotto of Our Lady, two miles from the Abbey.

Although his board and tuition were covered with scholarships, he raised chickens for pocket money. His mother started them in the spring and he continued their care in the summer. During his six years at Conception, Emil returned home each summer to help with the farm work, especially the harvest. Once, a neighbor noticed he was not wearing gloves and asked him why. In a matter-of-fact tone he replied, "I want to feel some of the pain our Lord felt when He was nailed to the cross."

After four years at Conception, the registrar recommended him as a suitable candidate for the priesthood, and he began to study philosophy. In

September 1936, he began his theology studies at Kenrick Seminary, Saint Louis, Missouri.

In a letter to his lifelong friend and cousin Emil Melcher, written shortly before his ordination, Emil Kapaun confides his almost overwhelming amazement at his call to the priesthood: "Think what it means! To offer up the Living Body and Blood of Our Savior every day in Holy Mass to absolve souls from sin in Holy Confession and snatch them from the gates of hell. These and a hundred more duties and responsibilities make a person realize that the vocation to the priesthood is so sublime that the angels in heaven were not given the honor, no, not even the Blessed Mother who was never stained with sin — even she was not called to be a priest of God — and here I am called!"

Emil Kapaun was ordained June 9, 1940, in Wichita, and he celebrated his first solemn Mass in his home parish on June 20. Ten days later, he was appointed assistant in his home parish; the aging pastor needed a helper who could speak Bohemian.

The kind, capable, energetic young assistant joined completely in the spiritual, social, and material activities of the parish. He particularly enjoyed working with the children and the youth, joining the children on the playground when he did not have other duties. He did a tremendous amount of manual labor in the yard: mowing, cleaning up rubbish, trimming the trees, and cleaning the cemetery.

Father Kapaun's first taste of military service came when he was appointed auxiliary chaplain at the Army air base in Herington, Kansas, sixteen miles from his parish. He served here from January 1943 to July 1944, and reported to his bishop that he served Mass there every Sunday, and that he enjoyed working with the men, who seemed glad to see a Catholic priest. He detailed all his responsibilities in a letter and finished: "In short, dear Bishop, I love that work."

Father Kapaun was appointed pastor of his home parish on the retirement of the old pastor, but he bared his soul in a letter to his bishop. With his sensitive nature, he felt that he might be a moral barrier to some of the parishioners who had known him all his life, and that the parish would be better served with a priest who was more of an "outsider." A week later, the bishop recommended him for an Army chaplaincy, and he left for training school in August 1944. He graduated from Chaplain School in October 1944, and was assigned to Camp Wheeler, Georgia.

During his military service, Father Kapaun kept up a regular correspondence with his bishop, faithfully sending a monthly report and a letter; the bishop as faithfully replied. He also maintained a lively correspondence with his family and friends, sending lengthy letters filled with news and his own homey brand of humor. The deep spiritual dimension of this humble priest is also shown in the collection of his extant correspondence.

Father Emil Kapaun in uniform.

In 1945 he was sent to Burma and to India. He reported: "Our work with the soldiers is sometimes strenuous, sometimes dangerous, but always worth the effort. My outfits are scattered over a long distance of jungles and mountains. I travel mostly by aeroplane, making a round trip of five hundred miles every week to reach my units during May." Here at last he came in contact with the missionary priests and sisters he had read about when he was a child. He wrote, "Yes, one cannot help but be impressed that the Catholic Church is one and the same the whole world over; even little children are able to notice that."

On June 4, 1946, Chaplain Kapaun was separated from military service and after assisting at two parishes during the summer, he began post-graduate studies at Catholic University in Washington under the G.I. Bill. He completed a master's degree in education in February 1948. That spring, he was appointed pastor at Holy Trinity Church in Timken, a predominantly Bohemian parish. Although he loved his work in the parish, and the parishioners loved him, Father Kapaun became aware of a crisis in the chaplaincy for the Armed Forces and volunteered to re-enlist. His bishop agreed, and from November 1948 to January 1950, he served with the Anti-Aircraft Artillery Corps at Fort Bliss, Texas. Here there were only two Catholic chaplains for thirty thousand soldiers. In January 1950, he was sent to Japan in a training unit. As he wrote his parents, ". . . in case of war we will go first."

On July 10, 1950, Father Emil Kapaun accompanied "his men" on the invasion into Korea. Notes from his correspondence show his feelings, and indicate that he has lost none of his gentle sense of humor: "Tomorrow we are going into combat. I have everything in order, all Mass stipends, my will, etc." "My hand is not steady as we have gone through a whole lot. Found this paper in a Korean house. I pity the people." "We are right in the front lines of fighting. This is the worst and hardest war I have been in yet." "My how nice it would be to sleep in a bed. These fox holes are anything but comfortable, but they feel good when the enemy shells start bursting around us." "War is terrible! I feel sorry for the Korean people who have to leave their homes. As the Reds approach, nearly everything is destroyed homes, lives and food. I hope these people can return in time to harvest their rice so they have some food for winter."

In the middle of the battle area, Father Kapaun said Mass on the hood of a Jeep; the Blessed Sacrament was reserved on his own body. His letters home reflected his gratitude for the prayers of his people; his award of the bronze star was only mentioned modestly under general remarks in his monthly report to his bishop.

His pipe was Father Kapaun's inseparable companion, even in the thick of battle. A minor casualty occurred when the bullet of a North Korean sniper demolished the stem of his favorite briar. He quit smoking only long enough to whittle another stem from bamboo. In another battle, his pipe was again knocked out of his mouth. One International News photo showed a smiling Kapaun holding his broken pipe.

In the wild and hellish confusion of the attack that preceded Father's capture, no one person could give a complete and accurate account. From later testimony of the brave men who fought for their lives along with the valiant priest, we have a picture of Chaplain Kapaun and proof of his daring and devotion. The reports of his ordeal as prisoner of war and his edifying death were gleaned from repatriated American soldiers after their release from prison camp during the Big Switch operation at Panmunjom. He was mentioned constantly by those who had seem him in battle and in the prison compound. He was their hero, their beloved "Padre." The reports all mention his bravery, his constancy, his love, his kindness, and his solicitude for his fellow prisoners.

Sometime in October 1950, Father Kapaun took the wheel of a Jeep loaded with wounded men when the driver was killed and drove the patients over fire-swept roads to safety. He acted as if this was all in a day's work; to the men he became a legend. In the heat of battle, he continued saying Mass, ministering to the wounded, and, when there was spare time, burying the dead enemies and assisting with the graves registration of his own men.

During the Red attack on November 1 near Unsan, Father Kapaun went back in the fighting to assist Dr. Clarence Anderson and was captured along with twelve hundred other men. The priest and the doctor had both elected to stay with the wounded, though they knew that capture meant certain death. The weather was cold, but the last word from escaping prisoners was that the chaplain had continued to minister to the sick and wounded in spite of badly frostbitten feet.

A lieutenant captured within days of Father

Father Emil writing a letter home.

Kaipaun testified that the priest carried a wounded soldier on a stretcher for the entire ten miles to a small Korean farmhouse near Pyoktong. The officers were put in the farmhouse and forbidden to see the men, but Father Kapaun would get out and sneak down to the sick and wounded first, and then visit and pray with the men. He continuously volunteered for the burial details.

The same officer relates that the men were nearly starving, so Father would go on a ration run to get cracked corn, millet, and soy beans. Before he went, he said prayers to Saint Dismas, the Good Thief. The lieutenant was confident Father Kapaun's prayers were answered because "he would steal, or get away with, sometimes two one-hundred-pound sacks of grain plus pockets full of salt which was very scarce. Pretty soon all of us were praying earnestly to Saint Dismas, but Father succeeded much better than the rest of us.

"Every night we held prayers and he prayed, not only for deliverance of us from the hands of the enemy, but also prayed for the Communists to be delivered from their atheistic materialism."

In January 1951, the officers were moved back to Yoktung. It was bitterly cold, about twenty degrees below zero, and Father would get up early and build fires to boil water to clean the wounds and to drink. He often stuck his head in the door and hollered "hot coffee" as he handed the men a nice hot cup of boiled water. People were dying at the rate of ten to twenty a day in the camp and Father Kapaun often sneaked past the guards to the enlisted men's section. In his nightly prayers with the officers, he prayed for his men and also for the enemy, that they would be delivered from their false philosophy. In indoctrination sessions as the Chinese yelled and screamed, Father Kapaun softly and calmly refuted their statements. When they taunted him that he could not see or hear or feel God and that thus, God did not exist, Chaplain Kapaun quietly pointed out that Mao Tse-Tung could not make a tree or a flower or stop the thunder and lightening. He also told them that his God was as real as the air they breathed but could not see, as the thoughts and ideas they had, but could not see or feel. After a while, they let him alone, since they were afraid of his arguments.

At Easter in April 1951, the men noticed that their "Padre" was limping badly. The two doctors cornered him and found that he had a blood clot in his leg and that it was badly swollen. They forced him to lie on the floor and put his leg in a makeshift suspension, forcing him to lie that way for over a month. His only complaint was that he thought he was a burden to the others. About May 19, the pain in Father's leg became unbearable.

An officer who was with Father Kapaun shortly before the priest was taken to the "hospital" where he died relates, "In his last hour, he heard my confession and told me to dedicate my life to the Blessed Virgin Mary, that she would intercede for me to Jesus, her Son. He told all of us the story of the Seven Maccabees. A mother had seven children, all of whom refused to repudiate God to the king. One by one they were killed. She cried, not tears of pain and privation, but tears of joy. Her children were with God. As he told us this, his own eyes were filled with tears of agony, I knew and he knew I knew! Father Kapaun said, 'As you see, I am crying too, not tears of pain but tears of joy, because I'll be with my God in a short time.' "

When the Chinese came to take Father Kapaun to the hospital, his fellow officers protested, but to no avail. The hospital was a place where they took people to die; only about five officers out of sixty had ever come back from there. The Chinese saw a good chance to get the man they feared, now that he was helpless. Father knew, as soon as he saw the stretcher, where he was going.

As Father Kapaun was raised on the stretcher, he told one of the men, "Walt, if I don't come back, tell my Bishop that I died a happy death." Three or four days later, on May 23, 1951, Father Emil Kapaun died among the men he served, up on a hill overlooking the Yalu River in a Communist hospital of death.

Father Kapaun had disappeared from the Korean War front November 2, 1950. He was still listed as missing in action when, on October 18, 1952, in a ceremony at his home parish in Pilsen, the Most Reverend Mark Carroll, Bishop of the Diocese of Wichita, Kansas, offered Mass.

Captain Dolan, left, and Chaplain Kapaun, right, leading an exhausted soldier to safety.

Two Army chaplains assisted in the presentation of the Bronze Star Medal and the Distinguished Service Cross. The parents of the hero-priest insisted that the citations be given to the bishop. They said, "The bishop should have them; we gave our son to the diocese."

On July 12, 1953, the Kapauns at last received the long dreaded notification of Father Kapaun's death. His grief-stricken parents forwarded the letter to Bishop Carroll, who immediately announced special services for the first gold-star priest of the Diocese of Wichita. The bishop celebrated the Solemn Pontifical Requiem Mass in the Cathedral of Saint Mary, Wichita, Kansas. At a luncheon following the service, Major George Hickey pinned a Gold Star medal on Mrs. Kapaun and presented the parents a fourth decoration given by the Defense Department, the medal for service in Korea.

Father Kapaun was posthumously awarded the Prisoner-of-War Medal in May 1989, making him the most decorated military chaplain in United States history.

If God wills, perhaps a higher honor awaits this humble chaplain. In June 1993, the Archdiocese for the Military Services, U.S.A., began an investigation which may lead to a cause for canonization.

Saint Gaspar del Bufalo

1786-1837

Missionary for the Precious Blood

"For God, it is necessary to do much, quickly, and well; to do much, because He deserves a lot; quickly, because our life is short; and well, because that is the only way to serve God," said Father Gaspar del Bufalo to his concerned friends. The great missionary and apostle of the Precious Blood had been advised to rest because of his health. In spite of the ever-increasing toll on his health, he continued his prodigious activity. "I will take a rest in Paradise," he said.

Gaspar del Bufalo was born January 6, 1787, in Rome. His father, Antonio del Bufalo, was an assistant chief at the palace of Prince Altieri. Gaspar was baptized the day after his birth and received the names that tradition assigns to the Holy Magi: Gaspar Melchior Balthazar.

When Gaspar was two, he was nearly blinded as a result of measles. His devout mother took him to the nearby Church of the Gesu, to the altar dedicated to Saint Francis Xavier, and begged the saint to intercede for her son. Gaspar's vision was saved and he grew up with a great devotion to this great missionary saint. As a young man Gaspar burned with the missionary zeal to save souls, and he later held Saint Francis Xavier as the model and special patron for his own missionaries.

As a child, Gaspar learned generosity and devotion from his mother. He was inclined to be stubborn and had a fiery temper, which the loving patience of his mother did much to control. At times, the effort to control his temper would be too great. His face would flush, he would tighten his lips, and he would whisper, "My Lady, forgive me! I don't want to get upset . . . but you know what's going on inside me!" Sometimes his efforts failed and he would clench his fists, stamp his feet, and shout, "I am angry because I am angry!"

Gaspar's parents often took him to the Church of the Gesu, where he was fortunate to hear the greatest preachers of his time. Back at home, he would imitate these preachers for the benefit of his young friends. He would stand on a chair or table and shout "Repent, you sinners!" or repeat part of the sermons he had heard at church. Once, after hearing a particularly stirring account of the missions, Gaspar, along with a little chum, determined to run away to the mission fields. Their plan was discovered and the runaways ruefully returned home. The young Gaspar loved to have his mother tell him about the Passion of Jesus and the lives of the saints. At an early age, he began to make sacrifices and do penances beyond expectation for someone his age. He was serious and absorbed in his devotions, and at times his mother worried about his overdoing things.

Gaspar attended elementary school taught by the Scolopi Fathers from 1793 to 1797. Then he was admitted to the school of the Collegio Romano, where he completed his education, studied theology, and was ordained in 1808.

Gaspar's father often brought home sweets and other delicacies from the Prince's kitchen. Gaspar gratefully took his share of the treat to his room, where he would slide it out the window into the waiting hands of the poor. Additionally, he often gave away his own supper. The news spread and an ever-increasing number of destitute people began to come to him for food. Once, when Gaspar was late, the indigents began knocking on his window with sticks. When his mother discovered this innocent subterfuge, she chided Gasper for giving up his food, because his health was delicate. Gaspar could only answer, "These poor people are hungrier than I."

As his studies became more and more demanding, Gaspar still found time to perform numerous deeds of charity. On feast days he would visit the sick, comforting them and giving them spiritual encouragement. For the most needy, he brought little gifts. He taught catechism at his parish church. He was a member of a number of organizations where he gave talks and taught Christian doctrine. Gaspar's charity work branched out in a number of directions, and side-by-side with his works of material charity he provided spiritual help by holding lectures, organizing retreats, and preparing children for First Communion.

In spite of his prodigious activity, he maintained a high scholastic average, and won the school prize for theology. He obtained permission to take Communion two or three times a week, at a time when this was rare, and other days he found time in his busy schedule for visits to the Blessed Sacrament.

During Lent of 1806, one of the most famous speakers of the time, the bishop of Famegosta, came to preach at the Church of Gesu. Police had to be called in to control the crowds that attended his lectures. He was fascinated to hear that a young cleric, Gaspar del Bufalo, was transcribing all his sermons after listening to them. The bishop sent for the young man, and recognizing his extraordinary qualities, offered to give him lessons to help perfect his preaching skills. Gaspar also attended the Academia Ecclesiastica, which was frequented by the most learned of the Roman clergy. Here he developed his fascinating style of oratory which deeply moved his audiences and touched many hearts. In 1807, Gaspar was ordained deacon. Shortly thereafter, he experienced a bitter testing of his soul, becoming terrified of the awesome responsibility of priestly consecration. In his humility, he thought about remaining in the diaconate, and going no further. Fortunately, Monsignore Vincent Strambi (now Saint Vincent) showed him that these thoughts were the work of the devil, and encouraged him to become a priest.

Saint Gaspar del Bufalo

Gaspar was ordained July 31, 1808, at the age of twenty-two. He began his missionary apostolate among the *barrozzari*, the teamsters and farmers from the Roman countryside. He had a number of holy priests as co-workers, and in collaboration with one of these, Monsignore Francesco Albertini, Gaspar established the Pious Union of the Most Precious Blood in 1808.

In Gaspar's deepening devotion to the Precious Blood of Jesus, he found the key to his sanctity, strength for his apostolate, and courage to endure in a period that was increasingly difficult for the Church. Gaspar had a deep personal appreciation of what Jesus did for us in His Passion and Death, and seeing the need for positive actions in compassion to our neighbors in need, began to preach devotion to the Precious Blood. He did not consider worship of the Precious Blood simply another devotion, but as the summary of all religion. He said, "All the mysteries are summed up in the infinite price of Redemption, as the lines of a circle to the center which they have in common!"

In 1809, Napoleon suppressed the Papal States, and in retaliation for his excommunication, he arrested the pope and sent him into exile. Not content with striking the shepherd, Napoleon began to persecute the flock. Members of the clergy were required to take an oath of allegiance to the emperor, under the threat of deportation. June 13, 1810, the young priest Gaspar, along with his father, stood before the magistrate. "I cannot, I must not, I will not!" was Gaspar's reply to the magistrate's request for him to take the sacrilegious oath. The judge tried to get Gaspar's father to convince his stubborn son. His father bravely replied, "Citizen, first shoot me and then my son, but don't ask me to do that."

On the morning of departure, Gaspar asked his mother for her blessing. He could not hold back his tears. He was driven away in a carriage escorted by mounted police. As his mother raised her hand in a last gesture of blessing and farewell, a friend standing nearby heard her say, "I prefer to die without my Gaspar than to see him a traitor in Rome." This was the foresight of a holy mother; she died before his return. "I had better call this city '*Dis-piacenza*' (displeasure) instead of '*Piacenza*' (pleasure)," Gasper wrote to a friend about their first stop. Gaspar and several companion priests were thrown into a cell infested with mice that crawled over them at night. Their scarce food was poorly cooked, and the air was damp and unhealthy. Although his heart was heavy, his faith was strong. "My sins deserve even worse, and what I am suffering for Jesus Christ is little," he wrote.

Within two months, his always precarious health deserted him, and he developed a violent fever which left him close to death. He requested Viaticum, and appeared completely resigned to death.

Monsignore Albertini believed that the time was ripe to reveal to Gaspar a prediction made by Sister Maria Agnese del Verbo Incarnato, who had died a holy death in Rome in 1810. She had told the monsignors, "You will get acquainted in the time of greatest anguish for the Church, with a young priest filled with zeal for the glory of God. Under the oppression of enemies and pain you will develop a deep friendship with him, and you will become his spiritual director. The distinctive character of this man is his devotion to Saint Francis Xavier. He is destined to be an Apostolic missionary and will establish a new congregation of missionary priests under the invocation of the Divine Blood. Through him, God will bring about a revival of moral principles for the salvation of souls, for the renewal of the diocesan clergy, and to turn all people from indifference and disbelief back to love and faith in Christ crucified. He is going to be the herald of the Divine Blood, to stir up sinners and sectarians in these difficult times for Christianity."

Gaspar's fever left him and his strength returned. For Gaspar, the suffering and confinement in the prison became a circumstance and a place for reflection on God's plan for him. At last, Gaspar was transferred from Piacenza to Bologna, where he was the guest of the Marquis Bentivoglio. He took advantage of the freedom he was allowed there, making his host's chapel a meeting place for retreats, lectures, and spiritual exercises. With Albertini, he studied a way to establish a congregation of missionaries, and began to draw up plans for an institute of sisters also dedicated to the Most Precious Blood.

At Bologna, he received the sad news of his mother's death, and shortly thereafter his friend Albertini was moved to Corsica and locked in the prison of Bastia. The French government was annoyed by the resistance of this handful of priests who refused to pledge allegiance to Napoleon. In 1812, Gaspar once again refused to take the oath. He was arrested and locked in the prison of San Giovanni in Monte for five months. In this fetid dungeon he and his fellow priests were not allowed to read, write, or celebrate Mass. Finally, after repeated petitions to the prison managers, they were allowed to celebrate Mass one at a time, but only in isolation. They resorted to all kinds of tricks in the middle of the night in order to celebrate Mass together. In May 1813, Gaspar was called and refused to take the oath for the third time. He and his faithful companions were moved to yet another dungeon and turned over to a jailer who had been labeled the "enemy of God and religion." Not all could stand the harsh conditions. Some died in prison and some submitted to the oath and returned to Rome.

In December, Gasper was asked a fourth time to pledge allegiance to Napoleon; again he refused. This time he was scheduled to be deported to the island of Corsica. While he waited in Florence for the order to proceed, news came that Napoleon's fortunes had changed in his ill-fated Russian campaign. Many prisoners took advantage of the confusion and fled into the countryside. Gaspar took shelter with a friend, and resumed his propagation of the devotion to the Blood of Jesus. At last, after four years of exile and prison, Gaspar returned to Rome and resumed his ministry with the Institute of Saint Falla, the Oratory of Sancta Maria in Vincis, and the other Roman pious institutions. In 1814, Gaspar applied for admission to the Society of Jesus. As he was making final preparations to leave for the novitiate, he received a summons from Pope Pius VII. In his audience, Pope Pius charged Gaspar to begin a ministry of the missions. Accepting the pope's word as the will of God, Gaspar abandoned his plans to join the Jesuits and began the fierce activity which would last until his death.

The twenty-three years of his missionary apostolate were marked by uncommon hardships and sufferings, but Gaspar was blessed by God with frequent supernatural interventions. According to the pope's wishes, Gaspar prepared to travel throughout the Italian peninsula to participate in the moral and religious renewal of the Papal States which had been so infected with anti-Christian ideology during the reign of Napoleon. Gaspar had joined Operai Evangelici while in Florence. This group of evangelical workers, begun in Rome in 1813 by Father Gaetano Bonanni, existed to promote the missions.

Gaspar was preaching in a village in Umbria called Giano during the winter of 1814. Near the town stood the old monastery of San Felice, abandoned and almost in ruins. Gaspar requested the property from the pope. In spite of a number of problems and misunderstandings, the property was finally turned over to Gaspar and his companions. In July 1815, Gaspar gave up his post as canon of San Marco in order to be free to devote himself entirely to the missions. Pope Pius VII blessed the new institute, and Gaspar, along with Father Bonanni, left for San Felice to begin the necessary renovations.

The Congregation of the Missionaries of the Most Precious Blood of Jesus was officially founded on August 15, 1815. The goals of the new congregation depended essentially on preaching. According to the original rule, the missionaries did not accept any commitment that would bind them to a fixed residence. It was not until the current century that the rule was modified to allow the members to participate in pastoral care, education, and other forms of apostolate to meet the current needs of the Church. Gaspar's original companions in the institute were faced with a difficult task. The Papal States were a mission area which needed to be liberated from godlessness and apathy, and to be won back to living faith in Christ. These sturdy mission priests traveled throughout the peninsula with this goal in mind.

Missions, usually lasting fifteen days, were held in cities, towns, and the countryside. The missionaries spread throughout the surrounding areas to invite the people. There were usually four sermons per day. In the evening, the missionaries went out into the streets, preceded by a crucifix, and gave short talks to urge the people to repentance and to invite them to come to the church the following day. Missions included penitential processions, devotions to the Precious Blood, and preaching sessions held in the prisons and hospitals. Special lectures were offered to the clergy, the intellectuals, religious institutes, and schools.

The missionaries lived a hard life. Travel in those days was much different from today. Coaches could travel only on some major roads; even then, the ride in these unwieldy conveyances was rough, and often ended in a spill when the coach overturned. The rest of the territory was navigated by foot or by riding a horse or a mule. Bandits and criminals abounded in the woods. There were no public address systems, so the missionaries had to speak loudly. Finally, the people were not always willing to hear their message. One of the priests wrote to the pontifical delegate in 1815, "I was sent into a forest infested by wild beasts rather than to intelligent beings . . . a mob of wretches without manners and without any discipline. It is a real miracle that riots did not break out at any moment of the day . . . I sneaked into this city . . . on foot and in disguise, in order to avoid a popular uprising."

Gaspar's program had but one objective: to win precious souls back to Jesus Christ, who had redeemed them at the price of His Blood. He promoted devotion to the Blood of Jesus in every way, and inspired people to turn with faith toward the Virgin Mary as their special protectress. The missionaries began in Benevento. Before they arrived, the walls of the city were covered with blasphemous posters that ridiculed the Eucharist, Blessed Mother, and other truths of the Faith. The enemies of the church stirred up the people to revolt against the pope and cast off the "chains" of religion. After fifteen days of the missionaries' work, however, a miraculous change occurred in the city. Even the authors of the sacrilegious posters were among the penitents who publicly confessed their sins. When the missionaries left at the end of their successful visit, a large crowd accompanied them for several miles.

Time after time, unusual happenings were reported as the missionaries preached in the towns. In Forlimpopoli, the local sectarians began a slanderous campaign. There were threats of murders and riots if the missionaries dared to enter the city. The courageous missionaries began their work in spite of the threats, and a great number of people were converted. This made the sectarians so furious that they hatched an assassination plot. Four men, chosen from among the most radical, were sent to execute Gaspar. As one of the would-be assassins stood in front of the missionary, ready to stab him, Gaspar quietly asked him, "Do you want to go to confession, brother?" Gaspar's voice was so filled with love and charity that the assassin dropped his weapon. His three accomplices, fearing the reaction of the crowd, began to flee in their carriage, without waiting for their companion. The carriage overturned in a ditch and the three drowned. When Gaspar learned of their death, he prayed with tears in his eyes that God would have mercy on them.

At Medola, some sectarians tried to poison Gaspar. A young druggist and a servant in the house where the missionaries were staying prepared a poisonous drink. During a long speech, Gaspar customarily took a drink to ease his throat, and he was holding the lethal cup when two of his missionaries came in and told him to throw the stuff away. The druggist had repented of his part in the conspiracy and revealed the plot. Gaspar smiled, blessed the glass, and drank the deadly potion. He then chided the druggist and his missionaries with the words of Jesus, "Oh men of little faith, why did you doubt?"

Bilocation was another phenomenon seen at Medola. Penitents going into church could see Gaspar hearing confessions. The same people, stepping out into the nearby square, could see the saint preaching there at the same time. Gaspar's long apostolic journey was often marked by such signs of divine intervention, which increased the fame of his sanctity and multiplied the persuasive power of his preaching.

At one town, a group of youths did not want to hear the saving words of the missionaries, so they organized a party out in the countryside. The voice of the saint reached them clearly and distinctly as if they were in the audience, in spite of the fact that they were over three miles away. In another town, a dove hovered over the saint's head the entire time he was speaking. At Comacchio, some German soldiers came to listen to the saint although they spoke no Italian. To their amazement, they realized they could understand all that was being said. A number of times bad weather was forestalled or stopped when the saint made a gesture of blessing in the air.

In 1822 during a mission in Vallecorse, Gaspar met the young Maria Mattias. She became aware of a divine call reaching out to her through the instrumentality of this holy missionary, although she had no idea what God wanted her to do. After two years of prayerful waiting, she approached Father Merlini when he returned to town for the Lenten services. Father Merlini, on the advice of Saint Gaspar, became her spiritual director. In 1834, Maria established the first community of the Sister Adorers of the Most Precious Blood. Today, this institute has spread to many countries all over the world, and Maria herself is a candidate for the honors of the altar.

Although missionary work formed the bulk of Saint Gaspar's ministry, his tireless activity extended to many other forms of teaching and preaching endeavors. Periods of time between missions were filled with spiritual exercises for clergy, nuns, prisoners, and other groups. He opened a seminary to train future priests for mission work, and taught theology to the students He drew up a constitution for the congregation, and on his visits to Rome kept up with the works he had been active in while he was a youth. Highway robbery was a plague in the papal states at this time.

The hill country in the provinces of Marittima and Campagna were infested with bandits who attacked travelers, held hostages for ransom, and were often guilty of rape and murder. A number of remedies had been tried, but nothing seemed to work. The city of Sonnino was considered a hotbed of the problem. In 1819, a decree was issued to destroy the city completely, and about thirty houses were razed to the ground. Respectfully, Gaspar wrote to the pope pointing out that to save Sonnino spiritually, the brigands must be socially redeemed. He suggested appropriate remedies, and closed by begging the pope to be merciful. The pope understood the solution proposed by the saint: those who had grown wild must be redeemed from evil by attracting them to good. Gaspar was appointed to head a project of ongoing missionary work in this area.

Refusing any armed escort, our saint took some of his best missionaries and went out to win the hearts of these wayward people. After months of patient work, when he had established an atmosphere of trust, a letter came from a group of the outlaws requesting the saint to intercede with Rome and obtain pardon for them.

Corrupt officials, dishonest police, and their accomplices who were guilty of the abuses that had caused a great deal of the problems in the area resorted to a campaign of slander. First they attempted to discredit the missionaries with the bandits, and then with Rome. In the maelstrom of hatred, Gaspar advised his companions to persevere, and told them, "Let us laugh to the glory of God."

After a great deal of opposition, Saint Gaspar was able to obtain pardons for the brigands, and these men were reintegrated into society and their souls were returned to Jesus Christ.

The whirlwind of slander lasted for some time. Whenever a group is doing great good, jealousy and hatred will crop up in opposition. After the death of Pope Pius VII, his successor Pope Leo XII called Saint Gasper to an audience in which he questioned him extensively, more in the manner of a judicial inquiry than a papal audience. At the end of the meeting, the good pope embraced the missionary and told him, "You have many enemies, but do not be afraid. Leo XII is with you!" After the saint left, the pope turned to his court dignitaries and said, "Canon del Bufalo is an angel!"

Two more popes reigned during Gaspar's life: Pius VIII and Gregory XVI. Gaspar's enemies continued their persecutions and his work was often called into question. Gaspar believed that his institute was God's work, and had faith that God would protect it. He asked for nothing for himself. "Let God do whatever He wills with my life, with my reputation and with my honor. If my abasement could serve His glory I surely shall count my being despised as my share of that same glory."

In spite of the opposition, Gaspar continued his work.

He said, "I only ask one blessing of God: to always be busily engaged in the work of the missions and to die while attending to this holy ministry."

Towards the end of 1836, cholera was spreading all over Italy. The pope ordered public prayers and a series of missions to be held in the churches of the city. Saint Gaspar was in a precarious state of health resulting from a recent high fever and persistent cough. Nonetheless, he accepted the task of preaching at the Chiesa Nuova. When his companions told him to refuse the assignment, pleading his bad health, Gaspar told them, "I am happy to do the will of God and to give my life for the sake of Jesus Christ." With an extraordinary effort, Gaspar was able to conclude this mission, the last of his life. Then he returned to Albano. When cholera broke out in Rome, panic spread among the populace, and many fled the city to seek shelter in neighboring locations. Gaspar, on the other hand, left Albano and returned to Rome. Weak and exhausted, he visited hospitals and homes, bringing help and consolation to the afflicted. Often he carried lifeless bodies to help those who were burying the dead. At last, totally exhausted, he could do no more and returned to his spiritual family at Ancona.

When Cardinal Franzoni learned of the serious condition of Saint Gaspar's health, he ordered him back to Rome in hopes that the native air would be helpful. His illness, however, was progressively worsening. He was able to stay on his feet until Christmas Eve, but afterwards was unable to leave his bed. The attending physician advised bloodletting. Gaspar had predicted he would die as soon as blood was taken from him, but he accepted the doctor's advice in obedience. Two bleeding treatments were given, and his condition worsened. Viaticum was administered and afterwards Gaspar spent the day in an ecstasy during which he was heard talking to his crucified Lord. Another saint, Vincent Pallotti, administered the last rites to Gaspar, and witnessed his death. As he later testified in the beatification procedures, "The countenance of the servant of God was shining with the splendor of gentleness, happiness, and peace. Considering everything in a Christian way, I had to say and to repeat again and again that the view excited a desire to be united with him in the agony of his death."

The body of the saint was laid out in the church of Saint Paul for six days, while thousands of mourners passed by. Miraculously, it remained fresh and incorrupt as if he had just passed away. Missionaries were stationed by the body to prevent excesses of piety, such as the woman who attempted to cut a finger off the saint. Most simply passed by, content to touch the corpse with rosaries and other personal objects of devotion. Some asked for and received wax drippings from the candles by the bier. Others had special requests and several cures were reported. One woman requested to be allowed to touch the hand of the saintly missionary to her face. Her request was granted and she was cured of an acute skin infection. A man who had been tormented by high fevers for a long time swallowed a tiny piece of wax from a candle near the coffin and was immediately healed. A young man who was partially blind implored the saint's help, and touched a handkerchief to the body. At home, he placed the cloth over his eyes. Not only were his eyes healed, but he also felt a great conversion and his entire life was changed.

Such a shower of miracles began that the investigation into his cause for beatification began shortly after his death. Gaspar del Bufalo was beatified in 1904, and was canonized by Pope Pius XII in 1954.

In 1960, before announcing the opening of the Second Vatican Council, Pope John XXIII went to pray at the tomb of Saint Gaspar, calling upon him to intercede for the success of the council. He called devotion to the Precious Blood of Jesus the "Devotion of Our Times."

Blessed Gianna Beretta Molla

1922-1962

Martyr for the Unborn

Chapter

II

"Save the child. Don't worry about me provided that all goes well for the baby." Discovery of a fibrous tumor in her ovary in her second month of pregnancy left Gianna Beretta Molla with three choices. She could remove the tumor and her uterus containing her unborn child, and certainly save her life. She could remove the tumor, and, by procured abortion, the child. This second choice would save her life and mean that she could probably have other children later. The third choice was to remove the tumor while attempting to save the pregnancy. This choice might save the life of the child, but would put the mother's life in grave danger. Because she was herself a doctor, Gianna knew full well the danger to her own life. She made a heroic choice, and asked the surgeon to operate in such a way as to save the pregnancy.

The baby's life was saved, and Gianna continued the rest of the pregnancy trusting in prayer, thanking God, and attending to her duties as wife, mother, and doctor with indomitable strength. A few days before the birth, with supreme trust in God's mercy and Providence, she told her doctor, "If you have to choose, there should be no doubt. Choose — I demand it — the life of the baby. Save him."

On April 21, Gianna Emanuela was born, and seven days later the heroic young mother died of complications in giving life to her fourth child.

Giovanna Francesca Beretta was born in Magenta (Milan) on October 4, 1922, the tenth of thirteen children born to Alberto and Maria Beretta. (Eight children survived childhood.) Alberto worked for the Cantoni Firm of Milan. Maria was a housewife who thought of marriage as a state of life to be dedicated to the service of God by serving her husband and all the children that God would give her. The family lived in Milan, and spent annual fall vacations in Magenta at their parental homes. Later, Gianna lived in the house where she was born for thirteen years, from 1942 until the time of her marriage.

The early life of little Gianna was spent in Milan and Magenta, in serenity stamped with seriousness. The loving parents taught their children a deep faith, a burning spirit of charity, and a generous and firm character. They consecrated their family to the Sacred Heart of Jesus. When their oldest daughter became ill, the family moved in 1925 to Bergamo, where they lived until her death in 1937. Daily, Alberto made the long commute of fifty-eight kilometers to the city. Each evening he returned to join his loved ones at supper and family prayer. Both parents were Third Order Franciscans who imbued their family life with Fransciscan spirituality. From her father, Gianna inherited the Franciscan attraction to prayer and compassion for the poor. From her mother, she gained strength of character united with humility. From both parents she learned a faith not made of formulae but of daily life with fidelity in even the smallest things, and the sacredness of work.

All of the Beretta children were lively, and Gianna and her younger sister Virginia were inseparable companions in many childish tricks and pranks. Because of chronic illness, the oldest sister, Amalia, had to stop her studies. She devoted herself to the care of the younger sisters and helped to prepare them for First Holy Communion. Gianna received the sacrament on April 4, 1928. From this time, she became a daily communicant, attending Mass with her mother or her sister, because Communion had become her indispensable daily food.

This same year, 1928, she began school at the Beltrami elementary school. She later attended three other elementary schools, where she obtained good marks in all subjects except physical education before beginning secondary school in 1933. For the four years of secondary school, Gianna was a student who had very little attraction for academic studies and who much preferred art, music, and painting to racking her brain on scholastic texts. She loved the outdoors, movement, and living with, and for, her dear family. Each year

The young Gianna (far left) with her family.

she barely passed her subjects; she had to repeat exams in Italian and Latin. Her last year of school her beloved sister Amalia died at the age of twenty-six.

Friends recall Gianna as a good girl, always happy and smiling, but with a natural reserved quietness. She was studious and paid attention to the explanations, but in preference to her studies her attentions were more directed to the demands of faith and religious piety. A morning meditation or a visit to the Eucharist were for her a source of joy, love, and strength. She always had her rosary in her pocket or bag and recited it daily. She was attentive to other people and preferred to sacrifice herself in order to see others happy. Her friends say that her faith was catching, and after being around her they were attracted to the life of the Church.

In 1937 the Berettas moved to Genova-Quinto al Mare so the older children could go to the University of Genoa. Gianna attended the fifth year of secondary school with the Dorothean Sisters. Here the entire family entered into the life of the local parish and Gianna became an active member of Catholic Action. In 1938 she attended a course of spiritual exercises which led her to a point of greater conscious and generous dedication to God. A notebook she wrote contains resolutions for herself, written at the end of each talk, as well as a number of prayers that reveal a striking spirituality centering around Jesus in His Mother and in His saints. In one of these she wrote a promise which she faithfully kept for the rest of her life: "O Jesus, I promise to submit to everything that you may allow to happen to me; only let me know your Will."

Gianna finished her fifth year with greatly improved studies, and after a year at home to strengthen her delicate constitution she returned to school and finished her classical studies in June 1942. In the three years of Lyceum she had brilliant results in her scholastics and excellent marks in conduct.

In 1942, both of the devout Beretta parents died. This same year, Gianna was admitted to the Faculty of Medicine at the University of Milan. In 1945, in her fourth year, she transferred to the University of Pavia, where she was awarded the diploma in medicine and surgery in March 1950.

As an active member of Catholic Action, Gianna held a number of offices with the group. In particular, she was attracted to work with the young girls whom she invited to be "living witnesses of the greatness and beauty of Christianity." Through her work with this group she found opportunity to display an exquisite charity to the poor, and to teach by her actions many lessons of charity and the value of suffering, all done in an atmosphere of joy. She also enjoyed playing the piano, singing, and painting. She loved all of nature and spent free time in mountain climbing and skiing.

In 1950, Gianna opened her consulting rooms at Mesero with her brother Ferdinando, also a doctor. She also served I.N.A.M. as a doctor from 1950 until her death. Mesero is a small town of two thousand people about five kilometers from the family home at Magenta. Daily she pedaled her bike, rode her motorcycle, or drove a car back and forth in her service to the sick, whom she considered as brothers. She told a friend, "There are far too many doctors who for the sake of money do every possible thing. According to me, the medical profession must be a mission." Although Gianna served many private patients, as well as those whose services were paid for by insurance, she also often exercised her profession as doctor without any reward in the free service to the poor. She continued her university studies to specialize in pediatrics, obtaining her degree from the University of Milan in 1952.

Dr. Gianna continued her assistance to the sick until the last day before entering the clinic for the birth of her last child. If the patient was poor, in addition to a free examination she often provided medicines and money. Sometimes if a patient could not continue doing the same kind of work because of health reasons, she helped them find a new job. She left her consulting rooms only after the last patient was examined.

The deeply religious Gianna had felt a call to be a missionary in Brazil, where she hoped to join one of her brothers, a priest, when she met Pietro Molla, an engineer employed by S.A.F.F.A. of Milan and a devout

Gianna on her wedding day ...

... and smiling on her honeymoon.

member of Catholic Action. The pair first set eyes on one another at the consulting room where Pietro was seeing Dr. Ferdinando because of an indisposition. The next year they met again in the hospital where Giana was treating Pietro's sister. Their third meeting was in the summer of 1950. Gianna's nurse lived in the same building as Pietro, and from 1950 to 1954 they came in contact from time to time with a rapid exchange of greetings and brief smiles. From that time, the couple began to see each other more often. Gianna began to question her vocation and, after much prayer, and consulting with her spiritual director, she became convinced that it was God's will for her to marry and raise a family. Pietro officially proposed to her on February 20, 1955.

A family outing with Pietro and Pierluigi.

On Saturday, September 24, 1955, Gianna Beretta and Pietro Molla were married in Magenta by Don Giuseppe Beretta, the brother of the bride. He blessed them and exhorted them to witness to sanctity. Extant letters from the period of their engagement and from their married days illumine a couple deeply in love, who saw in matrimony a special grace and a state which can sanctify those who are called to it.

Gianna wrote, "With the help and blessing of God, we shall do all in our power that our new family may be a little cenacle where Jesus may reign over all affections, desires and actions." "We become cooperators with God in the work of creation. Thus we can give Him children who will love Him and serve Him. Pietro, will I be able to be the type of wife you always wished to have? I want to be!"

After a month-long honeymoon, the Mollas began their married life in a two-story house close to the parish Church of Ponte Nuovo, a suburb of Magenta. The house was situated within the walls which enclosed the S.A.F.F.A. Works where Pietro had been promoted to director. Gianna continued with her medical practice.

Pietro, in his work, traveled frequently, and so there are many tender letters from Gianna which testify to her love for Pietro and, later, her happiness in her motherhood. In one letter written in 1959, Gianna tells her husband that she has been to church to thank God. "It is to thank Him for all the graces that He continuously bestows on you that I go to Church every morning. May He help me to be a good mother and to make you happy always."

Due to the fact that they were not young at the time of their marriage (she was thirty-three; he was forty-three), the Mollas wished to start their family as soon as possible. In spite of the fact that each pregnancy was a risk to her always fragile health, their union was soon blessed with sweet fruit. A son, Pierluigi, was born in 1956; Maria Zita was born in 1957; and Laura Enrica Maria was born in July 1959. After a number of miscarriages, Gianna began the pregnancy which resulted in the birth of Gianna Emanuela in 1962.

A devoted mother holding Pierluigi (left) and Maria Zita (right).

Toward the end of the second month of this last pregnancy, Gianna began to experience pain, and the doctor diagnosed a fibrous tumor in the ovary. She made her heroic choice, and the tumor was successfully removed while the life of the child was spared. As a doctor, she knew very well the risk she was running. The least she could expect was to submit to a caesarean section. Gianna appeared the same to those who saw her; she was determined not to make the uncertainties of her impending delivery weigh heavily on others, especially her husband. Her smile remained, if a bit more pensive.

In December, the Mollas attended a festive party with the Rotary Club of Magenta. Pietro was the founding president of this chapter. Gianna, wearing a fashionable dark evening dress, stood beside her husband while a photographer captured her serene and pensive expression in one of the last photographs of her.

Doctor Molla understood full well how her pregnancy was proceeding, but kept silent in order to keep others from suffering. She lived courageously in hope of getting through the delivery safely; each evening before leaving her office she had her nurse give her an injection which would help her "not to lose her child." Although she did not talk much with other people, she constantly spoke with God in prayer. Her husband later wrote a tender document for his children telling them how their mother suffered without complaint, praying, and offering her complete surrender to the will of God.

On the way to the hospital on April 20, 1962, Gianna broached the topic of her choice and told Pietro that she wished it was his choice, too, so they might be united "for life." She reminded her husband, "if they should ask you which of the two lives they should save, do not hesitate . . . first, the life of the child." At 11:00 a.m. on April 21, Gianna Emanuela was delivered by cesarean section.

Septic peritonitis set in and Gianna suffered greatly from atrocious abdominal pain. She begged the doctors not to give her stupefying drugs so that she could remain herself. She willingly submitted to all the treatments made to save her life. When the pain became too bad, she stuffed her mouth with a handkerchief and bit it in order to avoid crying out. In semi-delirium she cried out for her own dead mother. She told her sister Ginia, a religious, of her greatest suffering, having to die leaving small children. She almost died on the night of the twenty-fourth, but was brought back by the prompt and loving care of her brother and sister doctors. With a sweet calmness that seemed almost superhuman, she told Pietro, "I was already on the other side and if you only knew what I saw. One day, I shall tell you. But as we were too happy, too well, with our marvelous children, full of health and grace, with all the heavenly blessings, they sent me back here to suffer again, because it is not just that we should appear before the Lord without much suffering."

Pietro tells us, "I am sure that from that moment Gianna, in her sufferings and in her agony, has never ceased her colloquy with the Lord and her communication with Heaven. . . . She already belonged to Heaven."

On Thursday the twenty-seventh and Friday the twenty-eighth, Gianna was unable to communicate because she could not swallow, so she begged that the host be laid on her lips. Many times she repeated, "Jesus, I love you!" or called the names "Lord" and "Mama." She knew she was dying and she remained conscious almost to the end. On Friday night, the loving wife and mother who had willingly submitted her will to the will of God began her agony. She begged to be taken home and at four in the morning of April 29 she was returned to Ponte Nuevo to her bridal bed, near the room where her three treasures were sleeping. The baby remained in the hospital of Monza. In her silent dying, she heard the calls of her children; she was unable to answer because she was unable to speak. Then as a final sacrifice, she heard the children being taken away to the home of a relative. About 8:00 a.m., she too left on her journey to life.

The portrait of a loving mother.

The body of Gianna was laid on a bier in the drawing room which had served as a playroom for her children. Saturday, Sunday, and Monday were days of an endless pilgrimage of people who were praying, crying, and imploring. People of every type realized her great sacrifice and recalled her past kindness. A large number felt the need to go to confession before visiting the room where she lay in state. On Monday at 3:00 p.m., many people from the surrounding area gathered at the Molla house to accompany Gina to her last abode. The body was carried to the little church of Our Lady of Good Counsel, a few steps away, where a funeral board over the door carried the inscription: "Deeply moved, we remember Dr. Gianna Molla née Beretta, who in full awareness offered herself for the life of her daughter Gianna Emanuela." After the funeral rite, the procession formed again with the bier held at shoulder height to escort the beloved mother and doctor to the cemetery of Mesero. The casket, covered with red roses, was escorted by priests and ladies with lighted candles. Immediately behind walked Pietro holding the hands of the two oldest children. The long procession in prayer passed through the streets of Ponte Nuovo, Magenta, Marcallo, and Mesero to the cemetery. Here she was buried in the tomb of priests until November 1965, when her remains were transferred to the new chapel built by Pietro for his family.

The cause of beatification of Gianna was set in motion in 1972 by the archbishop of Milan, Monsignor Giouanmi Colombo.

In a postulatory letter to the pope written April 11, 1978, by the seventeen archbishops and bishop of the Episcopal Conference of Lombardy, they said, "God has wished to give us a stimulating and persuasive example of a wife and mother of our Church of Milan. The servant of God, Gianna Beretta Molla, has fulfilled . . . the commandment of love: that love which Jesus Himself said is the greatest and consists in giving one's life for those we love." They continued, "Such a mother-martyr for the love of God and in obedience to His commandment which forbids killing, witnesses and exalts the sublime heroism of a wife and Christian mother. Out of respect for every life which is always a gift of God to men she sacrificed her own young life to say 'yes' to the Christian duty of love." Gianna was beatified by Pope John Paul II on April 24, 1994, in the presence of her husband and children.

Saint Ignatius Delgado, Saint Vincent Liem, Saint Dominic Kham, and Companions

Eighteenth and Nineteenth Centuries

Martyrs of Vietnam

Chapter

12

In 1988, Pope John Paul II canonized a group of one hundred seventeen martyrs who suffered and died for the Faith during the eighteenth and nineteenth centuries in the region we know today as Vietnam. Ninety-six of the martyrs were Vietnamese; eleven were Spaniards; and ten were French. Fifty-eight of the group were associated with the Missions Etrangères of Paris (Paris Foreign Mission Society) and fifty-nine were members of the Dominican family. They were martyred at different times and places.

Untold thousands suffered and died to bring the message of Christ, have it take root, and bear fruit on Vietnamese soil. The history of Christian martyrdom in Vietnam runs concurrently with four centuries of recorded Church history in the area. In 1553, an imperial edict forbade the "false doctrine of Jesus" being preached by a certain Ignatius. From the outset, Christianity in Indochina came under official disfavor.

Christianity was brought to Vietnam in 1627 by the Jesuit Father Alexander Rhodes. He began his work in Tonkin, in the northern part of the country. Later in the same century, Dominican missionaries accompanied Portuguese exploration and mercantile ventures into the Indian Ocean. After failing to evangelize Buddhist Cambodia, these Portuguese Dominicans went to Vietnam, where they were better received by a population where the majority had no formal religion other than that of ancestor worship. By the end of the seventeenth century, Spanish Dominicans from Manila were also working in Vietnam.

During the first centuries, aliens were not allowed permanent residence, so efforts at evangelization came and went, as did the missionaries. In the seventeenth century, tolerant reigning dynasties allowed more fruitful work on the part of Jesuit missionaries. These Jesuits arrived in the region after the Japanese ruler forced them out in an attempt to eradicate the Christian faith from his empire. During the second half of that century, a second group of missionaries came from the Missions Etrangères de Paris, which was founded in 1659 to spread the gospel in Southeast Asia.

The political organization of Vietnam was much like China's: an empire ruled by dynasties that succeeded each other. Local viceroys and mandarins assisted the emperor, who was considered the "son of heaven," and was an absolute ruler.

In 1711, Emperor An Vuong issued the first Edict of Persecution of Christians. Many Christians lost their lives in 1745 and again in 1773.

Under the reign of Gia Long, from 1802 to 1820, Christianity was officially accepted and grew rapidly. By 1820, there were an estimated four hundred thousand Vietnamese Catholics, in three apostolic vicariates. The special development of catechists was characteristic of the Vietnamese Dominican Mission. They lived in community, in houses called *Houses of God*, and were dedicated to evangelization under the authority of the Apostolic Vicars. Women were organized and called sisters, and were consecrated to works of charity. Lay Dominicans and members of the Confraternity of the Rosary were numerous and of great help to the missionaries. A large infrastructure of social works began to be created in Vietnam.

After this brief time of peace, persecution again mounted and reached unparalleled heights during the reigns of emperors Minh Manh, Thieu Tri, and Tu Duc (1830 to 1864). This time period is known as the "era of the martyrs," and thousands were slain. After 1832, the Annamite king Minh Manh excluded all foreign missionaries and required native Christians to apostatize by trampling on the cross.

The tortures inflicted on the martyrs are beyond imagination. One particular type was the wearing of a *cangue*, two planks tied with chains, one on the shoulders and one on the feet. Christians were beheaded, burned, strangled, whipped, exposed to raw weather, crucified, and starved. Pliers were used to tear the flesh away bit by bit; Christians were placed in cages like animals, and some were continuously beaten with sticks.

A decree promulgated in 1854 by Emperor Tu-Duc was meant to eradicate the Christian religion from his dominions. Between the years 1856 and 1862, thousands of Christians died. In the province of Nam-dinh alone there were more than 30,000 martyred. In the 50 years before the establishment of the French Protectorate in 1883, an estimated 300,000 Christians suffered death or extreme hardship as their homes and villages were destroyed. It was possible to gather clear information on only 1,700 of them; for some, even the year of their death is unknown. By 1917, the causes of 1,315 were introduced. Representative groups of clergy and laity, both native and foreign, were beatified at various times since 1900.

Within the scope of a work such as this it would be impossible to detail even a brief history of the one hundred seventeen canonized martyrs. We must content ourselves with mention of only a few of these heroic martyrs, and hope that the reader may be inspired to seek out more information.

Dominican Fathers Vincent of Peace Liem, a native of Nam-dinh province, and Father Hyacinth Castaneda, a Spaniard, were martyred together in 1773. The Mandarin in charge of the execution ordered that they be taken out of the cages and allowed to walk in the streets because "We gain nothing toward destroying the Christian Religion by humiliating two such honorable persons." Father Vincent did not try to flee or defend himself. He said, "May God's will be done. If the Lord wants me to suffer I am ready."

A courageous farmer, Dominic Mao, was arrested and brought to trial by edict of King Tu-Duc. When the judge demanded that he renounce his religion and promised to free him to return to his wife and children, Dominic replied, "Why do you

A painting of the one hundred seventeen martyrs of Vietnam used at their canonization.

tempt me, judge? Am I a child that I shall tremble with fear of suffering or be seduced by the wiles of earthly pleasures, forgetting that I must never offend God? Had I wished to trample on the cross, I could have done so at home, when I might have been spared the outrage of imprisonment and the fatigue of my journey here. Do with me what you will, for I shall never trample on the cross or renounce my religion." Together with several other Christians, Dominic walked prayerfully to the place of execution and was beheaded.

Agnes Thanh Thi Le was a Christian housewife who refused to renounce her faith. On July 12, 1841, she was taken to a field to be trampled by an elephant. She requested beautiful clothes and an ebony fan. When she was asked why she wanted this elegant mode of dress at such a tragic time, she quietly replied, "I go to meet the Divine husband."

Father John Charles Cornay, a native of France, was ordained in Tonkin at the age of twenty-five. In 1837 he was framed when weapons were hidden in his garden and he was denounced for inciting a rebellion. He was kept in confinement for over three months, first in a cangue and later in a bamboo cage too small to lie down in. He was beaten and forced to watch some of his faithful Christians being tortured. He remained cheerful and even his persecutors gathered to hear him sing hymns in his fine voice. At last he was sentenced to death by being cut to pieces. In his last letter to his parents, written from his cage, he said, "I weep when I think of your grief, but the thought that by the time you get this letter I shall be able to pray for you in Heaven comforts me, both for your and for myself. . . . So be comforted; soon it will all be over and I shall be waiting for you in Heaven." Surrounded by a large crowd, he sang as he walked firmly to his execution. His sentence was to be cut to pieces, meaning that his limbs would be hacked off joint by joint and at last he would be beheaded by a sword. The presiding officer, apparently out of respect for such a courageous man, ordered that he be beheaded first and the mutilation carried out afterwards.

Father Peter Dumoulin Borie, another French priest, suffered in 1838. Beating him with bamboo sticks, his persecutors rubbed salt in his wounds in an attempt to make him disclose those who had sheltered him. When the official taunted him and asked, "Does it hurt?" Father Borie replied, "I'm made of skin and bone like other men; of course it hurts. But I was happy before and I am happy now." His spirit could not be broken. At the time of his execution, the official in charge expressed his regret that the priest had to die. Father Borie told him, "To show how grateful I am for the privilege of dying thus, let me prostrate before the man who has brought it about." The officer would not allow it and burst into tears. The executioner was drunk; after seven blows from the sword the head was only partially severed. With Father Borie, two Annamite priests, Vincent Diem and Peter Koa, were strangled.

The Spaniard Dominic Henares became a Dominican bishop whose virtues and knowledge gained him great respect even from the Mandarins. He was especially noted for his charity to the poor, and as a witness at the process of beatification stated, "At the hour of siesta instead of resting he mended clothes for the poor." One of the judges at his tribunal said, "The hand trembles and it does not dare to sign the sentence of this man." In 1838 he was beheaded and his head thrown into the river. Three days later it was rescued by a Christian fisherman. Francis Chieu Van Do, Bishop Henares's faithful lay-catechist, was executed along with the bishop. His last words were "Into your hands, Lord, I commend my spirit." Three days after his execution, a dew of blood appeared on the leaves of the trees at the place of his execution.

Another Spanish Dominican, Bishop Clement Ignatius Delgado, after serving in the Vietnamese mission for forty-eight years, finally fell into the hands of the infidels in 1838. Weakened by his advanced age and by being caged like an animal, he fell prey to sickness, and after suffering with incredible patience he fell asleep in the Lord before the death sentence could be carried out. The order for beheading was carried out anyway so that his head could be exposed to public view for three days before being thrown into the river. Almost four months later, it was recovered incorrupt.

Father Joseph Fernandez had been working in the Vietnamese mission for thirty years when the persecution of Emperor Minh-Manh broke out in 1838. He was forced into hiding and in one of his hiding places he met the aged priest Father Peter Nguyen-ba-Tuan. They journeyed together, sharing hardships as they fled from the persecution. Taken prisoners at last, Father Fernandez was caged and Father Tuan was given chains and a heavy cangue, which he wore along with his rosary. Father Fernandez limped to the place of his execution, where he was beheaded. When Father Tuan came before his judges and was ordered to step on the cross for forgiveness, he answered, "It is true that I am old and weak, but I know that God will give me the strength to suffer and even to die for him. I will not step on the cross. I just want the day to come when I will offer my head and shed all my blood for the Lord of Heaven, whose religion is the only true one." He died quietly before the sentence could be carried out.

Augustine Huy Phan, Nicholas The Duc Bui, and Dominic Dat Dinh were three Christians who were soldiers. Augustine had lived a disorderly and licentious life, but had repented and become a Christian; Nicholas and Dominic were his close friends. At one point a count of Christian soldiers was made by order of the emperor and then a purge was begun to make them renounce their religion. One by one they apostatized or escaped because of the tortures. They were punished by carrying a heavy cangue day and night, and at certain hours stocks were applied. Once a day, crucifixes were tied to their feet and they were forced to walk on them. At last, in order to avoid the misfortunes and torments that threatened their families, the three miserably gave way and stepped on the cross. They soon recognized their sin and crying bitterly, they confessed, repented, and determined to go to the capital to present themselves to the emperor. When the time came, Augustine and Nicholas went before the emperor and protested in his presence, "Death rather than step on the cross." Dominic was on duty, but told the others he would follow. In June, 1839, Augustine and Nicholas were sawed in half with a sickle and their bodies thrown into the sea. On hearing of his companions' death, Dominic took leave of his family and went to the capital, praying his rosary along the way. He was strangled in July 1839.

Francis Xavier Mau Trong Ha was so well-known for his natural goodness and joyful friendship, he won the friendship and admiration of all wherever he went. When caught and jailed, he catechized more than forty neophytes, several of whom also died for their faith. When someone asked how conditions in the jail were, Francis displayed his sense of humor when he replied, "The only thing missing is a mosquito net and a boy to fan us."

In 1839, as he led the group to the place where they were to be strangled, his face seemed resplendent and he joyfully said goodbye to those he passed. Every now and then he would raise his eyes to heaven and happily say, "I am going there." A witness for the beatification process testified that three years after his death, when his grave was opened to transfer his remains, a sweet scent was noticed by all present and that luminaries had appeared like lamps to light the work of the transfer, which had begun in the dark.

The young Thomas De Van Nguyen was a tailor and the father of a family when he learned his house was to be searched. He gathered his family and said, "Serve and adore our Lord. In this battle which I am about to enter, I only depend on the grace of God. . . . I will not return." Turning to his wife, he said, "If you love me, beg God to give me strength and . . . nothing more." Thomas De was strangled in 1839.

The aged catechist Thomas Toan was tortured and then jailed, where he was starved according to the command of the Mandarin in 1840. Once in a while, a non-Christian sergeant named Tham risked his life to bring Toan some food. He took him some clean clothing and saved the old as a pious relic. At last, when Toan was close to death, the sergeant, like the Good Thief, said to him, "Remember me when you get to heaven."

On July 28, 1858, the Spanish Dominican Bishop Melchior Garcia Sampedro and his two Vietnamese helpers left the jail in Nam-dinh about seven in the morning for the place of their execution. Surrounded by troops and wearing heavy cangues, they walked happily to receive their crown of martyrdom. On arrival, the youths were tied to stakes and the bishop was made to walk, wearing a heavy chain, through the more populated streets. He was escorted by twenty executioners with bared swords and five hundred soldiers, two elephants, four horses, and musicians playing "infernal" music.

As he passed the young helpers, Bishop Sampedro, himself only thirty-seven, exhorted them to be brave and not fear. Thereupon, the Mandarin, who was riding one of the elephants, ordered their heads to be cut off. The executioners threw the heads in the air like balls for the crowd to see. A small mat covered with a cloth was prepared and the bishop was made to lie face up on it. His hands and feet were stretched out and tied to stakes. On the Mandarin's order, five executioners armed with hatchets with dull edges cut off the bishop's legs, then his arms. It took twelve blows to sever the legs and the blood flowed freely. The victim at last had no more strength to repeat his litany of the name of Jesus. Fifteen blows were required to sever the head. At last the stomach was cut with a sharp knife and a hook pulled out the entrails. The pagan executioners ate the bishop's liver, believing they would get his valor in this manner. The mangled body was wrapped in the cloth and buried in a deep hole, covered with dirt. The Mandarin attempted to make the elephants step on the grave but the animals refused, seeming to know the respect due to the martyr. The head was torn apart and thrown into the river. A Vietnamese priest who was well camouflaged watched this execution and presented the testimony during the process of beatification.

Dominic Kham was born in the Christian community of Quancong. A rich man, he became one of those called *Notables*. Under the reign of Tu-Duc, he was accused of sheltering European missionaries. He urged his fellow townsmen not to apostatize and was jailed. Here he became an ardent preacher, attracting many to the Faith. With his alms, he helped many of the prisoners in their misery. He walked joyfully to his execution, praying with his companions. He died with the name of Jesus on his lips. Dominic's son Luke Cai Thin was also a rich Notable and a judge for three years. Neither bribery nor torments could make him abandon his religion. He carried a crucifix and prayed the Act of Contrition as he walked to his execution. He died with his father on January 13, 1859.

Two of our Vietnamese saints are called Joseph Tuan.

One, a fifty-year-old priest, was jailed by Tu-Duc. While in jail he showed such love to everyone, including his captors, that all admired him greatly, especially for his life of prayer. At his execution, he knelt and invoked the name of Jesus, commending his spirit to God before receiving the blow that severed his head. He was martyred in 1861.

The other Joseph Tuan was a poor farmer, honorable and pious. Imprisoned at the age of thirty-six, he was ordered banished. The prefect ordered him to step on the cross, but instead he knelt and adored it. Kissing it, he said, "I give you infinite thanks, my God. Be my refuge and my strength!" Thereupon he was sentenced to be beheaded. He joyfully walked to his execution, praying litanies all the way. He was executed in 1862, while invoking the name of Jesus. Another farmer, Lawrence Ngon, also adored the cross rather than step on it. He, too, was beheaded in 1862.

The young martyr Dominic Ninh was born in Trung-linh and entered a marriage arranged by his father, as is customary in many oriental countries. When the marriage proved to be a disaster, the couple separated, but Dominic never said an unkind word against his wife, giving a true example of patience. He began to study the Chinese language, and in 1862 he and four other youths of the House of God were taken prisoner. On hearing their sentence, all concurred and said, "This is the day of our return to our true home." Two of them were thrown into the air by an elephant and then stomped to death. The others were strangled, but in order to torture them before their death the executioners loosened and tightened the garrote for half an hour or longer until finally they gave the rope one last hard jerk to kill them. They then twisted their heads until they were completely turned around. They also burned the feet and left the bodies strewn on the ground.

Dominic Huyen and Dominic Toai were both fishermen and model family men. Imprisoned, burdened with the cangue and shackles, they endured every suffering with patience and resignation. They led a life of prayer and encouraged the other prisoners to do the same and to face death bravely for Christ. Sentenced to be burned to death, the two fishermen walked bravely to the cane-and-straw hut where they met their blazing death, offering their lives to God as the flames shot skyward. Two other fishermen and fathers were Peter Dung and Peter Thuan Van Dinh. They also were burned to death in 1862. Allowed to return home to say goodbye to their families before their execution, Peter Dung told his children, "Be happy that I am going to die for Jesus Christ."

Theophane Venard, a priest of the Paris Foreign Mission Society, was beheaded at Hanoi in 1861 at the age of thirty-one. Possibly the best known of the Vietnam martyrs, his fascinating letters, especially those written from a cage during his last two months, have inspired generations of French missionaries. In one letter to his family he wrote, "Can you fancy me sitting quietly in the center of my wooden cage, borne by eight soldiers in the midst of an immense crowd . . . I hear some of them say 'What a pretty boy that European is! He is gay and bright as if he were going to a feast.'" To his brother he recalled how his vocation began in their home village, when at the age of nine "I took my pet goat to browse on the slopes of Bel-Air, I used to devour [read] the life and death of Venerable Charles Cornay, and say to myself, 'and I, too, will go to Tonkin, and I too will be a martyr!'"

After seven years of apostolic labor in Indochina, Theophane was betrayed, captured, and sentenced to be beheaded. During his imprisonment, two Christian women, cooks for the prison, managed to sneak the Eucharist to him, and shortly before his death a priest in disguise came to hear his final confession. The march to the place of execution was impressive; led by a military commander followed by a detachment, the condemned man was escorted by twelve men with drawn sabers. Cymbalists and drummers preceded two Mandarins riding on elephants, who were to preside over the execution. A hundred soldiers brought up the rear. The long parade passed between two rows of onlookers and a murmer of sympathy and pity grew gradually. His hands folded and his eyes lifted to heaven, Theophane walked steadily in spite of the chains, singing the Magnificat. At the place of execution near the

Saint Theophane Venard

river, the soldiers formed a circle and removed the prisoner's chains. The family of a condemned man could render him a last service by providing a cloth so that the execution would not take place on bare ground. Theophane's "family," in the persons of a deacon and the two cooks, spread a cloth near the board where his sentence was written. Theophane turned and blessed the crowd, then knelt on the cloth and prayed. The drunken executioner ordered the young martyr to take off his clothes, and Theophane removed his tunic to bare his torso and stretch out his neck. His arms were tied behind his back and the drummers and cymbalists increased their din. From high on the elephant, the first Mandarin shouted the order into his megaphone and the drunken executioner performed several dance steps and let fall his saber. He only nicked the left cheek of the martyr. Four blows still did not detach the head and he was forced to use the saber like a saw to finish his grisly chore. Grabbing the head by the opulent hair, he brandished it before the Mandarins.

The widow Nghien, followed by some Christians and several pagans, soaked pieces of cloth in the blood of the valiant martyr. A brief shower, totally unexpected at that season, fell for a minute and then the sun reappeared. From the crowd came murmurs, "It is a sign from Heaven." The Christians put the body in a coffin and buried it, carefully marking the tomb. According to the sentence, the soldiers put the head in an openwork basket and suspended it from a well-guarded pole for three days, and on the third day it was thrown into the river.

After eleven days, the martyr's head was recovered by Christian fishermen who had been searching for it. His body was exhumed and was brought to the Christian cemetery at Doông-Tri, where it was reverently reburied. A month later, all the land where the execution had taken place was washed away by the Red River.

After his death, Theophane's letters were published in the Annals of the Propagation of the Faith and made a great impression all over France. The letters were reprinted by the religious weeklies, then by magazines and newspapers in other parts of Europe. One whose life was especially marked by these texts was the young Sister Thérèse of the Child Jesus. She who was to attain sanctity herself and who was one day named patroness of the missions said of her favorite martyr, "He is a little saint. There is nothing out of the ordinary in his life. He loved the Immaculate Virgin very much, his family too. And so do I. I cannot understand those saints who did not." Saint Thérèse wrote a long hymn in his honor, and near her death requested a relic of the martyr to console her in her own agony.

The blood of the martyrs of Vietnam have, like seeds, grown and blossomed into the sturdy faith of Vietnamese Catholics. Catholic Vietnamese communities thrive where the Vietnamese have immigrated to other parts of the world. Although the Church in Vietnam is still repressed by the Vietnamese government, from all accounts it is a strong one and growing.

Faces of Holiness

Names of the martyrs

The names of the one hundred seventeen Vietnamese martyrs canonized June 19, 1988, by Pope John Paul II are listed below. Eleven were Spaniards, ten were French, and ninety-six were Vietnamese. Fifty-eight of the group were associated with the Paris Society of Foreign Missions and fifty-nine were associated with the Dominicans. As always when dealing with saints whose names are in other languages, there are sometimes a variety of spellings; our list has been anglicized for North American readers. In Vietnam, names are written with the last name first. In our list, we show their Christian name, their Vietnamese first name, middle name, and last name (when known).

The Spanish-Vietnamese martyr-saints are: Peter Almato, Matthew Alonzo-Leciniana, Valentine Berriochoa, Hyacinth Castaneda, Clement Ignatius Delgado, Joseph Mary Diaz Sanjurjo, Joseph Fernandez, Melchoir Garcia-Sampedro, Francis Gil de Federich, Dominic Henares, and Jerome Hermosilla.

The French-Vietnamese martyr-saints are: Jean-Louis Bonnard, Jean-Charles Cornay, Etienne-Theodore Cuenot, Peter Dumoulin-Borie, Francois-Isidore Gagelin, Francis Jaccard, Joseph Marchand, Peter Francis Neron, Augustine Schoeffler, and John Theophane Venard.

The native-Vietnamese martyr-saints are: Paul Tong Viet Buong, Dominic Cam, Francis Xavier Can Nguyen, Joseph Canh Luong Hoang, Francis Chieu Van Do, John Baptist Con, Thomas Du Viet Dinh, Bernard Due Van Vo, Andrew Dung-Lac An Tran, Peter Dung Van Dinh, Vincent Duong, Paul Duong (Dong) Vu, Peter Da, Dominic Dat Dinh, John Dat, Matthew Dac (Phuong) Nguyen, Thomas De Van Nguyen, Anthony Dich Nguyen, Vincent Diem The Nguyen, Peter Duong Van Truong, Matthew Gam Van Le, Dominic Hanh Van Nguyen, Paul Hanh, Joseph Hien Quang Do, Peter Hieu Van Nguyen, Simon Hoa Dac Phan, John Hoan Trinh Doan, Augustine Huy Viet Phan, Dominic Huyen, Laurence Huong Van Nguyen, Michael Hy Dinh Ho, Dominic Kham Viet Pham, Joseph Khang Duy Nguyen, Peter Khanh, Peter Khoa Dang Vo, Paul Khoan Khac Pham, Thomas Khuong, Vincent of Peace Liem Quang Le, Luke Loan Ba Vu, Paul Loc Van Le, Joseph Luu Van Nguyen, Peter Luu Van Nguyen, Dominic Mao, Dominic Mau, Francis Xavier Mau Trong Ha, Philip Minh Van Phan, Augustine Moi Van Nguyen, Michael My Huy Nguyen, Paul My Van Nguyen, Jame (Giocobe) Nam Mai Do, Paul Ngan Nguyen, Joseph Nghi (Kim) Dinh Nguyen, Laurence Ngon, Dominic Nguyen, Dominic Nhi, Dominic Ninh, Emmanuel Phung Van Le, Peter Quy Cong Doan, Anthony Quynh (Nam) Huu Nguyen, Joseph Ta Trong Pham, John Thanh Van Dinh, Agnes Thanh Thi Le, Nicholas The Duc Bui, Peter Thi Van Truong (or Pham), Joseph Thi Dang Le, Thomas Thien Tran, Luke Thin Viet Pham, Martin Thinh Duc Ta, Martin Tho, Andrew Thong Kim Nguyen, Peter Thuan Van Dinh, Paul Tinh Bao Le, Dominic Toai, Thomas Toan, Dominic Trach (Doai), Emmanuel Trieu Van Nguyen, Andrew Trong Van Tran, Peter Truat Van Vu, Francis Trung Van Tran, Joseph Tuan (Hoan), Joseph Tuan Van Tran, Peter Tuan Ba Nguyen, Joseph Tuc, Peter Tuy Le, Peter Tu Van Nguyen, Peter Tu Khac Nguyen, Dominic Tuoc Dinh Vu, Andrew Tuong, Vincent Tuong, Dominic Uy Van Bui, Joseph Uyen Dinh Nguyen, Peter Van Van Doan, Joseph Vien Dinh Dang, Stephan Vinh Van Nguyen, Dominic Xuyen Van Nguyen, Vincent Yen Do.

Blessed Isidore Bakanja

circa 1880-1909

Martyr for the Scapular

"The White man did not like Christians . . . he did not want me to wear the scapular. He yelled at me when I said my prayers."

The Zairois catechist, Isidore Bakanja, groaned as he answered the questions of the Trappist missionary priest, Father Grégoire. The youthful catechist lay on his stomach, as his back was one large festering sore and his hipbones protruded from his skin. He promised the priest not to harbor hatred in his heart against Longange. This man, a white Belgian supervisor and avowed enemy of religion, had caused Isidore to be so cruelly beaten with an elephant-hide strap studded with nails that the young catechist was dying of his wounds. Isidore went further than forgiveness; he said, "Certainly I shall pray for him. When I am in Heaven, I shall pray for him very much."

The death of the young black man was not an isolated incident. In the Belgian Congo in the early 1900s, white colonizers often treated the native Africans in an inhumane and cruel manner. Agents, especially of companies dealing in rubber and ivory, perpetrated barbarous brutalities that today shame any fair-minded observer. King Leopold II of Belgium had requested Pope Leo XIII to send missionaries to the crown's colony, hoping that the humane activities of the missionaries would mollify the often inhuman treatment of the natives. At the pope's request, the Trappists of Westmalle, Belgium, sent priests to work in the central Congo. They began their work in 1895, close to present-day Mbandaka. These staunch missionaries had much work to do for the most elementary needs of the poor, sick, and illiterate populace. Soon they began to undertake apostolic trips to the interior of the region, where they often met hateful opposition from the white colonizers whose misconduct the missionaries denounced.

Isidore Bakanja was born into the Boangi tribe sometime between 1880 and 1890. There is no record of the exact date of his birth; natives were considered nonentities. His name first appears among the baptismal records of the missionaries. As a youth, he worked as an assistant mason in

Mbandaka, where he met the Good News of Christianity. He became one of the missionaries' most fervent catechumens and was baptized in 1906. Isidore, who was to die for refusing to discard his scapular, had been trained to see in this devotion the external emblem of the unsurpassed gift of faith. For Isidore, the brown scapular and the rosary were the badges that identified him as a Christian.

When his contract for work in Mbandaka finished, Isidore eventually went to work as a servant-boy to a Belgian colonizer, and followed his employer into the bush near the equator to work on a large rubber plantation. On this plantation there was an avowed anti-Christian and freethinker named Van Cauter, also called Longange. He often stated that religion was a farce and that priests were "stupid," "ignorant," and "zeros." He called the missionary priests by the pejorative name "mon père."

Isidore used his free time to teach the other natives about prayer and the Christian religion. He told his cousin that Longange had told him not to teach his people how to pray. His own master, Reynders, told Isidore that if he wanted to pray he should pray in his heart but not to let anyone see him praying with his rosary in public.

In such a tense, hate-filled, and antireligious atmosphere, things were

An artist's view of Blessed Isidore with his scapular and rosary.

bound to come to a head. One evening when Isidore and his friend Iyongo were serving their masters at supper, Longange spied the brown scapular around Isidore's neck and commanded him to remove it. Isidore, however, was too fervent a Catholic to discontinue wearing his scapular, his "habit of Mary," which, to him, marked him as a Christian. A few days later, on noticing that Isidore still had his scapular, Longange flew into a rage and had Isidore beaten with twenty-five strokes.

The other blacks, all non-Catholics, did not understand Longange's raging at the "animal of stupid priests." Yet all, to a man, were certain of the reason for the beating. The cook, Mputu, testified, "Only Isidore was Christian in Ikili. At that time we did not know what a Christian was. Longange always called Isidore 'animal of stupid priests.' We didn't know what 'stupid priest' was, we never heard anyone speak of it. When Isidore was beaten, we thought that Longange's rage was provoked by that piece of cloth which Isidore always wore around his neck."

February 2, 1909, Longange and two other Europeans were relaxing on the veranda, having afternoon coffee. Longange sent his boy after Isidore, who was walking toward the marshland nearby to say his prayers.

When Isidore asked Longange why he had summoned him, the Belgian accused him of teaching his workers about Christianity. He ripped the scapular off his neck and tossed it to his dog. He then grabbed Isidore by the neck and threw him to the ground, ordering one of his domestics to beat Isidore. This man, Bongele, was terrified of the Belgian and began whipping Isidore as hard as he could. Two other servant boys assisted, holding his hands and feet while Longange kicked the fallen catechist. Although Isidore begged for mercy, the beating continued until Bongele's arms could not take it any more. More than two hundred blows had ripped Isidore's back apart.

Fearing that Isidore would report him to some superior, Longange commanded him to get up, but the young catechist fell back into his blood that covered the ground. Longange then had him dragged to the rubber-processing room, chained by his feet, and laid on a tattered mat drenched with blood and covered with excrement. For several days he was left here with his wounds unattended. The cook Mputu and another domestic, Iyongo, secretly aided him, changing his position and leaving a bowl of rice and water near him. Isidore hardly had the strength to lift these to his mouth, and insects and the acrid smell of burnt rubber added to his torment.

On hearing of a pending visit by the company director, Longange panicked and ordered Isidore to go to a different town; he also sent Isidore's master, Loname, to get him away from the camp and the possibility of his mentioning the incident to the director. When Isidore protested that he could not walk, Longange threatened him and, doubled up with pain, the young catechist set off. Once out of view, he hid in the forest. Mputu found him and brought him some clothing, food, and a fire to ward off the night chill. When Longange discovered that Isidore had not arrived in the town where he had sent him, he attempted to find Isidore to prevent him from causing trouble. His search was interrupted by the arrival of Inspector Dörpinghaus on February 6, 1909.

A servant of the inspector found Isidore and listened to his story before presenting him to the inspector.

After hearing Isidore's story, the inspector called for Longange, who attempted to kill the young catechist. The inspector himself restrained Longange and took charge of Isidore, personally dressing his wounds. In a later court hearing, the Belgian accused Isidore of stealing wine, but witness after witness decried this as a trumped-up excuse by Longange to save face. Inspector Dörpinghaus took the invalid first to a different plantation and then to the central office of the company in Busira. The company provided medicine on a regular basis, but his wounds were too infected to hope for recovery.

In July, the missionaries came and administered the last sacraments to him. Father Grégoire heard his confession and gave him the anointing of the sick. The next day, the missionary brought him the Eucharist in the form of Viaticum.

The now-invalid Isidore was moved to the porch of the town catechist, Loleka. Here, throughout his final days filled with pain and suffering, Isidore was never without his rosary. Toward the end, because of the intense pain, Isidore was often in delirium. One Sunday morning at the first of August, Isidore threw up blood and those around him recognized the smell of imminent death. All of a sudden, the prayerful African stood up and walked into the banana patch beside the catechist's house, holding his rosary in his hand. Shortly, he returned and lay down.

The people did not know how to explain this brief walk by one who for months had been unable to stand alone, sit, or even lie on his back. Isidore took part in the Sunday prayer session held by the local Christians in the catechist's home. He requested something to eat and soon afterwards, he died quietly. The Christians buried him simply, still holding his rosary in his hand.

The life of Isidore Bakanja shows the heroic degree to which a solid scapular devotion can lead even a recently baptized convert. In him, the scapular devotion has its martyr. On his trip to Zaire in 1980, Pope John Paul II cited the example of Isidore as a source of pride for Catholics in Zaire. "I speak of a Zairois catechist, Isidore Bakanja, a true Zairois, a true Christian. After having given all his free time to the evangelization of his brothers as a catechist, he did not hesitate to offer his life to God, strong in the courage he found in his faith

A painting of Blessed Isidore with his rosary.

and in the faithful recitation of the Rosary. . . ." Through the life and Christian attitude of this modern day servant of God, the Universal Church has a new hero to emulate. Isidore Bakanja was beatified on April 24, 1994.

Saint Joseph Moscati

1880-1927

Doctor of Charity

Young Dr. Moscati, the recently appointed head of the department for incurables, called all his assistants to come to the autopsy room. It was not a day for postmortems, and all the assistants were surprised at the invitation. Nonetheless, they followed the doctor into the depressing and gloomy room. On the slab there was nothing. High up on the wall, however, there was a crucifix. Beneath it was the inscription, "O death, I will be thy death."

As one of the assistants, Dr. Pio, phrased it, "We had been invited to render homage to Christ, to the Life which was returning after too lengthy an absence, to that place of death."

Some time later, when called to perform a postmortem, Dr. Moscati approached the slab and remained some time in silent contemplation of the crucifix. Looking compassionately at the corpse, he was heard to exclaim, "Thus ends the pride of Man! Hatred, wealth, revelry, and then . . . this is what we are. How much death teaches us." In 1919, on his appointment, Dr. Moscati had thanked the president of the United Hospitals in a letter which included this statement: "I will endeavor, with the help of God and with all my strength, to correspond to the confidence placed in me." The young doctor began at once the reconstruction and economic reorganization of the department, which had suffered reverses during World War I. First on his program were spiritual matters, which had been neglected. His policy was to save souls by caring for the body. Dr. Moscati, as a scientist and a true Christian, won the esteem of all, even those who were indifferent or hostile to religion. As Pope Paul VI said during the beatification ceremonies on November 16, 1975, "Joseph Moscati's life was an example of harmony between science and faith."

Joseph Moscati was born July 25, 1880, in Benevito, Italy, a small town near Naples. He was the seventh of nine children of Francis and Rosa Moscati. He was baptized six days later, receiving the names Joseph Mario Charles Alphonse.

Francis Moscati was a lawyer who later became a judge. A number of promotions resulted in his moving to Naples in 1884 with his young family. Here he was named president of the Court of Assize. At this time, there was a great amount of anticlericalism and contempt for all religion, especially the Catholic faith. Going against the currents of secularism, Francis faithfully upheld Catholic teachings and beliefs, and imbued in his family a deep love for their religion. The family practiced daily attendance at Mass and had a great filial devotion to Our Lady. On frequent walks that he took with his children, Francis always included a short visit to the Blessed Sacrament in one of the beautiful churches that abound in Naples. This deep love for God in the Holy Eucharist grew in the heart of young Joseph so that even in later life when he had a hectic and busy practice as a doctor, he began each day with Mass and Holy Communion. On the rare occasions when he was unable to attend, he noted in his journals his deep sadness.

In 1890, Joseph made his First Communion in the church of the Servants of the Sacred Heart. His first education was at home where he was taught by his parents. In 1889, he entered the lowest class of the Secondary and Grammar School of Victor Emmanuel. At school, he was quiet although friendly to everyone, and well-liked by his companions and his teachers. Each year he scored such high marks that he was exempted from expenses. He obtained his grammar school diploma in 1894 at the age of fourteen. He continued his studies in the Lyceo and obtained a first-class Classical Diploma in 1897.

Joseph's home was close to the Hospital for Incurables. Daily, the sight of the sick and suffering, and his practical love for the poor, drew Joseph toward a career in medicine. After much prayer, he finally decided on his career and enrolled at Naples University.

In December of his first year at the university, his father died. Full of grief himself, Joseph became the consoler for his family. He wrote to a friend, "God takes the place of those whom He has taken to himself."

Joseph studied assiduously and continuously scored high marks. He had a serious, composed, and attentive attitude, and in 1903 he obtained his degree in medicine and surgery with first-class honors. His final thesis on hepatic urogenesis was considered good enough to be printed. He applied for and was chosen second of twenty-one general assistants in the United Hospitals.

At the age of twenty-two, young Dr. Moscati began practicing medicine. He saw God within each of his patients who were suffering and desperate. He said, "Happy are we doctors, who are so often unable to alleviate sickness; happy if we remember that, as well as the body, we have before us the immortal soul, concerning which it is essential to remember the gospel precept to love them as ourselves. The sick represent Christ for us."

In 1904, Joseph's brother Albert died at the young age of thirty-four. He had been ill for some time, and had gone to live with the Hospital Brothers of Saint John of God, offering himself to God and devoting himself to prayer and penance. Joseph wrote, "Beauty and the enchantment of life pass away; there remains alone eternal love surviving in us, which is our hope and religion, for love is God. The grandeur of death is not the end, but the beginning of the Sublime and the Divine, in whose presence flowers and beauty are as nothing." Joseph remembered a scene from his childhood, ". . . looking at the hospital from our terrace, I was seized with wholesome perplexity and began to think of the transience of all things, and passing illusions, as the falling petals from the flowers of the orange trees around me. . . ."

In his writings, collected for the introduction of his cause for beatification, Joseph expressed the guiding sentiments of his life of heroic charity. He wrote, "Let us daily practice charity. God is love. He who loves is in God and God in him. Let us never forget to offer every day, nay, every moment, our actions to God, doing all things for love."

In April 1906, the Mt. Vesuvius volcano began a period of activity. A branch of the United Hospitals for elderly invalids was in Torre del Greco. Dr. Moscati became alarmed and without regard for himself he quickly left for the city, reaching it in a thick rain of ash, dangerous to human life. He decided to evacuate the hospital at once, and he began moving the most helpless patients himself, encouraging and comforting them. Shortly after the last patient was evacuated, the roof of the hospital collapsed.

In 1911, he passed the examination for medical coadjutor of the United Hospitals, and in July he was chosen for the university chair in chemical physiology. He began lecturing on a number of

A drawing of Dr. Joseph Moscati.

subjects dealing with clinical medicine. At thirty-six, he was reaching to become the head of the medical world of southern Italy. Joseph continued to keep up with all developments in medicine, reading journals from a number of countries to learn of new developments in science. In later years, he was named to a number of other prestigious posts. In addition, Joseph traveled to a number of international medical conferences where his scholarship, his papers, and his discussions caused him to be noted as one of the most outstanding scientists among his peers.

For a time, Joseph was in doubt whether or not to marry. He spent long hours in prayer and finally concluded that he should remain celibate, consecrating himself to an apostolate within his medical profession. He thought about entering the Company of Jesus, but the Jesuit fathers advised him that he would better follow the will of God by continuing his work as a doctor.

In 1914, Joseph's beloved mother died. Grief-stricken, he wrote in his diary on November 25, "At five o'clock in the evening, my mother went to heaven, dying as she lived, like a saint."

The next year, Italy declared war against Austria. Joseph volunteered for service, and was given the rank of major, and appointed head of the Reparto Militare and director of the office for assistance to soldiers who were wounded or ill. Many soldiers were assisted by the young doctor, receiving not only good medical care but also the kind and intuitive care of his apostolic heart. He spent himself without counting the cost of his excessive labor, and his health began to suffer. His greatest delight was to see the soldiers becoming good and devout, assisting at Mass and receiving the sacraments.

After peace was declared, Joseph became the head of the department for incurables. Both at the hospital and with his private patients, he showed an apostolic concern for their soul as well as for their body. He held a deep conviction that the first condition of well-being was to be in a state of grace. With shrewdness and delicacy he convinced his patients to return to the sacraments, sometimes obtaining that which relations and friends had been unable to bring about with lengthy arguments. He wrote, "I feel my heart breaking at the thought of so many souls so far from God; I would wish to lead them all to the feet of Our Lord, I would wish to convert them all."

There are numerous stories of the good he accomplished for his patients, rarely taking any fees for his services. A poor workman said to be tubercular went to Moscati who, after examining him, diagnosed a different condition. He advised the man, "Pray to Our Lady and go to the Sacraments." Following this unique treatment, the man was cured. When he went to pay his account to the doctor, Moscati refused any fee, saying, "If you wish to pay, go to Confession, for it is God who has cured you."

In 1927, a well-known doctor was giving a lecture at the university. Suddenly he felt ill and fell. The dying man looked at Moscati, who felt drawn to him. At once he sent for a priest, meanwhile bending over the doctor and holding a crucifix. Moscati suggested that he pray, "My Jesus, have mercy." The priest arrived barely in time to administer Extreme Unction before the doctor expired. Writing to the doctor's niece, Moscati said, "I still can feel the impression of that look which sought me out, among so many who were present. [Your uncle] knew well my religious feelings, having known me since I was a student. I ran to him, suggesting words of penitence and faith, while he tightly clasped my hand, being unable to speak. . . . I did not wish to go to that lecture . . . but that day a superhuman force, which I could not resist, urged me to go." Although the rich and famous often sought his medical expertise, the poor, the homeless, religious, and priests were his favorite patients, and he would not accept any fees from them. His outstanding and sensitive charity was well-known.

Once he was called in to examine a railroad worker. He explained the man's serious condition to the relatives and advised them to call the priest because, "One must first attend to the salvation of the soul, and only then to that of the body." He prescribed remedies, encouraging all present to have faith in the cure. The man's friends were standing off to the side, and they began collecting money to be offered to the doctor. Guessing what they were doing, Moscati approached and said, "Since you, scraping together part of your hard-earned money, have come to the aid of your sick friend, I also wish to associate myself with your humanitarian actions and to contribute my share to this subscription, so that by means of this sum the invalid may be able to afford the necessary remedies." Thereupon, he gave them some money, and escaped before the surprised and admiring group could overwhelm him with their thanks. Often, in order not to embarrass poor people, after treating them free of charge, he would surreptitiously leave money behind. One found enough *lire* folded in her prescription to be able to buy the medicine; another found a sum of money under his pillow. Near the door of the consulting room at his apartment sat a small basket on a table with the invitation, "If you can, put whatever you wish; if you cannot and are in need, take what is necessary."

Joseph did not become a priest or religious because the guidance of his confessors had indicated his apostolate to be in the work among the poor and the suffering. He retained, however, a sincere esteem and veneration for priests and religious, and sped to their aid as often as he was called. To him, no invalid more truly resembled the image of Christ than a suffering priest. He encouraged others to share his esteem for the priesthood, and advised them to pray for them because, "It is necessary to pray for priests because they are easily forgotten by the living, since Christians often consider that priests do not need prayers."

Once, after examining a priest, he sat at his desk as if to write a prescription. Instead, he picked up a small copy of *The Imitation of Christ*, and read, "In thy cell thou shalt find that which thou mightest lose outside. The cell when continually dwelt in becomes sweet, and when it is ill cared for engenders afflictions." God himself had suggested to him the remedy best adapted for that soul; the priest got the message and changed his way of living.

The famous tenor Enrico Caruso became ill in 1921. He was misdiagnosed and operated on in America, and returned to Italy very sick. He sought the best doctors of Rome and Naples, but none could help the dying tenor. Doctor Moscati was invited to see him, and made an accurate diagnosis. Knowing the end was near, he reminded Caruso that while he had been consulting with various doctors, he had neglected to consult the most important physician — Jesus Christ. To this, the celebrated singer replied, "Professor, please do whatever is necessary." Immediately, Dr. Moscati called a priest to administer the last sacraments, and a few days later the great tenor died at age forty-eight.

"Let us love the Lord to the limit, that is to say, without measure whether in suffering or in love." Joseph Moscati took his own advice, and lived a busy life of intense labor. Such a schedule could not fail to affect his health. In 1923, a Jesuit professor asked him to come and visit a boarder who was ill with pneumonia. As he met Dr. Moscati at the train, the professor noted that Moscati staggered and was hardly able to stand. He admitted that on the trip his sight had darkened and he had been tempted to return to Naples. His sense of duty and charity had caused him to continue.

Joseph had often mentioned that he felt his life would be short. He did not fear death, and had praised the beauty of a sudden death for one who was properly prepared. "After all, what is life? Is not earthly life just death? Only death itself can unveil to us the treasures of the real life."

On April 12, 1927, Joseph Moscati began his day as usual. He rose, spent time in meditation, and went to church where he served Mass and took Communion. He worked at the hospital and returned home to begin examining the many patients who were awaiting him. At three o'clock, he felt ill and stopped work, retiring to his bedroom. He called the servant and asked for a little laudanum. Then he sat down in his favorite wingback chair and crossed his arms. Without agony and without speaking again, he gently fell asleep in the arms of his Lord. As soon as the news of his death became known, his corpse, laid out on his bed, became the object of continual pilgrimage. His funeral, two days later, was an impressive and moving ceremony attended by a large group of mourners. Almost immediately, people began speaking of him as a saint.

During life, Moscati's presence at the bedside of his patients brought them comfort and peace. After his death, those who suffer have frequently obtained graces and cures. Often, a petitioner seems to see the holy doctor standing near at the time of his cure. A number of moving episodes which have no human explanation confirm this. A blacksmith dying of leukemia said Dr. Moscati appeared to him in a vision and told him "you are well." Immediate medical tests showed his leukemia had been cured. A man sent home by the hospital doctors with a diagnosis of terminal Addison's disease prayed at the portrait of Dr. Moscati. Falling asleep, he dreamed that the doctor operated on him. The next day he returned to the hospital where the doctors confirmed that he was cured.

Joseph Moscati was beatified in 1975 by Pope Paul VI, and canonized by Pope John Paul II in 1987.

Louis and Zélie Martin

1823-1894; 1831-1877

Saintly Parents of a Saint

Chapter

15

"God gave me a father and mother more worthy of heaven than earth" — Saint Thérèse of Lisieux.

What part does family background play in influencing a person to become a great saint? Although there are records of persons from completely non-religious backgrounds who have attained sanctity, Pope John Paul II says that it is through the family that "the primary current of the civilization of Love" passes. "To the family is entrusted the task of striving to unleash the forces of good."

That the venerables Louis and Zélie Martin, parents of the Little Flower, handled their responsibility well is shown in the life of their daughter Thérèse. Parents of a saint, they may one day be declared saints for parents.

Saint Thérèse herself thought of heaven as a re-creation of her home. "There we shall all be together again, never to part. For all eternity we shall enjoy the bliss of family life; we shall see again our dearest father surrounded with honor and glory for his perfect fidelity and especially for the humiliations of which he has had to drink so deeply; we shall see our good mother, who will rejoice at the trials which were our lot during our earthly exile, and we shall take great delight at her happiness as she gazes at her five daughters — all of them nuns. Together with the four little angels who are awaiting us up there, we shall form a crown which will encircle forever the brows of our beloved parents."

With the Holy Father's insistence on the place of the family and the importance of family values, the two separate causes of canonization of the Martins have been presented to the Congregation for the Causes of Saints in a joint study. To give greater emphasis to the matrimonial bond that united the Venerable Servants of God in their earthly life, the faithful are invited to invoke Venerable Louis Martin and Venerable Zélie Guérin, together, to obtain favors and miracles through their joint intercession. United and faithful in marriage, they have left us an example of Christian living and evangelical virtue. In raising a large family through trials, suffering, and bereavement, they put their trust in God, constantly seeking His will.

Louis Martin was born in Bordeaux, France, August 22, 1823. At the age of nineteen, he began training as a watchmaker. At twenty-two, he sought admission to religious life, but he lacked a knowledge of Latin. Returning home, he tried hard to learn the language, but abandoned the idea within two years. After a three-year stay in Paris, he returned to Alençon, where he acquired a large house and shop, meanwhile living an intensely spiritual life. At the age of thirty-five, he met and married the devout lacemaker Zélie Guérin on July 13, 1858, in a quiet ceremony at midnight in the Church of Notre Dame in Alençon.

Zélie was born on December 23, 1831, the second of three children of a retired soldier, who became a policeman in Alençon. Her devout mother was considered too austere and severe in her ways, causing the sensitive daughter much childhood sadness. Although her older sister became a nun, when Zélie applied for admission to the Sisters of Saint Vincent de Paul, she was refused. The superior told her that God had plans for her, but not as a religious. We do not know if this superior had a special light in regard to Zélie's future or whether the young woman's delicate health was the reason for the refusal. Zélie then determined to marry in order to fulfill God's will, begging Him to give her many children which she would then consecrate to Him. In particular, she prayed for sons that would become missionary priests, and who would save many souls. Both her sons died in infancy, but God answered Zélie's prayers to give a missionary to the Church through her

Saintly parents Louis and Zélie Martin.

daughter. Thirty years after her death, Thérèse, who never left her cloister, was named by Pope Pius XI as "Principal Patroness of all Missionaries . . . and of all missions throughout the world."

Zélie had the marvelous gift of harmoniously combining a practical business ability with a tender maternal heart. Although she established a profitable business making Alençon lace, which she engaged in until the last months of her life, she faithfully fulfilled all the duties of a wife and mother. An excellent housekeeper, Zélie rose early, attended daily Mass, and prepared breakfast for the family before beginning her lacemaking work for the day. She was the last to retire at night. Saint Thérèse related that her mother "admonished all the little faults of her daughters, heard their prayers, and from their earliest years taught them how to make little sacrifices to please the good God." Thérèse points out that, surrounded by such inspiring example, one could not help but be good.

On the deaths of four of her children, and despite the sharp pain of loss, Zélie found comfort in the realization that her little ones were chosen to be angels in heaven. She showed the same wholehearted acceptance of the Divine Plan in her reaction to the fatal breast cancer that caused her untimely death at the age of forty-five. At the cost of great sacrifice, and in spite of tremendous pain, she did all she could for her beloved family until the final days of her life.

The Martins had nine children. The surviving five, all girls, became nuns. Four of the sisters became Carmelites in Lisieux. The fifth, Leonie, became a Visitation nun.

After the death of his wife, Louis devoted himself to the care of his daughters, suffering heart-rending separation as each left for the convent, while blessing and encouraging their vocations. Overwhelmed with gratitude to God for His blessings, Louis offered himself as a victim that he might share intimately in the bitter sorrows of the Passion of Jesus Christ. His offering was accepted and his life was crowned with the trial of mental illness. Hospitalized for three years at the asylum of Bon Sauveur, he was brought home in 1892, paralyzed and subdued, to the loving care of Céline, the only one of his daughters remaining at home. Céline tenderly nursed her father until his death in 1894, after which she joined her sisters in Carmel.

The Martins are excellent models for Catholic parents, who are entrusted with the responsibility of instructing their children both by word and example in the practice of our Holy Faith while also providing for their temporal needs.

After the early death of Mrs. Martin, the self-sacrificing father moved his family to Lisieux in order to be near to his brother-in-law's family, the Guérins. Here, Louis withdrew from his business in order to devote himself to the upbringing of his children. He saw to their education, made their toys, and took long walks in the country with them. Here, too, he practiced his private charities and became a zealous member of the Conference of Saint Vincent de Paul. Other than the Guérins, and an occasional priest who came to dinner, the family had few visitors, although every week a crowd of poor people would arrive to be given money or food.

The seclusion of life at Lisieux, the almost complete withdrawal of the Martin family from the world, are not something we can or should try to imitate; almost all of us must be involved with the world and its daily hurly-burly. At the same time, the strong alliance of the parents and the family values taught by the Martins are imitable goals for all Christian parents. Through them we are shown what a marriage can and should be.

Together, the Martins prove that holiness is not confined to souls who dedicate themselves to God in religion. Holiness is the blessed portion of all God's children in every walk of life, and it is the secret of a happy home.

Mother Lurana Mary Francis White, S.A.

1870-1935

Woman of Unity

Chapter 16

Today, the word *ecumenism* is heard more and more often in the Catholic Church as God's people struggle for unity. Mother Lurana Mary Francis White, foundress of the Franciscan Sisters of the Atonement, was a forerunner in the effort to reunite all Christians in the True Faith. Promoters of ecumenism today can learn much from the life of this remarkable foundress.

The "Decree on Ecumenism" (*Unitatis Redintegratio*) was promulgated by Vatican Council II on November 21, 1964. The decree urges all Christians to pray for the unity of the Church and to work toward that goal according to the mind of Christ (UR, n.7). The life and work of Lurana White began to preach the same goal half-a-century before the council.

As a young woman, Lurana White sought to express her love for Our Lord in a lifestyle modeled after the example of Francis of Assisi. With the Reverend Lewis T. Wattson, an Episcopal priest, she cofounded the Society of the Atonement in 1898. Father Wattson (later known as Father Paul, S.A.), Mother Lurana, and the fledgling members of their society entered into the Roman Catholic Church in 1909. From the beginning, they followed a special vocation of atonement.

Mother Lurana explained the society's twofold definition of the word. "It means, of course, the righting of a wrong and making reparation for the wrong. But also, divided into syllables to read 'at one ment,' it means a making one of several parts." The mission of Mother Lurana and her sisters was to pray and work toward this "at one ment" of all the branches of the Catholic Church. Today, her sisters follow in Mother Lurana's footsteps, praying for unity while working in pastoral ministries, religious education, social services, retreat and hospitality services. From the beginning of her call, Mother Lurana desired to establish a threefold community: priests and brothers in the first community; sisters in the second; and tertiaries (lay persons) in the third. During her lifetime, she saw her vision realized in the Society of the Atonement.

Lurana Mary White was born April 12, 1870, in New York City. She and her younger sister Annie were baptized in Christ Church, Warwick, in 1873. Her parents were devout Episcopalians, and the girls were brought up in a deeply religious home. Even as a child, Lurana was a deep thinker. One of her earliest disillusionments came when she was seven — her grandmother told her the truth about Santa Claus. Making an immediate and logical connection, Lurana cried out, "Is all you have been telling me about God a lie, too?" Her grandmother hastened to reassure her, for she saw that the very foundations of the child's faith had been toppled.

Later in life, Lurana recalled incidents which showed that God had found in her a special vessel for His will. She remembered at the age of ten hearing a voice one day which told her that "one day you will die." From that time, she thought often about the brevity of life, the certainty of death, and the account she would have to render one day to God. She was not, however, an overly pious child, and spent a happy and carefree childhood. There were trips to Florida, vacations on the Jersey shore, and exciting excursions on a favorite uncle's yacht. Her family was well-to-do, and Lurana had the additional benefit of loving relatives and a good education.

Unlike most little girls, Lurana did not like to play with dolls because, as she put it, "they aren't really real." She had a deep love of all living things and in her tiny baby carriage she pushed, instead of a doll, a fat, happy pet chicken. First, she would place the hen for a while in a barrel of shelled corn, where it could have a substantial snack. This effectively "buttered up" the chicken so that it actually seemed to enjoy its rides.

Lurana was a good student, and enjoyed her studies. The only subject she disliked was algebra. After completing grammar school she attended a finishing school in New Jersey, and later transferred to an Episcopal high school, Saint Agnes Academy in Albany. Here she developed a great love for the liturgy and was influenced by the sisters. After her graduation, Lurana was actively involved in the social life of New York so favored by her mother. Social calls, traveling, horseback riding, and parties filled her days. Suddenly, Lurana informed her family that she wished to return to Albany and join the sisterhood.

Overcoming her mother's reluctance, she became a postulant to the Sisters of the Holy Child on October 17, 1894. After nearly a year, however, she began to doubt her vocation to this community of the Anglican sisters. One of her main hesitations was that although they were good religious women, the community did not take a vow of poverty.

At this time, Lurana began corresponding with Father Wattson. She had learned of him through family friends before joining the sisters.

Acting on the advice of a friend of her bishop's, Lurana left the Sisters of the Holy Child and traveled with her aunt to Europe to seek a stricter community. In England, Lurana received what she felt to be the answer to her prayers and, filled with a sense of security, she realized that she was not to join an existing community but to begin one. She requested the Sisters of Bethany in London to allow her to stay with them and receive religious training before returning to America to found a group of mission sisters dedicated to the principals set by Saint Francis of Assisi. In particular, the sisters would be devoted to a love of corporate poverty. In her correspondence with Father Wattson, she discovered that he, too, shared many of her aims, and wished to start a group of priests which would be a preaching order.

After some time with the sisters in London, Lurana was given a brown habit modeled after the Franciscan pattern. She then traveled with her sister through several cities in Europe. In Rome, before the statue of Saint Peter, Lurana was inspired to make an interior act of devotion and allegiance to the Prince of Apostles. In Assisi, she begged the prayers of the Franciscan Friars. When they gave her assurance of their prayers, she smiled and said, "But would you promise so willingly if you knew that I am what you would probably consider a heretic?" Their superior replied, "We shall pray all the more willingly."

Lurana as a young woman.

On her return to America, Sister Lurana was at first joined by two of her former companions from Albany. A time of waiting and indecision ensued. Finally, she went to establish a convent at Graymoor near Garrison, New York, close by an abandoned church which had been discovered and restored by three pious ladies.

Lurana rented a house known as the Dimond House, a half-mile from Saint John's Church, and began the building of a convent, which she called Saint Francis House. On October 4, 1899, Bishop Leighton Coleman of the Delaware Episcopal Diocese dedicated the convent at Graymoor. Mother Lurana and two companions moved in.

Also in October 1899, Father Paul arrived at Graymoor. His first residence was a paint shack offered to him by a local contractor. Father Paul called the shack the Palace of Lady Poverty.

Later, other "pioneers" joined the little band and together they laid a foundation for the Society of the Atonement. That God was calling the Society of the Atonement into existence was evident, but the specifics took a while to solidify. Here in Graymoor, the small group began their mission of social service and unity. The first years contained much of the holy poverty that Sister Lurana had been searching for. Potatoes, oatmeal, and bread were the usual menu. The rough existence was well worthy of the name "pioneer."

Slowly but certainly, the two founders realized that the particular mission that God was calling them to was to preach Christian unity, and to call their Episcopal brethren into the fold of the Roman Church.

From the beginning, Lurana realized that this mission would bring persecutions and hardships, but she was determined to live the will of God for her life. Through all of the trials inherent in such a mission, she never lost her zest for life or her keen sense of humor. Once, when a caller asked to speak to the superior of the group, Lurana informed him that she was the superior. Although she was tall (five feet, eight inches), she was slight, and at age thirty-two had a youthful appearance. When the visitor refused to believe that she was the superior, complaining that she was "too young," Lurana began to chuckle. "Well, Dear Lord," she said, "That is certainly one fault I have which will be remedied in time!"

Lurana as a postulant.

In order to find the exact path the will of God was leading them to, both Lurana and Father Wattson sometimes resorted to the old custom of opening their Bible and interpreting the scriptures found at random to read God's will. In 1904, inspired by the scriptural quote "Gather up the fragments lest they be lost" (John 6:12), Father Paul began the Union-That-Nothing-Be-Lost, a charitable missionary society whose twofold objective is corporal works of mercy and the salvation of souls.

The social-service works of the society included many things: they fed indigents in the area, worked with the unemployed, and cared for children, helping all in any way possible. Mother Lurana even adopted two little girls in 1905.

From the initiation of the Society of the Atonement, Father Paul and Mother Lurana worked toward Church unity. In August 1909, the Franciscans of Graymoor requested acceptance of the Society of the Atonement to the submission of the Catholic Communion. In their letter to the Holy Father, transmitted by the Apostolic Delegate, the founders also requested that the Holy See commission the members of the Society of the Atonement for works of "(1) reconciling sinners unto God through the precious Blood of the Atonement, (2) the winning of Anglicans and other non-Papal Christians to the obedience of Saint Peter, and (3) the conversion of the heathen."

On October 30, 1909, in the first instance of corporate reception since the Reformation, the Society of the Atonement was received into the Roman Catholic Church by Monsignor Joseph Conroy, later bishop of the Diocese of Ogdensburg, New York. The moving ceremony took place at Our Lady of the Angels chapel at Graymoor. Two friars, five sisters (including two novices), six tertiaries (including a married couple), and four children knelt and made their profession of faith. "Thank God," Mother Lurana wrote that evening, "we are all safe in Saint Peter's boat."

Among other problems the young community faced was a law suit by the original trustees to reclaim the property where Graymoor was built. Although the property had been given to the sisters and not to any denomination, the suit claimed that the property should belong to the Episcopal Church. Mother Lurana believed that in their mission of unity it would be wrong to counter-sue. Instead, she wrote a letter of justification of their position. After a number of years, the sisters lost the suit and were in danger of eviction. Instead of being distraught, the sisters all felt that this was God's will and would be most pleasing to their model Saint Francis, the "Poverello." At last, through the efforts of good Episcopal friends and after a bill by Mr. Hamilton Fish went through the New York legislature, the trustees agreed to sell the property to the sisters for two thousand dollars.

From the beginning, the members of the Society of the Atonement carried on a printing apostolate to publicize their work. Their hospitality was extended to "Brothers Christopher" (wandering, out-of-work indigents), and to many different groups of missionaries. Their works of love and mercy to the poor were constant, and by 1930, the sisters had begun giving retreats. Filled with Franciscan joy, the society had grown and spread to several states. It had survived the great flu epidemic, a major world war, and the Depression. Later, when someone asked Mother Lurana how the Depression had affected the sisters' bank account, she laughingly replied that their account had not had a great deal to be affected.

Through the years, one of the greatest joys that Mother Lurana experienced was the happiness at the reception into the Catholic Church of any person, especially those who had been alienated by being away from religion altogether,

Lurana in the habit of the Sisters of the Atonement.

or those who came in a spirit of unity from some other denomination. Mother Lurana was privileged to see her own mother received into the Catholic Faith shortly before her death. Her beloved sister Annie also became a convert.

Mother Lurana's health broke and in April 1935, after a long period of illness, she quietly passed to her reward. Her body was carried to the little brown church, Saint John's in the Wilderness, the same spot to which she had been led in her determination to follow God's will for her thirty-six years before. Today, her sisters follow in the footsteps of their mother foundress, who has been called "Woman of Unity," as they actively work for the development of Christian faith communities.

Sister Maria Aparecida, O.P.

1901-1974

An Indian Who Married a King

Chapter

17

In the story of the tortoise and the hare, it was the tortoise who won the race because of his slow, steady pace. In Brazil, the Dominican nuns tell a story of another race — a race to heaven. They tell of a little Indian nun, who began life sleeping in a tortoise shell. In the jumpy manner of a rabbit, she began the race for heaven, and finished it in a tortoise pace of obedience.

Curupira Ida Tuba was born in the Brazilian Amazon in 1901, an Indian of the Tupi Guarani. She was baptized at the age of three. After the death of her father, she was adopted at the age of fourteen by her godmother and taken to live with her at Belém, later moving to Rio de Janeiro.

From the time of her First Communion at the age of eighteen, Curupira was attracted to the religious life, and in 1935 she was received as a postulant by the cloistered Dominicans of São Paulo. She was clothed as a lay sister in 1936 and pronounced solemn vows in 1944. The monastery was later transferred to São Roque, where Curupira died a holy death in 1974.

Curupira's entire religious life was one of constant struggle to overcome her impetuous indigenous temperament, overflowing with arrogance and the desire for freedom, and to make it adapt to the demands of monastic life. A chosen soul, she mystically lived with God while constantly fighting against her lifelong horror of humiliations. She begged Our Lady, "My Mother, Mary most holy, obtain for me the grace to become a saintly bride of your Son Jesus." In following the ordinary path to sanctity of obedience, she wrote, "I hear at every step that the saints did this or that, but what did they do that we cannot do? . . . Do we not have the Sorrowful Virgin to help us? Jesus Crucified to encourage us?"

Here is Curupira's story told in a simple manner, much as her translators took it from her own writings in her diary. It is a story of love combining with Love to overcome all obstacles so that a little Indian might marry and live forever with a King.

On January 22, 1901, deep in the Amazon jungle, a tiny baby girl was laid in the hands of her grandmother. Her father, as was the Indian custom, cut the cord which had held her to her mother. The entire village had been awaiting the birth. They formed a procession and, dancing and singing, wound their way through the forest to the river. Here the decision of life or death would be made for the infant — Tupa, their god, would decide if the child would survive its first bath. Curupira, as the little girl was named, was marked for survival, for she came out of the water safely. Laughing, singing, and joking, the happy extended family returned home where the tiny girl was rocked to sleep in a beautiful cradle made of a turtle shell, decorated by her father. The cradle was hung in a tree to swing in the wind, safe from harm. For many years the child swung in the wind, and God kept her safe from harm until she went to live as His spouse.

On January 22, 1904, Curupira received a second birth by water — the water of baptism. A French missionary came to the village of Carariaca and talked to the people about baptism. All of the Indians wanted to be baptized, and to receive a new name. Again Curupira was marked by water. She received the name of Flaviana.

The common custom at the birth of a Caitete Indian was to espouse her to one of the boys of the village. In Curupira's case, this was not done, and later her proud father, an Aimore Indian, defensively said that his daughter was not espoused at birth because she was destined to marry only a king. The eight-year-old Curupira remembered his words for the rest of her life.

Curupira was a happy child, carefree, laughing often, and rarely serious. When she outgrew her turtle-shell cradle with its beautiful and bright decorations, the little girl dashed about the village, climbing trees, singing, and perfectly at peace with the wild climate of the Amazon forest. Tiny, though healthy, at birth, for the rest of her life she remained small of stature. She loved beautiful things, and loved to make them with her own hands. From her grandmother, she

Sister Mary in the yard of the Dominican convent.

learned how to make lace. From her father she learned to paint with beautiful colors.

The little Indian was particularly fond of turtle eggs. Once, she asked her mother to fix her one — then two, then three. Since Indian parents deny their children nothing, Curupira kept eating. At last, after having eaten six of them, she became ill. Her worried parents were uneasy because she fell asleep and slept soundly for two days. When she awoke, unharmed, Curupira had learned two things: first, that gluttony is often repaid poorly, and second, that she had lost all taste for eggs. For the rest of her life, she would not willingly eat an egg.

Eventually, she had seven younger brothers and sisters to keep her company and to play with her. One day, however, sadness came into the life of the happy little Indian. Her father, Pery Ido Tuba, asked his wife (as was the custom) for permission to go away and to take a barge load of merchandise down the river. The barge was later found empty and abandoned. Father Ido Tuba, whose name means "Happy Place," was gone, probably drowned. His young wife and all of his children and relatives were sad and wept loudly; Curupira, her father's pet, cried and wept the loudest. There was no consoling her!

At last, a lovely European lady, Curupira's godmother, came to take the unhappy little Indian home with her to Belém, and have her educated. (They later moved to Rio de Janiero.) The tiny Indian girl, won over by her godmother's kindness, dressed carefully in pretty clothes with a bow of red ribbon in her jet-black hair. Sadly she went with the kind woman, leaving behind her grief-ridden family. Although Curupira had left on the road to her King, she never forgot her loving Indian family, nor they her. To the end of her life, she wrote them long, large, loving, and decorated letters. Her family, too, remembered their happy little sister, and once, when one of her brothers was near, he came to visit with her, bringing presents of fish and flour. Because of the distance, this was the only visit with a family member she ever had.

When Curupira first arrived at her godparents' home, she was still sad about the loss of her father. She remained in a depression, crying and refusing to eat or bathe, until she noticed the tears in the eyes of her beautiful, angelic godmother. Then, the little Indian tried her best to cheer her godmother — laughing, hugging, and kissing her with abandon. The loving heart of the little Indian could not tolerate sadness, and no one could be around her for long without being affected by the contagion of her happy heart. She was very happy living with her godparents. Her godmother was beautiful, smiling and good. Her godfather was good, but was of a serious nature, which was something different for the little Indian girl. Indians are always laughing and happy, or impassive, concealing all emotions. With her nature and her cultural background, Curupira was joyful and playful, but she concerned herself more with the sheer joy of life itself than with the European notions of study, work, money, and seriousness.

Although Curupira learned to read and write very well without ever having given any indication of studying, her godparents worried about her lack of seriousness. They were waiting for her to achieve a little more maturity to allow her to make her First Communion. At last, long before her godmother was comfortable about the matter, she made her First Communion at the age of eighteen. This same day, she seemed to feel the call to be a religious. Shortly after this big event, which made her very happy, another sadness entered the life of the little Indian. Her beloved godmother died, and as Curupira saw it, her angel had returned to heaven. Soon, she confided a secret to her godfather. The little Indian told him that she wanted to become a nun.

"Being a nun is a very serious thing," he said, "My daughter, to become a nun requires that you study and learn to work." But the loving heart of the little Indian would not be denied, so her solemn, but kind, godfather sent her to school with the Spanish sisters to learn how to work and to study. Here, she did not seem to improve on her work-study skills, but she did develop a great love for the Immaculate Mother.

Curupira charmed all who met her. Her ebullient nature caused her to make immediate and intimate friendships with everyone she met. No one knows how, but she met many politicians and their wives, church dignitaries, and even the president of the Republic. Curupira, however, made no difference between these famous and important persons and her humble companions, the poorest of the poor. Curupira became very devoted to the mother superior of her school, and followed her around like her shadow.

At last Curupira confided her desire to be a religious to a holy monsignor and to Mother Clare. They told her to work at mortifying her self-love and egoism in order to prepare to enter the novitiate.

One day, her beloved superior disappeared. Finally, the other sisters explained to the unhappy little Indian that the superior had gone on a trip to São Paulo. Somehow, she convinced a companion to go with her, and talked the president of the Republic, Getulio Vargas, out of two railroad passes, in order to follow Mother Clara to São Paulo. How greatly surprised the superior was to open the door and find her little Indian, shivering from the cold!

Mother Clara told Curupira that they were going to Mass at the convent of Christ the King. She never noticed the surprise on the face of the little Indian, who remembered her father's prediction about marrying a king. With the typical curiosity of the Indian, Curupira was entranced with the mystery of the King hidden in the convent of the Dominican nuns. Mysteriously, from the grate behind the altar of the little chapel came a lovely hymn to Tupa (the Indian word for God) in an unknown tongue (Latin).

Then and there the curious little Indian decided that this was the house where she would serve, and await, her King.

Later, after speaking with a half-deaf maid, the little Indian returned to the Dominican convent with a large bunch of bananas. When the French superior came to the grate, all she could see awaiting her was a large bunch of bananas! At last, in the dim light, she discerned a small Indian girl crouched behind the bananas. Without rising, the squatting girl then explained to "Ma Mère" that she wished to become a nun and live in this house to wait on her King. After asking her name, the superior told Curupira, "We are waiting for an Indian whom we asked of Our Lady of the Apparition, patroness of Brazil, as a sign that we should make this foundation in Brazil. We were considering returning to France, as we have had many difficulties. Here our life is truly austere. We fast a great deal, we rise at midnight for prayer. Do you want to endure all this?" With an Indian's simple logic, Curupira only asked "Don't you endure it?"

But the clever superior remained mysterious and tantalized the prospective little postulant in order to test her. "Then come back some other day," she said.

Day after day the little Indian returned until eventually she overcame all obstacles and was admitted. The reception was fine until hunger made itself felt. Curupira was an Indian, through and through. As an Indian, the natural way, which she took a long time to overcome, was to eat when you were hungry. These strange European nuns did not eat well, often, or decently! They never ate meat, and for an Indian this type of fast is something unbelievable. Although Curupira tried to adjust rapidly to the dictates of another culture, and made all sacrifices to understand the theology of their hunger, she followed the natural course of being cross when hungry. This and other cultural adjustments which the little Indian could not seem to make led the sisters to consult and decide that she could not stay. Tactfully, the saintly mother superior tried to tell Curupira that she would have to leave. She told her that the sisters from her previous school missed her and would be soon coming for her. She hurried away with tears in her eyes — how she loved that impossible little Indian! When the time came for Curupira to leave, the superior had to hunt for her. She found her in the garden doing one of the most hated chores. Smilingly (another miracle), the little Indian removed her veil; there stood Curupira, completely bald! She had shaved her hair to nothing. "Your Reverence cannot send me away like this," she said. The superior, convinced of the perplexing but firm nature of the little Indian's vocation, left speedily. She hid her tears, and sternly told Curupira that she might have won a battle, but certainly not the war.

While the sisters waited for her hair to grow, the cagy little Indian wrote to the bishop of Araguaia, "Great Dad, they want to send me away. Do not let them." Curupira's appeal struck home. In spite of her faults, and she had many, her contrition was sincere. Due to this, the intervention of her bishop, and the tolerance of the loving Dominicans, Curupira stayed with the cloistered Dominicans for the rest of her life.

"Ah, how I like those corrections of 'Ma Mère.' " Curupira's ability to be truly contrite for all of her many faults was the one thing in the beginning that convinced her sisters to allow her to stay. To solve the little Indian's problem about eating, the sisters finally allowed her to work in the refectory. Slowly, as a tortoise, Curupira grew in virtue, especially those virtues which were so against her nature — humility and obedience. When she fought with her sisters, or lost her temper or her sense of humility, she would humbly apologize, saying, "I love you very much, and I thank you for your charity. It was all because I am an Indian. Forgive me." No one could doubt or deny her sincerity.

All her life, Sister Maria of the Immaculate Conception Aparecida retained much of her native Indian culture. She loved colorful and beautiful things. She wrote marvelous cards, a meter square, painted with large well-formed letters of red, green, and blue, and with colorful cutouts from magazines glued on them. Her natural sense of joy and happiness never left her. With her ebullient sense of humor, she played tricks on her sisters. To test the vocation of new novices, she put salt in their coffee. She mischievously put stones under the superior's quilt, saying that as she was a saint she must do penance. She joked that she would be the first native Brazilian saint, as she was full-blooded Indian unless you wished to count a drop or two of the European blood of the first Franciscan missionaries — whom her ancestors had eaten.

The sisters outgrew their first monastery, and moved to a new monastery on the slopes of the São Roque mountain. At first, Sister Aparecida kept to her room, as she was afraid of snakes. At her request, a group of seminarians who had helped the sisters move lengthened the legs of her bed so that she would not be so afraid. The people of the countryside came to visit the new monastery. Here, they were charmed by the little Indian nun who mystically seemed to be able to talk to them without ever leaving the presence of God.

To Sister Mary Immaculate Aparecida, all things in life were holy. Since everything is created by God, what is not so is only because we corrupt it. She accepted and lived with this sense of holiness so well that she could even count things like the corrections of her superiors or, later, an operation, as "beautiful." After the changes brought about by Vatican Council II, she was thrilled to be allowed, along with the other lay sisters, to sing the beautiful and mysterious Latin hymns. Joyfully she marked the pages with large, boldly colored holy cards. And when the office was changed to Portuguese, she soon realized there was even more mystery in hearing words which she understood. Now she realized that the mystery was not in the obscurity of the words, but in the light of truth that the words revealed.

Sister found great joy in the Holy Bible. She read it constantly, and her knowledge of and delight in the Holy Scripture was incredible. She carried her Bible about with her like a Protestant minister.

Curupira's rosary was a favorite joy of her heart. A series of personal meditations which she wrote for the mysteries speaks to all of Mary's children.

At last, Curupira fell ill. After an operation in the hospital in São Roque, she went for treatment to the large hospital in São Paolo. Before the operation, the sisters were amazed at her supernatural calm and courage. Everyone in the hospital came to know the holy little nun. Ever since her childhood, she had detested eggs. Her doctor had prescribed several egg drinks a day. These she would drink, murmuring prayers on behalf of those priests and religious who had ceased to be religious. Finally, she returned to her monastery in the mountains. She passed long hours without being able to do anything, not even to paint her famous cards with the profound quotations from Sacred Scripture. In her chair, in front of an open window, she passed long hours absorbed in God. "My prayer is nothing more than that of people watching a clock." As long as she could walk, she managed to drag herself to her beloved Divine Office, but that was all. At last, holding her crucifix and her beloved rosary, Curupira passed to her reward.

"After my birth I was counted among the souls that You had chosen. Why? I do not know. God knows. I will be judged by charity, on love, a charity that springs from the depths of my heart. If my Lord finds this virtue in me for all my sisters without reserve, I will be counted among the chosen."

Maria de la Luz Camacho

1907-1934

Martyr for Catholic Action

Chapter 18

"There is no God! God is dead!" Sixty angry young men, full of cognac, shouted and shuffled their feet. They had orders to burn the church, but they hesitated. On the steps of the church stood a young woman with her sister and a small group of Catholics. Obviously the leader of the group, the young woman was encouraging those with her to defend the entrance to the church. A children's Mass had begun, and the young woman hoped to occupy the marauders long enough for the priest to consume the host and escort those in attendance out the back way. Each time the mob uttered blasphemies, Maria de La Luz Camacho shouted loudly: "*¡Viva Cristo Rey! ¡Viva Cristo Rey!* [Long live Christ the King! Long live Christ the King!]"

At last the young men would be held back no longer. Shots rang out. Bullets splattered against the adobe of the church walls.

"*¡Viva Cristo. . . !*" A final triumphant declaration of faith in the One King, and the young woman fell. The red blood spilled over her green dress with its white collar; red, white, green . . . the colors of Mexico. The colors reminded observers of the reason that the stalwart defenders stood in front of the parish church. God was not dead, and the sturdy Mexican Catholics would defend their beliefs, even at the risk of death.

Shortly before the firing began, a young man approached the young woman standing so fearlessly in front of the church. "Miss Camacho, please go to safety," he begged with tears in his eyes. He risked censure from his companions, but wasn't this the same lady who, misguided though she was, had prepared him so lovingly and carefully for his First Communion? Truly, God was only a myth, but Miss Camacho had been kind. He could not bear the thought of killing her, even if her foolish beliefs led her to take such a stand against the power of the state. "Please leave," he begged.

Maria de la Luz refused his tearful request with sad reproachfulness in her beautiful eyes. There were children in the church, and time must be bought for their safety. Her brave stance indicated that any who entered the church with evil intent would do so only over her dead body. Within minutes she was indeed dead, along with several others who had stood with her,* but those inside the church left safely. The Red Shirts fled when they saw the death of the defenders.

Maria de la Luz Camacho was born May 17, 1907, in Mexico City. Her beautiful name means "of the light," and is from a famous name for Our Lady which is common in Mexico. Her father was a businessman; her mother, Teresa Gonzales, died when Maria was only a few months old.

For a time, Manuel Camacho and his pretty baby girl lived with his mother-in-law. Then he remarried, and Maria had a younger brother and sister to love. As a child, Maria had a heart of gold, along with a terrible temper and a stubborn nature. Tantrums were common in her early years, but she usually recanted completely and sincerely, and rushed to the loving and forgiving arms of her parents. When Maria was eight, she boarded for a time in a convent school in Puebla. One of the other students carelessly broke a tool used in their arts and crafts class. Maria was blamed, scolded, and told to pay for the damages. She spoke no word in her own defense. Naturally, when called upon to "pay up," Maria's father learned of the charges. After a discussion with his daughter, he was convinced of both her innocence and her goodness, and he was proud of her learning to suffer in silence.

In 1918, Maria's stepmother died, and the family again went to live with her maternal grandmother and aunt. After four years, Maria's father married this aunt, who became another dear mother for the children.

Maria's early years were spent in the company of a happy, loving family, strong in their Catholic faith. Her father's business produced a comfortable income. Maria's school years were happy, and she did well academically. Drama and art were her favorite subjects. At home, she delighted in presenting little plays of her own, with her brother and sister as fellow actors.

Although Maria was a good student, she was also a trickster, full of fun. One favorite trick was to take a coin attached to a thread and drop it from the window just as an unsuspecting person passed by. The person would of course, stoop to pick up the coin when "presto," it would disappear!

Maria was born at a time in Mexico's history when there was relative peace in the country.

Maria at her First Communion.

Then came the first wave of persecution of the Catholics, and for many of Maria's early years the country was in a state of turbulence. Some of the laws regarding religion in Mexico during this time have been called the most vicious laws ever enacted against the Church. Churches and convents were turned into barracks for soldiers; priests were thrown into prison or murdered.

Mexico, at heart, is a Catholic country. In spite of all persecutions, the sturdy Mexican Catholics built an ever-stronger faith. When the churches were closed in protest against the Calles laws, many of the Catholic homes became a home for Our Lord in the Blessed Sacrament. The sacrament was reverently kept until the priest, hunted as he was, came to say Mass. Here in the church-homes, the priest was hidden, sheltered, and made welcome. Catholic Action has rarely been stronger in any country or in any age. Maria, caught up in the whirlwind of patriotism and love of God, joined in readily.

In 1924, when Maria was seventeen, a National Eucharistic Congress was held in Mexico. Some of the Mexican bishops were arrested and thrown into prison. By 1926, things were intolerable. Bishop Manrique wrote, "Let them (the faithful) face the Wolf. Die as martyrs if need be, for the Faith and for Liberty. . . . Churches are closed! Never mind, let every home become a sanctuary! If a school is closed, let teaching be done in a house near-by. If they can't gather under a roof, let them pitch tents or shelters under the trees. Young and old unite to do battle for Christ."

Similar to the penal days in Ireland, this period in the history of Mexico brought repression, and bravery on the part of the common people determined to keep the Faith alive. All over the country, Eucharistic stations appeared. In the homes of the faithful, the people kept watch, and at night, a priest came in disguise. Friends of the house gathered to watch all night before the Blessed Sacrament. At dawn, Mass was said, all received Holy Communion, and the priest left on his dangerous way. When the "Great Friend," as the Mexican people called the Divine Presence in the sacrament of the altar, came to Maria's home, she hardly ever left Him, preferring to watch all night by the light of candles. All day she had prepared for His visit, putting flowers by the homemade altar. Once, she was caught sprinkling perfume on the flowers. A childish act, perhaps, but her justification was sincere: "I want Him to remember that Maria of Coyoacan is the same as Mary of Bethany."

At this time, there was only one priest in the country for every four thousand people. A priest in

Maria dressed as a nun for a play.

the Federal District organized young men and women to teach the catechism. In Mexico City alone there were thirty thousand children under instruction at one time. At the young age of fifteen, Maria trained as a catechist, and established a center in her own home. Most Saturday nights about eighty children came to hear her teach the truths of the Catholic faith. She told other workers in the catechetical field, "Study, study hard! Only then shall we be able to instill the love of God and of His Church into the hearts of the children!"

In addition to her catechetical work, Maria helped with the housework at home, singing and laughing. She loved music; she played the violin and sang beautifully. At times, she was heard singing in her sleep. Maria enjoyed gardening and projects to "fix" things around the house. Her father teased and said that if she had only been born a boy she could have been a gardener, a mechanic, and a furniture maker, all in one. Maria kept notes of her conferences and instructions to the children, and to her fellow catechists. Her spirituality was based on a well-balanced doctrine, a strong line of virtue, and methodical prayer. Religiously speaking, Maria was down-to-earth and very practical. While she entertained her young charges with laughter, jokes, and marionettes, Maria thought philosophically as a mature adult.

Maria as a young catechist.

One of the most interesting facets of Maria's life was her affection and aptitude for the theater. In addition to the little plays which she put on at home, she had studied the subject in school and did very well. She determined to put her theatrical aptitude at the service of God in a new apostolate, and for a time she wrote and presented a number of plays for the people of Coyoacan.

Although Maria was an attractive girl, marriage was apparently not in her plans. When one of her friends asked her about this, she told her that anyone contemplating marriage should consider well the responsibilities entailed in such a vocation.

In a loving letter to her father the year she was twenty-five, she writes that she wants to enter with the cloistered Capuchin sisters, and tells him, "I will work at some employment, but I would not like to impose that expense [the dowry] on you. . . . The ideal I have forged out for myself is [one of] sacrificing myself for God Our Savior. " She had no illusions about a religious life, calling it ". . . an anvil on which God hammers his saints into shape with the hammer of sacrifice. . . ." She planned to live at home, helping her sister with the housework, and also work to save the money for the dowry needed to enter the convent.

Maria had a vivacious and outgoing personality. In spite of her warm and generous nature, she also was often impetuous and high-spirited. There was a time when she, like many saints before her, suffered interior trials and scruples. A number of jealous persons made comments which Maria took severely to heart. She endured a "black night of the soul." In her hurt, she suffered alone. "Do good and let people talk," she told her spiritual director. "When one can bear the pain alone," she said, "why make others suffer?"

Maria became a member of the Third Order of Saint Francis in February 1930. One of the other Franciscans later described her tireless efforts to collect clothes and funds. She was not reluctant to spend time among the very poorest and destitute of the city. In addition to her love of teaching catechism to the children, Maria also taught the adults, not just their religion, but also reading. She wanted all of them to be prepared, in their simple faith, to face their inquisitors.

For a time, the religious persecutions let up, and the persecutors became lax in their war against the Faith. In 1932, the persecution of Catholics began again. Two churches were set on fire, and in one fire two religious were burned to death.

"Sorrow is as necessary as love," wrote Maria in her diary. Again, sorrow had come to Mexico City. Again, the Catholics lived in fear. About this time, Maria had a strange dream that later her

Maria looks pensive in her pictures, but she was known for her cheerful demeanor.

friends took to be prophetic. She seemed to see herself lying in a park, filled with red poppies. For a long time, the memory of this dream haunted her, and she mentioned it to several people.

"What would you do if you had to choose between dying for your faith to be happy in this world, or living in the other world by dying to preserve your faith?" asked one of her friends.

"God would give me the grace to be faithful to him," she answered. "Besides, if I had the misfortune to deny my God, I should die of grief."

The Tenth Annual Congress of the Red Syndicate was held in Mexico in 1934. In Coyoacan, Maria's home district, Anti-Catholic Hours were held every Sunday. On December 30, such a gathering was held in the park across from the church at ten o'clock in the morning. Fifty or sixty youths in the red and black uniforms of Thomas Garrido Canabal's "Red Shirts" gathered.† They planned to burn the parish church of Coyoacan in broad daylight. All morning, they enhanced their "courage" by drinking quantities of cognac.

The children's Mass was just ready to begin. The terrible news of the threat began to spread. Word was carried to the Camacho home.

Quickly, Maria dressed in her best dress — green with a white collar. When her sister Lupita questioned her as to why she dressed so carefully, Maria said, "We are going to defend Christ, our King." Then the Camacho sisters left their quiet and peaceful home and hurried to the church.

Maria stood at the church door with her sister. Her sister whispered her fears, and Maria told her that anyone in their situation would be a fool not to be afraid. Her fear, however, remained hidden. In response to a taunt from one of the Red Shirts that it was not good to be Catholic and that the Catholics that day would see terrible things, Maria responded, "We are not afraid. If it becomes necessary, we are ready to die for Christ the King. Those who wish to enter this church must first pass over my body." Then, in her lovely clear voice, she called out, asking any who were brave enough to join her in protecting the church. About twenty people, seeing her brave stand, joined the Camacho sisters at the church entrance. There were some young women, some workers, and some mothers holding their children by the hand.

They also began to shout, "Long live Christ the King! Long live the Virgin of Guadalupe!"

At last with a shout, "Long live the Revolution!" the Reds charged. They fired as they came.

For the last time, the brave young catechist began her response, "Long live Christ. . . ." A bullet struck her breast and she lay dying. As the priest anointed her, she peacefully closed her eyes and went to meet the King she had so valiantly defended.

Observers looked at the park across from the church where the Red Youth had congregated. Some remembered Maria's dream of the red poppies. As one, the unarmed, outnumbered defenders turned on the persecutors. The Red Shirts, not having anticipating any resistance, turned and ran to the municipal palace where they felt that city official Homer Margalli would protect them. Their plan to burn the church had failed.

After the routine autopsy, required by law, Maria's body was returned to her father's house. On the last night of 1934, over two thousand people passed in procession by the virginal body of the young martyr who was surrounded by a bed of flowers, predominantly white lilies, and whose lovely face gave the appearance of one sleeping. They came to pray and to touch their rosaries and handkerchiefs to the body of one they already acclaimed a saint. The Third Order Franciscans came, as did the members of the J.C.F.M., Maria's Catholic Action circle. They brought the flag of Catholic Action to drape her coffin, and several members begged pardon for their previous actions. Perhaps the most moving were the little children to whom the brave catechist had so lovingly taught the love of God and the principles of the Faith. In tears they brought flowers to show their gratitude. During the night, a priest friend entered, carrying some palms to place beside the body. Several people began crying when they saw this, and he told them, "There is nothing to cry about. It is not death which has entered this house but rather a blessing from Heaven." When some people thought to recite the *De profundis*, the psalm in which we pray for the dead, the priest stopped them. "No," he said. "We do not need to pray for a martyr. Rather, it is she who must pray for us." Then, in a voice full of devotion he said, "Maria de la Luz, virgin and martyr, pray for us. Maria de la Luz, virgin and martyr, pray for our beloved Mexico!" Some people spent the entire night in the presence of the body of the young martyr. The next morning, they prayed to her, asking that since she had accepted the palm of martyrdom she would intercede to bring peace and happiness again to her native land.

The happening at Coyoacan on December 30 had caused a great stir throughout the country. Newspapers in the capital and throughout the country published an account which irritated the entire nation, provoking many protests against the most radical groups. Telegrams piled in a mountain on the desk of the president of the Republic.

The martyr of Coyoacan on her funeral bed of flowers.

The funeral of the martyr was announced for five in the afternoon on January 1. By three, the park across from the church was full. Many people had come from the capital and the surrounding areas to share with their brother Catholics of Coyoacan, and lined up along the way from the Camacho home, to the church, to the municipal cemetery of Xoco. The crowds parted to allow the procession to pass. First came a hundred children dressed in white, carrying palms, followed by a group of young women from the J.C.F.M., also dressed in white. Maria's white casket was carried by her father and by a group of youth from A.C.J.M. Thousands of white flowers were carried in the hands of thirty thousand persons from all social classes who escorted the young martyr to her resting place. As they wended their slow way, the crowd prayed and sang.

The archbishop of Mexico, His Excellency D. Pascual Diaz Barreto, came to meet the procession. On seeing the valiant profession of faith, without fear of the government, on the part of thirty thousand souls who came to render homage to the heroic young woman who gave her life for Christ, he was overcome with emotion. On seeing the flag of Catholic Action covering the coffin, he exclaimed, "Hail to the first martyr of Catholic Action!"

"Hail," the crowd repeated, as they had repeated Maria's own shout of faith, *"¡Viva Cristo Rey!"*

Maria de la Luz Camacho had lived, and died, the motto of the Mexican Catholic Action which she had chosen for herself: "Apostolate, Eucharist, Bravery."

Notes

*There was great confusion immediately after the shooting. Six people, including two Third Order Franciscans, were killed. It is thought that several children may also have been killed, but the mothers grabbed them immediately and hid the bodies to avoid the odious autopsy required by law.

† Garrido Canabal, known as the "Scourge of Tabasco," had been named the Minister of Agriculture. He was a vicious persecutor of the Catholics and after his tenure as governor of Tabasco had left the Church in his home state in flaming ruins — with only two churches left standing. An atheist who stated that he believed in nothing but "results," he parodied baptism in socialist style when he named his children Lenin, Lucifer, and Libertad. He brought with him, and recruited other members, a group of young Communists known as the *Red Shirts*, from the uniform they wore.

Sister Maria Troncatti, F.M.A.

1883-1969

Mother to the Savages

The elderly missionary sister, her legs hard and swollen, climbed with difficulty into the Jeep for the short trip to the airport. She, along with two other sisters, was on the way to her annual retreat in Quito. "Don't cry, I'll be back very soon," she reassured the Shuar children clustered around her in the mission compound.

Half-an-hour later, Sister Maria Troncatti returned to her mission hospital, her lifeless body lying on a slow-moving tractor. The plane had crashed in a sugar-cane field. Sister Imelda was stunned; Sister Blanca had broken her back; and Sister Maria, the *Mamacita* of the Shuars, was dead. From all the surrounding villages her children came to mourn the heroic missionary who had given so much to them. For many, this included life itself.

Maria Troncatti was born in Corteno (Brescia), a small Italian village in the Alps, a few miles from the Swiss border, on February 16, 1883. As a child, she loved the Alpine meadows where the family goats were pastured; she and the children of the other families took turns watching the livestock.

One day, the goats disappeared. Maria went in search of them but found herself in the midst of a thick fog which covered the top of the mountain. Unable to see, she quickly lost her way. When the goats returned without their young herder, Maria's father and some of the men searched the mountain by the light of their lamps all through the night. At dawn, they found Maria under a bush, fast asleep. When they asked her if she was frightened, she calmly replied, "No. Our Lord protected me because I still had the grace of my Communion in my heart. When I realized that I was lost, I said my prayers. I told my guardian Angel to go in search of the goats, and then I lay down to sleep." This childlike reliance on the providence of God became a hallmark of Maria Troncotti's personality.

In the fall, the children returned to their villages. At the small village school Maria attended, the teacher received the *Salesian Bulletin*, which she used as a reading supplement for the class. She read about the work of the missionaries in lands far away, and began to dream of going to the missions. In particular, work among the lepers attracted her.

At seventeen, Maria confided in her older sister Catherine that she wanted to become a sister and go to work in the missions. Later she told her pastor, who cautioned her to wait and pray. At last, she applied to the Daughters of Mary Help of Christians and was accepted in 1905 as a postulant by the sisters in Nizza Monferrato. The pastor had worked hard to convince James Troncotti, Maria's father, to allow her to go. As Maria bid her family goodbye, her father issued a piercing cry and fainted.

The painful parting, her strong love for her family and home, a sensitive nature, and the radical change in her lifestyle made the adjustment difficult. When the other sisters asked Maria if she was happy, she often answered in monosyllables because of a lump in her throat; tears of homesickness often came, unbidden, to her eyes. The sisters wondered if Maria were truly called to religious life and began thinking of sending her home.

When Maria realized that she might be dismissed, she made a fervent novena to Saint John Bosco. Although her health declined, she was allowed to make her vows for a year. Her health had to improve before she would be allowed to renew them.

She made her vows in 1908, and the Provincial sent her to Varazze, where the climate was favorable to her health. In 1915, she attended a course for Red Cross nurses given by the city, and during World War I worked in a military hospital there, nursing the wounded. In June of that year, during a violent storm, Sister Maria and another sister were caught up in a flash flood when the wall of the dining room of their residence fell in. In her fright, Sister Maria begged Our Lady Help of Christians to save her, and promised that if her prayer was answered, she would go to the missions.

In 1922, Sister Maria was transferred to Nizza Monferrato. One of the pupils of the teacher-training college, Marina Luzzi, was dying of

Sister Maria Troncatti

pneumonia. Knowing that she would probably not recover, Marina had asked to remain with the sisters and to be accepted in the sodality of the Children of Mary. On the night of her death, Sister Mary asked Marina to greet Our Lady when she saw her, and to request the favor that she be sent to the missions to work among the lepers. The dying girl was silent a few moments. Then she whispered, "No, Sister Maria, you will go as a missionary to Ecuador." Three days after Marina's burial, Mother General Catherine Daghero unexpectedly asked Sister Maria, "Have you made a request to go to the missions?" When Sister Maria answered in the affirmative, the superior said, "Good, you will go to Ecuador."

Sister Maria with some of her beloved children of the mission.

After a last, difficult visit with her family, Maria left for the mission fields. Her heart ached with love and nostalgia for her family and home. Time and again she opened her small notebook to read the farewell thoughts given her by Mother Enrichetta Sorbone, one of the first sisters of the congregation: "As we take leave of our country and relatives, we must do so with a sense of peace. Jesus walks before us cutting down the branches, but He wants us to follow Him with courage. So let us forge ahead."

During the ocean passage the sisters studied Spanish, and Sister Maria constantly prayed her *Ave's*. From this point, her life would be a continual rosary.

The sisters entered the country at Guayaquil, where they spent their first Christmas on the missions before traveling to Chunchi, a small town on the Cordillera mainly inhabited by natives. Sister Maria had been appointed superior of the little group, but above all she was the "doctor." She prepared a small makeshift pharmacy called the *botiquin*, and a dispensary. Here she greeted the natives with a smile, taking care of their bodies and worrying about their souls. Soon, the people in the surrounding areas began to send for their "doctor" from quite a distance. She mounted a horse and traveled to her patients. She wrote her parents, "When I enter the miserable huts where the natives gather, all kneel down and ask for my blessing. I am the 'doctor' of this village. They call for me at any time, even during the night. Poor people!"

After three years in Chunchi, Sister Maria wrote, "Now I am about to go into the wild forest, among the savages, and these poor Indios are crying." Her beloved natives cried at the loss of their *Madrecita* (little mother), thinking the sisters would be eaten alive by the savages.

On November 9, 1925, Sister Maria, already in her mid-forties, began her great expedition towards the wild Amazon forest on horseback. In the group were two young sisters assigned for the mission, two sisters who would later return, Monsignor Dominic Comin, Father Albino del Curto, and some hired helpers. The journey was so difficult and rugged that at one point Mother Mioletti asked herself why she had exposed the sisters to such danger; at one stop, Sister Maria fainted. Monsignor encouraged the sisters saying, "Courage, Sisters. Prayer alone is not sufficient to convert the Kivari; the sacrifice of our entire selves is necessary." Although she was terrified of the foreboding, mysterious jungle and the unknown future, Sister Maria Troncotti willingly gave her fiat to this sacrifice. Shortly before reaching Mendez, the center of the vicariate entrusted to the apostolic care of Monsignor Cumin, a gunshot signaled the arrival of Father Corbellini, who was accompanied by several Kivari. Here, for the first time, Sister Maria saw representatives of the people with whom, and for whom, she would spend the rest of her life. Their only attire was a very short skirt, which they placed on their head when they forded the Paute River. The sisters crossed in a canoe.

When the group reached Mendez, the mission was surrounded by about eighty Kivari, armed with arrows, lances, and large knives. A tribal chief's daughter had been caught in the crossfire between two warring tribes and the witch doctor had not been able to cure her. They brought her to the mission; a bullet had grazed her arm and embedded itself in her chest. The chief threatened the frightened missionaries. They must cure his daughter immediately or he would kill the entire group. All turned to Sister Maria, as Monsignor commanded, "Operate, Sister Maria. We will pray." The other sisters went to the tiny mission chapel to plead for Our Lady's aid; Sister Maria examined the girl on the mission's only table. The bullet, lodged in her chest for several days, had caused an infection and high fever. Sister Maria sterilized her pen-

Sister Maria with a group of First Communicants.

knife with boiling water and swabbed the girl's chest with iodine. With a fervent "Mary Help of Christians, pray for us," she resolutely made an incision. The bullet bounced out as if pushed from behind. Three days later, the jubilant Kivari walked out of the mission compound and were swallowed immediately in the dense

Working in the dispensary.

jungle. Almost immediately, tom-toms began to beat out the message: "A witch doctor better than all the witch doctors has arrived; let her and those with her pass." The right-of-way for the missionaries was assured.

In early 1926, when the caravan started back, leaving the three sisters in the "Green Hell," the three cried their eyes out. In the middle of the forest, with snakes, beasts, and the hidden danger of the jungle tribes all around, the three were being left to spend the rest of their lives. The colonists welcomed the sisters eagerly. Little by little, under the protection of Mary and by examples and words, the sisters earned the love and trust of the natives. The Shuars would come to Sister Mary to be healed, but they kept their hands on their lances and remained ready to run off again into the jungle. "It is for them that we came; the Pope wants it," sighed Sister Maria.

One day, a young girl of about nine came to the door. She declared her intention of staying with the sisters for good. From her, they learned the Shuar language. Sister Maria asked a missionary to translate a little catechism and from then on when she went to the Indian villages to cure the sick, she would bring the book with her. Soon a large number of young Indian girls came to board with the sisters. Shuar law required that each malformed or illegitimate baby be killed. Soon, though, everyone learned that Sister Maria was asking for those babies. They would bring the babies to her, asking for something in exchange, such as a mirror or other trinket.

One of these children remembered Sister Maria by saying, "From the time I reached the age of reason I didn't know I had another mother on earth other than Sister Maria Troncatti. I received affection, tenderness, a home, and education from her. I feel that I can honestly say she gave me my life."

Sister Maria Troncatti lived in the forest for forty-three years. She went where she was needed, day or night. She healed the people, buried the dead, rocked the newborn babies, prepared the young women for marriage, and, in general, was a true *Mamacita*.

Once, Sister Maria saved a young girl of the Achuara tribe who was dying of pernicious anemia. After that the Achuaras idolized her. The chief of the tribe brought her a crown made out of bird feathers.

From a homesick, fearsome young girl, Sister Maria grew to one who was filled with love for God and for her fellow man. In 1969 during a civil distruption, when flames turned the Shuar federation headquarters into a raging inferno, Sister Maria spoke with tears in her eyes: "If there has to be a victim, Lord, take me." She told a former student, "I wish to die before other ugly things happen, before the Fathers or your husband are killed." Through her tears and prayers, her work and sacrifice, Sister Mary Troncatti brought the Shuar to Christ. Following the advice of Saint Don Bosco, co-founder of her order, she asked "Give me souls, I am not looking for anything else."

Blessed Sister Marie Clementine Anuarite Nengapeta

1939-1964

Faithful Virgin of Zaire

Chapter 20

"I don't want to commit this sin! If you want to, kill me. I forgive you because you don't know what you are doing."

The drunken Colonel Olombe viciously hit the young nun in the head with the butt of his gun.

"*Naivyo nilivyotaka! . . .* This is just as I wanted it." Sister Anuarite fell to the ground, and Colonel Olombe called to a nearby band of rebel Simbas armed with large knives.

"Get her!" Olombe demanded.

Two of the rebels began to strike the sister in the chest with their knives. After a few moments, as blood streamed from her wounds, Olombe aimed his revolver and shot Anuarite through the heart.

The other sisters who had witnessed the attack from the verandah of the house where they were being held captive were told to remove the body. Inside, Sister Uwenze held the head of Anuarite on her lap as she tearfully tried to get the stricken nun to speak. There was no answer, and the valiant martyr expired at one o'clock in the morning of December 1, 1964. She who had vowed her virginity to Christ had held true to her promise at the price of her life.

Anuarite Nengapeta was born December 29, 1939, at Wamba, a small town in the northeast part of the Belgian Congo (now Zaire.) She was the third of five daughters of Amisi Badjulu and his wife, Isude. At the time of her birth, her father was away at war.

While he was away, Amisi visited Palestine and was impressed by what he saw and heard of Christianity. He wrote home, telling his wife to take the children to the Catholic Mission and to become baptized. Anuarite was baptized and given the name Alphonsine.

A few years after his return from war, Amisi became angry that his wife had not given him a son, and took another wife. Isude left him rather than tolerate living with a polygamous husband. This situation was very painful for the young Anuarite, but she simply said, "All the same, he is our Papa, even if he doesn't want to know us."

Growing up, Anuarite was very close to her mother and to her grandmother Anjelani. It was her grandmother who taught her to pray and to respect the poor, the elderly, and the sick. From her, Anuarite learned to serve people in order to make them happy. Her lifelong motto became: "Serve and make others happy."

Anuarite began school at the mission in Wamba when she was nine years old. She was not a good student and had to struggle hard to learn her lessons. She repeated the fifth year in order to be accepted to high school.

Anuarite's selfless service to others became the hallmark of her personality. Often she would be seen helping a poor neighbor by carrying water, sweeping the compound, or cooking. If the sisters asked her to do a job, she finished her work and disappeared quickly. When the other students helped the sisters, they stayed to receive some treat or small form of pay; Anuarite wanted to help, but didn't want to be paid for the things she did. Her reward was in making the others happy. Although she grew up with suffering and poverty, she was a generous and caring person.

Blessed Anuarite Nengapeta

The sisters at Wamba had started a convent for young African girls at Bafwabakka, and Anuarite began thinking of the religious life. When she mentioned the subject to her mother, she was told to think about it carefully. Anuarite was certain about what she wanted to do, and joined a group of other girls at the school who had the same idea, but the sisters discouraged her because they were afraid she could not make it to profession because of her low academic performance. The determined young aspirant gained her D3 at the end of 1956 and became eligible for secondary school. The sisters had suggested that she attend the domestic science school at Wamba but Anuarite was adamant; she wanted to become a sister.

When the time came for her to leave for the convent at Bafwabakka, Anuarite's mother had still not given her definite consent. The big lorry with the other girls was ready to leave; at the last minute, Anuarite raced to scramble aboard. Her mother was forced to accept that her determined daughter was leaving to join the sisters.

As a postulant, Anuarite taught in the primary school. Her continuous good humor and her liveliness, along with her simplicity and patience, made her a favorite among the students. After two years, she was admitted to the novitiate. At her clothing, presided over by the bishop, she was given the name of Sister Marie Clementine Anuarite.

As a novice, Anuarite paid the utmost attention to conferences and advice from the other sisters, and worked hard to put into practice all that she learned. She learned to accept corrections in a joyful spirit. She kept the good of the others foremost; she willing took on tasks that the other sisters disliked.

Sister Anuarite was not robust, and she suffered from continual headaches. It took a great effort for her to remain in good spirits. She wore glasses because of a squint in her eye, and she had a slight speech impediment. Her selfless nature helped her to overcome these difficulties; in thinking always of the good of others, she forgot herself.

At recreation, the sisters used their talents to entertain the others. Anuarite had no talent for singing or dancing, but she had a special knack for making others laugh. At one memorable recreation, Anuarite got up on the table with a costume similar to a traditional dress and began to give a spontaneous display of one of the old-fashioned war dances. The entire community was reduced to tears of laughter at the sight of the sister-comedian.

One Saturday, as the sisters were returning from teaching catechism at a nearby village, they were walking in two groups. A young man with impure desires came up to one of the groups and began making unseemly proposals. When Sister Anuarite, who was in the other group, realized what was going on, she returned and began speaking to the youth.

"*Sababu gani?* What is this? Why do you want to do bad things with my sisters? Go away! We forgive you, but go away."

The young man hung his head with shame. He left and did not return to bother them again.

Anuarite loved to hear the stories of the saints, and among her favorites were Saint Cecelia, Saint Agnes, and Saint Maria Goretti, three martyrs of purity. She told a fellow sister that if her own purity was challenged, she would remain faithful to death itself.

Anuarite cherished a special devotion for Mary, and often spent time at a little grotto in the convent garden, praying her rosary. As she read books about Mary, she copied passages from them into her own notebook. The works of Saint Alphonsus Liguori were among her favorite books.

Anuarite professed her first vows on August 5, 1959, as a sister of the African Congregation of Jamaa Takatifu (Holy Family.)

In 1962, Anuarite completed her college education and began to teach the fourth year in the primary school. She was a popular teacher because of her liveliness and happy spirit. She sponsored a group of Xaverians and encouraged them to undertake Catholic action. Sister Anuarite was most concerned with the girls who were wayward, and she continuously tried to bring them back to the right path.

She was popular with the other sisters, as well as with her students. Quietly and humbly she continued her goal of serving others to make them happy.

Because of her responsibility, Anuarite began to be assigned to more and more duties in addition to her teaching. In 1963 she was put in charge of the boarding section of the school. She spent long hours caring for the girls, especially when they were ill. Often she would stay up all night, taking care of one of the students. She worked so hard that she became ill herself, and had to take a few months of rest to restore her failing health.

At the end of 1964, civil war broke out in the country. A group of rebels known as Simbas tried to overthrow the government. Although they were eventually stopped, they killed and wounded many people, including Catholic priests and religious, and Protestant missionaries.

On November 29, 1964, while the sisters were eating their lunch, a big lorry pulled up outside and a group of rebels invaded the convent. The leader told the sisters that the soldiers had come to protect them from the Americans, who would soon be arriving; he demanded that they pack their bags and accompany his group.

During Anuarite's novitiate, one of the other sisters had brought some little statuettes of the Virgin with her on her return from a trip to Italy. Sister Silvana had given one of them to Anuarite, who received it joyfully, exclaiming, "*O Bikira Maria, safi mno!* Oh, Virgin most pure!" Anuarite had thanked Sister Silvana profusely, and the little statue became one of her most treasured possessions.

When the Simba demanded that the sisters accompany them, the sisters suspected a trick. The men were armed, so the sisters obeyed their orders. Anuarite put a few clothes in her bag, and took some food because the sisters had heard that food was scarce in the rebel-occupied towns. Then Anuarite carefully put her little statuette of Our Lady in her pocket, and with the other sisters boarded the cotton truck.

The sisters prayed the rosary as the Simbas sang and danced in the back of the truck. With horror, the nuns realized the rebels' true plans as they heard the words of the obscene song the Simbas were singing:

Oh the Little Wives of the Fathers

> Where will they go tonight?
> Oh! Oh! Oh! Each one of us will have one for himself and
>   amuse himself this night.

As the truck rolled along through the African countryside, the rebels occasionally stopped at villages to terrorize, loot, and drink. By nightfall, they had arrived at the abandoned mission of Ibambi. The rebels broke into the rectory and told the sisters to sleep on the floor. The next day, they started toward Isiro.

About midday they met the car of the commanding officer of the Simbas: Colonel Yuma Deo. He became angry at the sight of the sisters' rosaries and demanded they take them off.

Yuma Deo said, "Get them (religious objects) off! There is only one God for the blacks and that is Patrick Lumumba. You should now dress like other women." The sisters were stripped of their religious items, including their rosaries, and these were thrown into the bush. Somehow, they failed to find Sister Anuarite's little statue, which stayed safely in her pocket.

The lorry began again; they started down the road to Bafwabakka, but turned to regress toward Isiro. They arrived at the headquarters of the Simba rebels at Isiro and parked outside the villa of Colonel Ngalo. The sisters were ordered to go to a nearby house. As they were being led away, one of the officers demanded that Anuarite stay behind. Reverend Mother saw his look and took Anuarite by the hand. She insisted on staying with Anuarite. When Colonel Ngalo finished his supper, he came into the garden and announced that he intended to take Anuarite for his wife. Mother Superior protested that Sister Anuarite had taken a vow of virginity; this caused Colonel Yuma Deo to fly into a rage. "For the Fathers you are always ready. For us, your brothers, you have nothing but disdain. This is politics and you belong to the enemy!" He then slapped the superior and took both sisters into the house.

Colonel Ngala started making advances toward Anuarite, but she protested. "What you are asking is impossible. I cannot commit a sin. Kill me instead." He grew angrier and snatched off her veil. The Colonel slapped the sisters a number of times, and then he received word that the other sisters were refusing to eat until the other two were returned to them. Abruptly, he dismissed them and sent them to join the other sisters.

Reunited with the group, Sister Anuarite and the superior were given supper. Throughout the meal, Sister Anuarite asked the others for prayers, saying, "My virginity! Pray for me, help me with your prayers. I prefer to die! Pray for me."

After they ate, a man came for Sister Anuarite and Sister Jean-Baptist Bokuma. They were told to get into the back seat of a car, but the drunken Colonel Olombe couldn't catch them; each time they went in one door and out the other. The man began to beat the sisters with the butt of his gun. He broke Sister Bokuma's arm; Sister Anuarite was killed for remaining faithful to her heavenly Bridegroom.

All night one of the other officers tried to get the sisters to lie down with him but they resisted, strengthened by the example of their slain sister. In the few quiet moments, the sisters tried to prepare Anuarite's body for burial. They replaced her veil, but they could not change her habit because her head was so terribly swollen. They were able to change her blood-soaked overcoat, replacing it with a coat belonging to one of the other sisters. In the morning a car came for the body. The Simba driver promised to take care where he buried it, but he dumped the body in a common grave.

Six days later, the rebels took the sisters to Wamba. Within a week, government forces freed the sisters.

When the priest, Father Odio, heard about what had happened, he determined to find the body of the virgin-martyr. He traced it to the cemetery at Dingilipi. In a common grave, he found one body slightly away from the others and with the arms crossed over the chest. Through the help of the Blessed Virgin, the identification of Anuarite's body was made certain; the little statuette was still in the pocket of her faithful devotee. The remains of the faithful virgin-martyr were reburied.

Anuarite's influence continued to be felt in her congregation, and her story influenced the faith of those who came in contact with the sisters. Eventually her story came to the attention of Church authorities and in 1978, an official investigation was made of Anuarite's life and death. Her body was exhumed and reburied in a beautiful tomb at the Cathedral at Isiro. During the time the coffin lay exposed before its reburial, it was covered with pieces of paper — handwritten petitions asking for Anuarite's help and intercession.

On his visit to Zaire in 1980 to celebrate the hundred years of Christianity in the country, Pope John Paul II personally approved the cause. He returned to Zaire in 1985 to beatify the martyr Anuarite at a solemn High Mass in the capital city of Kinshasa. Africa now has its own martyr for purity and a powerful advocate for its people.

Blessed Marie Léonie Paradis

1840-1912

Heavenly Housekeeper

Chapter

21

"If we wish to do God's work, we must not only say Lord, Lord, but we must do God's will in the Church. To do the will of God is to imitate Jesus. He who does the will of My Father will enter the Kingdom of Heaven."

Mother Marie Léonie Paradis had a unique desire to work in obscurity for the priesthood. This desire bloomed in her spiritual daughters, The Little Sisters of the Holy Family. Begun in Canada in 1880, the order met a crucial need of the times; they were mandated to dedicate their lives to the domestic services required for seminaries, colleges, bishops' houses, and clerical residences. Therefore, they are religious women exclusively devoted to the priesthood. Today, their houses span two continents, but they remain exclusively faithful to their original mission.

Mother Léonie wrote: "Our mission is one of material and spiritual assistance to the priesthood. No matter where they are missioned, the sisters shall have the same deep respect for the priest as they would have for Christ himself. They shall keep in mind the mission of the holy women of the gospel as they minister to the Lord. Perceived with the eyes of faith, this ministry will become for them a sublime apostolate."

In 1984, Pope John Paul II traveled to Canada. At Mother Léonie's beatification in Montreal, he said: "This woman is one of you, humble among the humble, and today she takes her place among those whom God has lifted up to glory. . . . Never doubting her call she often asked, 'Lord, show me your ways,' so that she would know the concrete form of her service in the church. She found and proposed to her spiritual daughters a special kind of commitment: the service of educational institutions, seminaries, and priests' homes. She never shied away from the various forms of manual work which is the lot of so many people today and which held a special place in the Holy Family and in the life of Jesus of Nazareth himself. It is there that she saw the will of God for her life. It was in carrying out these tasks that she found God. In the sacrifices which were required and which she offered in love, she experienced a profound joy and peace. She knew that she was one with Christ's fundamental attitude: He had 'come not to be served, but to serve.' She was filled with the greatness of the Eucharist and with the greatness of the priesthood at the service of the Eucharist. That is one of the secrets of her spiritual motivation."

As the pope reminded his audience that the life of this humble foundress is an inspiration and a model for all, he said, "The Lord counts on you so that human relations may be permeated with the love that God desires. The ways of accomplishing this service may differ from that chosen by Blessed Marie Léonie. But in the most evangelical sense which transcends the opinions of this world it is always a question of service, which is indispensable for humanity and the church."

Alodie* Virginie Paradis was born May 12, 1840, in the village of L'Acadie, Quebec, and baptized the same day in the parish church of Saint Margaret. She was the only daughter of Joseph Paradis and Emilie Gregoire. The couple also had three sons; two other children died in infancy. Joseph farmed land inherited from his father in order to provide for his family.

When Elodie was five, the farm could not produce enough to feed the family, so Joseph rented a mill near the village of Laprarie and moved his family into a house "twenty feet square."

Sister Léonie in the habit of a Holy Cross sister.

A happy child, Elodie learned much from the example of her parents that would imprint her personality through life. Her father worked hard and always tried to improve his family's situation. Her mother, too, worked at the care of the little family. From her mother she learned lessons in charity and a simple but strong faith in God and a devotion to the Blessed Virgin. Elodie also developed a deep veneration for Saint Joseph the Workman.

When she was nine, her mother enrolled Elodie as a boarder with the Sisters of the Congregation of Notre Dame. Elodie was her father's pet and he missed the sound of her laughter; he visited her at the boarding school and brought her home. Her mother promptly returned her to school. A few weeks later when her father again visited and suggested she come home for a visit, Elodie refused, telling her father that her mother would not approve.

In 1849, things were not going well at the mill and Joseph Paradis decided to join the gold rush to California in hopes of striking it rich and being able to better provide for his family. Emilie and the children moved in with her parents in Napierville, and for a time Elodie attended the village school. She attended catechism classes at the parish church and made her First Communion in the spring of 1850. After this day, her mother again sent her to the boarding school at Laprairie.

In his discouragement at not finding gold quickly, Joseph rarely wrote his family. Emilie became worried and decided to make a pilgrimage to the shrine of Saint Anne at Varennes. Her oldest son and a neighbor's son, Camille Lefebvre, accompanied her. On the return trip, Camille found a notice in a Montreal newspaper telling of a program of studies given by the Holy Cross Fathers; poor students could work off their tuition by teaching at the college. At home, Emilie was overjoyed to find a letter, containing a check, from her husband. Saint Anne had answered more than one prayer!

In January 1854, while he was home on school vacation, Camille, who was actively pursuing the priesthood under the Holy Cross Fathers, spoke in glowing terms of the religious life to Elodie. Elodie, not yet fourteen years old, became so enthusiastic that she applied for admission at the Novitiate of the Holy Cross Sisters in Saint Laurent. She received a favorable answer from the foundress herself, Mother Marie des Sept Douleurs, and on February 21, 1824, at the age of thirteen years and eight months, Elodie became a postulant of the Marianites of the Holy Cross Congregation. Because of her young age, Elodie was required to remain a postulant for a year before assuming the white veil of a novice on February 19, 1855. She was given the name Marie de Sainte Léonie, which was usually shortened to Marie Léonie.

On her father's return from California, the joy of his reunion with his loved ones was marred by the absence of his beloved daughter. At last, his usual sound judgement was overwhelmed by his affectionate nature and he went to the convent and peremptorily demanded the withdrawal of his child. With tears in her eyes, she reassured her father that she was extremely happy and wanted to stay. Nothing could bend the iron will of the sturdy miller, and the cautious expostulations of the superiors and the tears of his daughter had no effect; he continued to demand the return of his child. As a last resort, Sister Marie Léonie ran and flung herself at the foot of the statue of the Blessed Virgin, asking to be allowed to die rather than to be torn away from her beloved novitiate.

Our Lady's answer was swift and startling; the young sister collapsed. She had suffered a pulmonary hemorrhage. The frightened and loving father realized that his daughter no longer belonged to him, but to God alone.

Because of her fragile health, the superiors deferred the time for Marie Léonie's first vows. They felt that because of her poor health it would be difficult to accept her for profession. Fortunately, the founder of the congregation, Very Reverend Basil Moreau, came for a visit to this religious house in Canada. An older sister, whose name is not recorded, counseled Marie Léonie to petition the founder, telling her that the kindly priest could never resist tears. Courageously, the young novice tearfully put her request to the holy founder. He gave his sanction and on August 22, 1857, Sister Marie Léonie made

Sister Léonie in the Holy Cross habit.

her first vows of obedience, poverty, and chastity. She was seventeen years old. In later years, she repeatedly told her sisters, "I shall never find words adequate enough to express the bliss I felt on that day."

By the time she was thirty, Marie Léonie had served in a number of houses of the Marianite Sisters as a teacher and in corporal works of mercy, such as her time at Saint Vincent de Paul Orphanage in New York City. Still, her heart yearned for what had so attracted her to religious life: the domestic service offered by the sisters to the Holy Cross Fathers teaching in colleges. She longed to take Martha's role in ministering to the Master in the form of His priests. She was working as a teacher in the French department at Notre Dame du Lac, as always bending her will to the will of God, when a fortunate request from her old neighbor, now Father Camille Lefebvre, began the series of events that led to the eventual founding of the Little Sisters of the Holy Family.

Father Lefebvre was the pastor of Saint Thomas Parish at Memramcook, New Brunswick, as well as the superior of Saint Thomas College. In 1871, he was appointed Provincial for Canada. In 1872, the overworked priest attended a general council of the community at Notre Dame in Indiana. He examined the school minutely, including the kitchen, the laundry, and the refectory. He immediately requested sisters to help him with the domestic work at his own college. Presented with four recruits, he realized with dismay that none of them spoke French. On further appeal to his superior general, the wise and holy Very Reverend Eduoard Sorin, sent Sister Marie

Léonie and another sister, putting Léonie in charge of the little group. At last, her true apostolate was beginning.

When Father Sorin missioned Sister Léonie to Memramcook, she imagined that she was being sent to the most uncivilized region in the universe; this impression was immediately modified upon her arrival there. She soon grew to love deeply the region and its Acadian people. They returned her affection in full measure. She realized how forsaken these French-speaking people were and how threatened they were by anglicization on the part of both state and Church. There was no existing French-speaking religious community of women to receive those aspiring to religious life. Simple in both speech and manners, Sister Léonie was kind to everyone, rich or poor, learned or ignorant. She was considered a counselor and a saint by the Acadians. Many young Acadian girls were attracted to the religious life, especially that of domestic service to the priests and priests-to-be in the colleges and seminaries. Acadia was not the only place requesting the services of religious women for the management of the domestic section of an institution. Every new college in Quebec needed such workers. At last, Bishop Edward Charles Fabre of Montreal asked Sister Léonie to found a small community for the domestic service of colleges.

Sister Marie Léonie discussed the idea with Father Lefebvre. There were many difficulties and obstacles which would need to be overcome. Until a solution could be worked out, a convent workshop was founded to receive young Acadian women as auxiliaries. On August 26, 1877, fourteen Acadian girls adopted a uniform habit, different from that of Holy Cross. The general chapter of the order accepted the idea of a new foundation in 1880, and the official document was drawn and signed by Father Lefebvre on May 31, 1880.

After twenty-one years in Acadia, the motherhouse and novitiate were transferred to Sherbrooke. The order continued to grow and at the time of Marie Léonie's death comprised forty houses.

Mother Léonie as the foundress of the Little Sisters of the Holy Family, in 1895.

From 1894 until her death in 1912, Mother Marie Léonie was afflicted with throat and liver ailments. In spite of her poor health, she continued to work and travel on behalf of the order. Her constant reply to those who advised her to slow down was, "We shall rest in Heaven!"

On May 3, 1912, Mother Marie Léonie started her day as usual: Mass, breakfast with the community, council meeting, and with the help of her secretary, the correction of the Book of Rules, which was finished and sent to the print shop. After an hour of prayer and the rosary in the chapel, she went to visit the sick sisters in the infirmary. To one of them, she made a prophetic remark: "I'll see you in Heaven." After supper, she went upstairs with two sisters, who noticed an unusual weariness and pointed it out to her. She replied, "I will go to bed immediately; I feel sleepy." As soon as she lay down, she became so pale that the sisters called the doctor and a priest. Peacefully, Mother Léonie breathed her last as the priest was administering the last rites.

Note

*Spelled "Alodie" in the baptismal records, she was known as "Elodie" throughout her life.

The reliquary in the chapel of the motherhouse of the order which guards the remains of Blessed Marie Léonie.

Blessed Mary of the Cross MacKillop
1842-1909

The Cross Down Under

At 8:00 a.m., the bishop arrived and demanded the presence of the sick superior. Wan and drawn, she entered and asked for his blessing. He refused it, then turned to the assembled sisters and announced that because of her disobedience and rebelliousness, Mother Mary of the Cross was to be excommunicated. Instructing her to kneel before him, Bishop Sheil read out the stern sentence of excommunication.

As Mary MacKillop knelt, dazed and silent, on that September morning in 1871, the bishop of Adelaide informed the sisters that anyone who had further dealings with her would suffer the same penalty.

Mary recalled, "An awful scene, one that I can never forget, followed. When I was ordered to leave . . . my poor sisters followed, and some . . . seemed bereft of all reason . . . utterly unable to control themselves . . . but it did not last long. The Bishop called [them] back, and then one after another asked to be dispensed from their vows, saying they could not follow any but the [original Constitution]. At first he listened to a few, but seeing all of the same mind, ordered the rest back to their places, positively forbidding them to think of leaving without permission. . . ."

Mary left the convent immediately, and for the next six months lived quietly with friends. Within weeks, most of the sisters in Adelaide had been either expelled or dispensed from the order, and the convent turned over to a different group.

The true grit and goodness of the character of Australia's first native saint was brought out during this time. In spite of the fact that priest friends advised her that proper procedure had not been followed and the excommunication was invalid, Mary did not protest. She refused to speak up in her own defense and would not willingly let others do so. Instead, she accepted the bishop's actions as a cross given by God; she felt it was a trial that she and the sisters were intended to endure. She waited patiently for it to reach its natural resolution.

Mary never spoke or wrote a word, in public or private, against the bishop; instead, there is a clear written record showing that she continuously defended him, asked others not to blame him, and said only that she felt he had made a mistake or was misguided by his advisors.

A report appeared in the Catholic newspaper and a veritable storm of gossip and misinformation broke.

The wildest sort of rumors circulated. Mary said, "[Once] all the disturbance in the papers commenced, had it not been for a kind few who encouraged me, I would have fled from the place altogether." The human in Mary wanted to flee; the saint stayed, silent and prayerful.

In mid-February, shortly before his death, Bishop Sheil's mind seemed to clear. On the same day he received the last rites, the bishop, who had once been a friend and supporter of Mother Mary, instructed a trustworthy priest to find her and remove the sentence of excommunication.

Although the sentence was devastating to the woman who had worked so hard to aid the poor and downtrodden of her native land, she never held ill feelings against the bishop who pronounced it. With a magnanimous generosity of spirit, she wrote, "Our late and much loved Bishop was far too kind a Father to the children of the [Order] for any, much less myself, to forget his memory now. I think he thought too kindly of us, and when some who did not understand our struggles and intentions spoke, perhaps too hastily of us, he believed what he heard and consequently felt bitterly disappointed in us."

Mary MacKillop was born January 15, 1842, in Fitzroy, Melbourne, Australia, barely fifty years after the first Europeans had settled in the country. She was the oldest of eight children of Alexander MacKillop and Flora MacDonald, recent Scottish immigrants.

Although Mary's father was a good, religious man, devoted to his children, he was a poor provider. His reckless business deals often resulted in the family being supported by relatives. At sixteen, Mary became the main provider for the family, working first as a governess, then a shop assistant, and finally a schoolteacher.

From her earliest years, Mary had a

Young Mary MacKillop, circa 1870.

sense of God's presence and was attracted to religious life. The welfare of others always concerned her. Her sister Annie said, "She took charge of us all."

Once, her mother came home to find eleven-year-old Mary dressing her baby brother and the hired nurse nowhere to be seen. When she inquired regarding the nurse's whereabouts, the "little mother" said, "I sent her away. I sacked her. She was drunk."

Mary's childhood was not a happy or carefree one. She accepted responsibilities at an early age and death, financial worries, and family problems marred her early life.

For a time the family lived in a rural area near Melbourne and made their living by raising sheep and cattle and farming. Here they lived close to Mary's MacDonald grandparents and Mary became very attached to her grandfather, who called her his *"gnothach miadhail* [precious thing]." From him, Mary picked up a gentle Scottish lilt that stayed with her the rest of her life. Her favorite pet was a calf named Blorac that Grandfather MacDonald gave her, and he taught her to ride a pony at a tender age.

When Mary was five, Grandfather MacDonald drowned in a tragic accident. Six months later, her much-loved baby brother died.

Shortly thereafter, Mary went to stay with an aunt in Melbourne. On her first night there, her aunt went in to check on her, thinking she might be homesick. Mary was sitting up in bed, wide awake. She told her aunt, "A beautiful lady has been here and told me she would be a mother to me always." This aunt believed the little girl had seen a vision of the Virgin. As an adult, Mary wrote a prayer that seemed to confirm this: "Ah, my Mother, think of the day when I knelt but a child to ask you to be my Mother and to let me love no other mother but you, and I remember your gentle whisper when you said that you marked me as your child since my birth. . . ."

On Mary's return home, she took up her chores — housework, caring for the younger children, light farm chores — and spent her free time on horseback.

When there was enough money, the children attended school. This was rare, because money was usually very tight, so Alexander taught the children at home. Before he married, he had studied for the priesthood, so he was able to give the children a well-rounded education. Mary was intelligent and an eager student.

In those days, to abandon a religious life was something of a disgrace and Mary began to feel that she should take her father's place. ". . . From the time I came to understand that he had been intended for the Church, and had not persevered, I began to desire [to] leave all I loved and live for God alone."

Mary heard and read about the sad predicament of many families caused by the gold rush (1851 to 1861). Women and children were left behind on bush property or in dismal city slums. The misery of those left in loneliness, fear, and abject poverty pricked Mary's social conscience, and she became committed to the idea of somehow helping these struggling Australians.

At sixteen, Mary worked for Sands and Kenny stationers in Melbourne. She had a warm and genuine nature, and the owners' families became close friends. She did not like the job, however, because it had nothing in common with the charitable work she hoped to perform as a nun. Also, the way that some of the wealthy customers sometimes treated her raised her hackles. Mary hated the prejudice that could allow people to be judged by their social status, race, religion, occupation, or wealth.

In 1860, Mary began teaching at Penola. Here she realized the beauty and the perils of the Australian bush country. The people lived hard, rugged lives; many became social degenerates and alcoholics. This lifestyle was, in many ways, a legacy from the gold rush, when the huge influx of immigrants caused a population explosion that left many destitute. In this pioneer era, life was tough in the bush and even tougher in the colony of South Australia, which struggled with a recession and rising unemployment. Often people looked to the Church for relief, but there were few priests and no religious orders involved in social welfare.

At Penola, the parish priest was an English emigrant, Father Julian Tenison Woods. He and Mary seemed to connect on an intellectual level, both being humanitarians, devoutly religious, and committed to improving the lot of ordinary Australians. Both felt that if the children of poor families could receive a Catholic education they would acquire a knowledge of God and an opportunity to improve their lot in life.

Mary and Father Woods realized that many of the poor children in Australia were not attending school, and were discriminated against when they did. By 1860, all the other colonies had at least one order of nuns. In South Australia there were no sisters because of extreme poverty, harsh living conditions, and a small proportion of Catholics. A group of sisters was needed who would be flexible, well-educated, committed, used to Australian conditions, and who would be willing to live in the same poverty as those they served. The people were scattered, so the sisters would have to live in small groups out in the country; frontier hardships would be their daily lot. Father Woods and Mary began to plan the establishment of just such an order — an order not based on European ideas, but an order of Australians for Australia.

In 1860, Father Woods was a young, newly ordained priest of twenty-eight. He was handsome, intelligent, and creative, with a charismatic personality. His human faults included gullibility, nervousness, and vanity, which eventually caused problems for Mary and for the order they jointly founded — the Sisters of Saint Joseph of the Sacred Heart. In spite of their eventual rift, Mary always acknowledged the good in Father Woods. At the time of his final illness, she visited him and sent little comforts to him. After his death, she wrote a biography of him, highlighting the best parts of his nature. This, in spite of the fact that he had often acted against her.

In 1863, Mary moved to Portland where she taught in the Catholic Denominational School and helped her mother run a boarding house.

After work, Mary often went to church to pray. One evening when she did not return home at the usual time, the family became worried and went to look for her. Mary had been so deep in prayer she did not hear the church being locked for the night, and was locked in.

In Portland, a wealthy young man fell in love with Mary and wanted to marry her. In spite of his persistent advances, Mary resisted, determined to become a nun.

Mary's teaching job in Portland ended over an ugly incident with the headmaster, a Mr. Cusack. An inspector came to examine the children, and the teachers' pay depended on the result of this exam. Shortly before the inspection, Mr. Cusack took over the classes that Mary and her sister Annie had so carefully prepared and gave them the poorly prepared students he had been instructing. During the examination, he held the answers up on cards, behind the inspector's back. When Mary's father heard what had happened, he stormed to the school in angry protest, and a nasty scene ensued. Although the headmaster was eventually terminated, much gossip was spread about. In charity, Mary kept silent, which led to her being blamed for the entire problem. Years later, Mary encountered this same headmaster in Sydney, waiting for a ferry. He was old, crippled, and in rags, obviously leading a miserable life. Mary had long since forgiven him, and she offered him the little money she had with her, touched to see him in such condition.

Father Woods had kept up with Mary's problems at Portland and decided that it was time for Mary to return to Penola and begin her preparations to become a nun.

Mary's family was still deep in debt, and Father Woods rashly agreed to settle their debt. In her innocence, Mary never questioned how a poor parish priest would accomplish this. She wrote, "At last I began to think that my obligations to my family were nearly fulfilled . . . and that I could freely turn to God alone."

As it turned out, Father Woods never paid a penny of the family debt; not from bad intentions, but because he was broke. It was eventually settled by money inherited from deceased members of the MacKillop and MacDonald families.

Father Woods outlined a plan that would, in effect, split the MacKillop family, overriding Mary's objections by telling her that her family would never be safe as long as the improvident Alexander was living with them. For a time, Alexander was to move to his brother's property near Portland, while Flora stayed on in Portland. One child would stay with relatives, one would look for a job, and Mary and her sisters Annie and Lexie would go to Penola to open a school. Those were the last days that Alexander would spend with his family; he died three years later.

Father Woods and Mary agreed that poverty should not prevent any child from attending their school, so fees were paid only by those who could afford them. Mary found an old stable which she turned into a schoolhouse with the help of her brother John, a carpenter. Opened in January 1866, this is considered the first school of the Josephites. Two months later, on the feast of Saint Joseph, Mary publicly declared her commitment to become a religious. She wore a simple black dress and hat, and began signing her letters "Mary, Sister of Saint Joseph." That day is regarded as the founding date of the Josephites.

Although they were not the first Australian order, the Sisters of Saint Joseph were the first group founded specifically to teach Australia's poor. For the first few years, Father Woods made all the important decisions regarding the sisters, considering them his special charge. Mary, the nominal head of the group, took the name Mary of the Cross at Father Woods's insistence. Perhaps the choice of name was prophetic. Her acceptance of the crosses in her life with silence and charity, never blaming others and faithfully resisting her natural urge to retreat, is the hallmark of her sanctity.

To understand the life of Blessed Mary of the Cross, it is necessary to understand the culture and the time in which she lived. She began a work of education and social welfare in a pioneer time. The awesomely rugged climate of the country and the poverty with which she underpinned her work engendered many hardships. In true gospel spirit, the sisters lived as, and with, the poor they served. Australia, at this time, was a country filled with prejudice: there was racial prejudice, prejudice based on wealth and status, sexism, and prejudice within the Church. Mary spent her life gently combating this prejudice by her own example, seeing God in every human. Mary and the Josephite order exemplified those qualities at the very heart of the colonial spirit: justice, equality, and a fair go for all. Mary's egalitarian approach to religious life upset many of the clergy used to European models. They were familiar with religious orders of women where "choir" sisters from upper-class families lived a genteel life of prayer and "lay" sisters from the lower classes did the menial work. The Josephites had no such class distinctions. Their sisters were forbidden

Sister Mary of the Cross

to speak of their early lives in order that none might be considered "better" than any other. These sisters did not hide behind high walls of city convents. They lived where they worked; if the work was in the bush, or in the slums, that is where they were sent. They lived in small groups of two or three, in makeshift huts or whatever housing was on hand.

The original constitution of the Josephites called for two startling things: poverty and central government. The prohibition against the order owning property was later amended in Rome. After many long battles, Mary finally won approval for the central government, which meant the sisters would be governed by a superior elected from their number and individual bishops could not make changes which would change the mission of the order. The male-dominated Australian Church of the time believed the nuns required a man to properly interpret spiritual and theological matters, and to offer guidance and consistently fought the idea of a central government.

All fledgling religious orders face problems. Many of the problems the Josephites faced came from the clergy. Time and again, the strength of will, extreme charity, and silent suffering of Blessed Mary of the Cross led to eventual victory for the order.

Blessed Mary's life was filled with crosses. She wrote, "The Cross is my portion — it is also my sweet rest and support. I could not be happy without the Cross — I would not lay it down for all the world could give. With the Cross I am happy, but without it would be lost."

In mid-1867, the sisters extended their work to Adelaide, and on August 15, 1867, Mary made her first vows. In a moving ceremony orchestrated by Father Woods, Mary wore a crown of thorns on her head and a cross on her shoulders. She promised the traditional obedience, chastity, and poverty, and added a fourth vow: to promote the love of Jesus Christ in the hearts of children.

In addition to their work in education, Mary directed the Josephites to help alleviate a multitude of other social service problems. They visited hospitals, sickrooms, and jails, and sheltered the homeless. By 1868, there were eight Josephite schools as well as an orphanage and a home for women in "moral danger," which accepted former prisoners, prostitutes, and unwed mothers. Government social welfare programs were practically nonexistent in Australia before the 1900s. In spite of a drastic shortage of money, the Josephites started an additional crises center in Adelaide which served neglected children, young people in "moral danger," old people, and homeless migrant women of all races and religions. It was named "The Providence" because the sisters relied on the providence of God to provide the means to run it. The sisters knocked on doors daily, begging donations, and did plain sewing for a small fee. At first, only women and children stayed there while looking for work or a permanent home; men were given food and clothing but had to find their own accommodations. If one of the destitute died there, the sisters always scraped together enough money for a proper funeral.

In 1869, the sisters opened the Solitude to provide for the aged, the terminally ill, and alcoholics. By this time, the order had grown to seventy-two sisters who operated twenty-one schools throughout South Australia.

Aware of the difficult adjustment to a new lifestyle that the new sisters faced, Mary wrote regularly to each of them, encouraging them. She was generous with her praise and gentle with reprimands.

Another of Mary's greatest crosses was her lifelong, chronic bad health. Stress and her rigorous travel schedule contributed greatly to the disintegration of her constitution. She had mild heart problems and severe bi-weekly attacks of dysmenorrhoea, accompanied by migraine headaches, dizzy spells, fever, and nausea. In her early fifties, she developed rheumatism (arthritis) in her hands and legs, and bronchial problems. A stroke in 1902 left her in a wheelchair for the last seven years of her life. In spite of her health, she continued her exhausting schedule. After her stroke, her right hand was paralyzed, so she taught herself to write with her left hand in order to continue her correspondence.

In her younger years, Mary's headaches were so debilitating that, under her doctor's direction, she took medicinal doses of brandy. Having lived with a father who often overindulged in alcohol, and seeing the prevalence of alcoholism in the society with which the sisters worked, Mary was well aware of the thin line between use and abuse. She recognized the risk of becoming alcohol-dependent, and as a prevention against anyone misconstruing the facts, she assigned a sister to measure out her prescribed dose and then lock away the bottle. This was a providential precaution.

Sister Mary was co-founder of the Sisters of Saint Joseph of the Sacred Heart.

In 1884, a commission was held in Adelaide to investigate allegations by three Australian ecclastics that Mary was an alcoholic, and an embezzler, among other charges. Sydney's Archbishop Moran was in charge of the investigation, which absolved Mary of the charges. His report was submitted to Cardinal Simeoni in Rome in March 1885. Although the report cleared Mary, Archbishop Moran felt the matter would reflect badly on the bishop who had brought the charges and advised that his report be kept confidential. Accordingly, the report was hidden away in Rome. This led to a hitch in Mary's beatification process in 1931, because no official documentation of her clearance could be located. It was twenty years before Archbishop Moran's report was located and her cause could proceed.

The last eighteen months of her life, Mary spent in continual pain, virtually bedridden. Her nurses testify that she suffered without complaining. Shortly before her death, Cardinal Moran visited and told the sisters, "Her death will bring many blessings, not only on yourselves and your Congregation, but on the whole Australian Church. . . . I consider I have this day assisted at the death-bed of a saint."

Mary died quietly and calmly on the morning of August 8, 1909.

At the exact time of Mary's death, Father Thomas Lee was celebrating Mass in Adelaide. At the Consecration, he saw Mother Mary standing at the right side of the altar, smiling at him. His shocked hesitation was noticed by the congregation.

When he arrived in the sacristy after Mass, the sisters came to ask if he were ill. He replied, "No. Mother Mary is dead."

Asked how he knew she was dead, he replied, "Because I saw her."

Immediately after her death, expressions of sympathy began to arrive from all parts of the country, and even from the pope in Rome. Her body was laid out in the motherhouse in Sydney, and a veritable flood of people came to visit and pray by her remains. The feeling that a saint had died was so prevalent that in spite of the fact that the Australians had no

This is a detail from a painting of Mary MacKillop by artist Mary Brady, O.P. (1993).

experience with such a thing, the people began to bring rosaries, crosses, and other objects to touch to the body. They asked for remembrances, and took soil from her grave. The ordinary Australians, who usually shied away from any public display of feelings, openly shed tears at her funeral. This special woman was remembered for her utter selflessness, her kind heart, her steely determination to attain the best for her fellow Australians, and her life of sacrifice. She was honored for her invaluable contribution to the lives of the poor and for her role in establishing the sisters who would carry on her work.

On January 19, 1995, Pope John Paul II raised Mary MacKillop to the honors of the altar at a solemn Beatification Mass in Sydney, which was attended by thousands of her countrymen. He said, "In the vastness of the Australian continent, Blessed Mary MacKillop was not daunted by the great desert, the immense expanses of the outback, nor by the spiritual wilderness which affected so many of her fellow citizens. Rather, she boldly prepared the way of the Lord in the most trying situations. With gentleness, courage and compassion she was a herald of the Good News among the isolated battlers and the urban slum-dwellers. Mother Mary of the Cross knew that behind the ignorance, misery and suffering which she encountered there were people . . . yearning for God and His righteousness. She knew, because she was a true child of her time and place; the daughter of immigrants who had to struggle at all times to build a life for themselves in their new surroundings. Her story reminds us of the need to welcome people, to reach out to the lonely, the bereft, the disadvantaged. To strive for the kingdom of God and his righteousness means to strive to see Christ in the stranger, to meet him in them and to help them to meet him in each one of us!"

Blessed Miguel Pro, S.J.

1891-1927

Martyr for Christ the King

Miguel Augustín Pro Juarez was born January 13, 1891, in Guadalupe, Zacatecas, Mexico. The oldest son of a mining director, Miguel grew up concerned with the status of the workers, and planned to be an engineer in order to help them. His childhood and youth were marked with high spirits and a true sense of joy. His sense of humor and his practical jokes found an outlet in his large and loving family and many friends, who learned to respond in kind. Along with his happy nature, Miguel had a deep spirituality and was devoted to Christ the King and to Our Lady of Guadalupe.

Although he had an intense desire to help the workers and could have made a lucrative career in the business world, Miguel became convinced of a call to the priesthood and applied to enter the Jesuits in 1911. He studied in Mexico until 1914, when the political situation in the country forced the novitiate to close. The seminarians were sent first to Texas, then to California. Miguel later went to Nicaragua, Spain, and finally to Belgium, where he was ordained in 1925.

Miguel developed a serious stomach disorder. In order to hide the pain this caused, he told jokes in order to have an excuse to grab his sides while laughing. A number of operations did not improve his health, and his superiors finally acceded to his wish to return to his beloved and troubled homeland.

Miguel arrived in Mexico City in 1926. Within twenty-three days of his arrival, an order suppressing all public worship was issued. Priests were

As a young boy, Miguel nicknamed himself "The Little Miner" in solidarity with his father's workers.

Miguel often adopted disguises in his hidden ministry in Mexico City.

subject to arrest and prosecution. In addition to celebrating Mass and administering the sacraments in secret, he also collected and distributed food and supplies to the poor of the city. He ministered in secret and had many close calls with capture. Father Pro's life and escapades during this time read like the best of fictionalized espionage novels. In order to carry out his ministry, the valiant young priest adopted a number of disguises. His messages sent to the underground Catholics were coded. These messages signed "*Cocol*" reminded the people not only of the type of sweet bread favored by the heroic priest, but also of the Sweet Bread of the sacrament he brought them. The undercover priest might show up in the middle of the night dressed as a beggar in order to baptize an infant, or, dressed as a policeman, slip unnoticed into police headquarters itself to hear confession and distribute Viaticum to Catholic prisoners before their execution.

In November 1927, there was an assassination attempt on a former president. The car used by the assassins had once belonged to Pro's brother. Although all three of the Pro brothers had solid alibis, they were marked men and were betrayed within a few days. With no due process or trial, the order for their execution was issued, and in spite of a stay of execution obtained by Miguel's sister and an attorney, the brothers were led to their death. A phone call from the Argentine ambassador saved the life of the youngest brother, Roberto, who was exiled to the United States.

The first to be led out, Miguel blessed the firing squad and expressed forgiveness. As his last request, he humbly knelt in front of the bullet-pocked walls and prayed, a rosary in his hands. Rejecting the traditional blindfold, he stood up and stretched his arms out in the

This photo was taken by the police the night before Miguel's execution.

form of a cross. As the rifles fired, his last words were clearly heard: "¡*Viva Christo Rey!* [Long live Christ the King!]"

A number of newsmen were invited to attend the execution in order to photograph the cowardice of the condemned Catholics. Contrary to expectations, Father Pro and the others met death heroically. These photographs today bear mute testimony to their heroism.

What motivated the heroism of Blessed Miguel Pro? A fragment of a poem he wrote the year before his death gives us a clue to his deep spirituality and exuberant joyfulness:

Father Miguel praying, as he had requested, before his exeuction.

> O Lord! take all I have, but give me souls, I pray;
> Take health and earthly goods, and even my friend's esteem;
> But let zeal's flames devouring, higher mount each day,
> That in my heart from Thine a dim reflection gleam.
> Let sorrow, loneliness, and exile encompass me;
> Let friends be absent when my heart is crushed with pain.
> My mother's kisses take — earth's sweetest ecstasy — But grant, dear Lord, I pray, that sinful souls I gain.

Father Miguel Pro, S.J., was beatified September 25, 1988, by Pope John Paul II, as the first of this century's wave of martyrs from Mexico to be so honored.

Father Miguel, without a blindfold, held his arms in the shape of a cross, saying, "Long live Christ the King," then was executed.

Montserrat Grases

1941-1959

Sanctity with Serenity

The life of Montserrat Grases is an inspiration for those who, in any walk of life, try to give their existence a higher meaning. Through the everyday things of life, Montserrat became a holocaust of love for God and an instrument to make others happy. The life of this young Spanish girl proves that sanctity isn't something removed from ordinary life; rather, that sanctity lies in serene, cheerful, simple, and yet heroic correspondence to the will of God. Montse, as her friends called her, died when she was only seventeen years old. Her brief years, lived with love and simplicity, and united to suffering, show that the way to true happiness has God as its beginning and its end.

Montserrat Grases was born July 10, 1941, in Barcelona, Spain, the second of nine children of Manuel and Manolita Grases. She was baptized nine days later in the church of Our Lady of Pilar. According to local custom, she was confirmed, along with two of her brothers, in 1944, when she was almost three years old.

The Grases family was a close one, and the older children helped their parents with the multitude of tasks involved in raising such a large family. The parents taught their children the value of work and study, and provided for them a sound basis for a Christian life.

In 1952, Montse's parents came into contact with Opus Dei, an institution of Catholic laypeople whose spirituality teaches that sanctity is directed to all men. Opus Dei, from the Latin "work of God," is the Church's first personal prelature, whose mission is to help ordinary faithful live a deep awareness of their Christian vocation by practicing a life of prayer and active apostolate through their daily work and family, social and civic activities. Founded by Blessed Josemaría Escrivá, Opus Dei originated in Madrid, Spain, in 1928. This group and its ideals influenced the Grases family greatly, and because of it their home was loving, bright, and cheerful.

At the age of five, Montse began her education at the Colegio de

Montse with her mother.

Jesús-María. She made her First Communion in the little chapel of the school in May 1948 at the age of six.

As a young teenager, Montse was a pretty girl: tall, strong, and athletic. She had a cheerful, outgoing personality, and a ready smile. She was dynamic, open, sincere, and simple. Along with her outgoing nature, Montse had a quick temper that caused her to get angry easily, and to argue with her brothers. Little by little, through a daily struggle with her nature, she developed a more tranquil and serene character. In school, Montse displayed average intelligence, but was very self-motivated. She was a good athlete and played basketball, tennis, and Ping-pong. Her favorite recreation was outings with her friends. With them, she climbed most of the mountains near Seva, the village where her family spent the majority of their summers. Montse was good at manual and artistic tasks, and she applied her talents to her household duties. At get-togethers, she sang and played the guitar.

When she was thirteen, Montse went for the first time to Llar, a center directed by the women's branch of Opus Dei in Barcelona. A group of girls attended a meditation directed by a priest in the oratory of the center. After this, the girls had a lively get-together in the living room of the center. When Montse arrived home, she bubbled with happiness, and told her mother that she wanted to go back. From this time, Montse returned again and again to Llar; a new phase had begun in her life. She learned how to grow in her interior life with a few minutes of prayer, of conversation with Our Lord every day. Close to the tabernacle, she told Our Lord all her joys, her work, her struggles. When her studies allowed her some free time, she helped with chores at Llar, she organized excursions, and she sang and played the guitar at the get-togethers. Montse's interior development began to show at home. Her family noticed that she was more cheerful, and more aware of her family. She was controlling her temper, and fights with her brothers were becoming rare. The spirit of Opus Dei was reflected more and more often in her daily actions.

In October 1956, at the age of fifteen, Montse entered the Professional School for Women in Barcelona. Her classes included domestic formation, cooking, life drawing, dancing, and artistic trade.

This same year, Montse attended a retreat at the Opus Dei conference center, Castelldaura. Her previous two years had seen her grow in interior life. At this retreat, in direct conversation with God and in the silence of prayer, she discovered that she wanted to be more generous and to put more love into her life. The possibility of total dedication to God occurred to her. After the retreat, she was happy but uncertain. She discussed it with her mother, who encouraged her to simply have faith and do whatever God might ask of her. Montse prayed and waited. Finally, a little before Christmas, she became convinced that God had asked her to give her all. She told her parents of this, and the three of them asked God, in prayer, for whatever would be best for Montse.

On December 24, 1957, Montse went to Llar and asked to become a member of Opus Dei. Externally, nothing had changed. Her daily activities were much the same. Only her heart had changed. More and more she lived in a spirit of apostolic impatience in her search of Love.

In January 1958, Montse went skiing with a group of friends. She fell, and the fall left her leg sore. Thinking she had sprained it, she went to a doctor, who didn't consider it a serious problem and who recommended the use of a knee pad. The pain, however, continued and increased. The doctor prescribed rest. Montse got up later in the mornings and did less around the house. Montse considered this enforced rest as a special mortification because it made things more difficult for her mother.

In spite of the rest, the leg did not improve, and a cast was put in place. On her trips to Llar her friends kidded her about the bulky leg. She laughed with them, although her leg ached. When she prayed in the oratory, Montse had to prop her leg on a stool. Once, a tired-looking girl entered the room and all of the chairs were taken. Montse inched her leg off the stool and smilingly invited the girl to be seated.

Always smiling, always a joy.

In June 1958, the doctor gave tragic news to Manuel Grases. His daughter was suffering from Ewing's sarcoma, bone cancer. The progress of the disease was irreversible. Radiation treatments might

Montse as an old woman in a school play.

slow the cancer, but it would certainly be fatal. Her stricken parents could not talk about it.

Montse did not know what was wrong, but she began to suspect that her condition was serious. Then, the radiation therapy sessions began. She pleaded with her mother, "Can't I know what's happening? What disease I have?"

Her mother told her that she thought it best not to talk about it just yet. She calmed her daughter by promising to talk about it later. Montse asked again and again, and at last extracted a promise from her father to tell her about it when they arrived at home one night. They arrived late, but Montse remembered her father's promise. She walked into her parents' room and said to them with great calmness, "Well, now that you've settled down, let's see if you can tell me everything."

Sadly, her father explained to Montse that she was suffering from cancer of the bone. "And if they cut off my leg?" was her only question. Her parents were amazed at the calmness of her reaction. They answered her question by telling her to leave everything in God's hands. Montse understood, and did not seem to be frightened. Instead, she calmly returned to her room and after making her daily examination of conscience went to bed.

On checking, her mother discovered that she held fallen asleep peacefully almost immediately. It is hard to explain Montse's serenity unless one understands that she had organized her life as a loving dialogue with her Lord, and that while still a child she had learned a difficult and important lesson: to embrace lovingly the will of God.

The following day, Montse went to Llar. After a brief prayer in the oratory, she knocked at the door of the directress's office, telling her that she wished to speak with her. While Montse waited, she did a little ironing. Then, in Mexican style, she sang: "When I lived most happily without thinking of affection, you wanted me to love you, and I loved you with a passion. And I will continue to love you until after death. I love you with all my soul, and the soul never dies."

The directress relates, "I went first to the oratory and then called Montse. I had feared this moment and now that it had arrived I tried to appear calm, but I didn't succeed because Montse said to me, 'Were you crying, Lia?' Then she immediately said, 'You're clever. So you knew everything and you didn't tell me a thing. But now I know because yesterday papa told me.'" When Lia asked her what next, Montse replied, "I'm ready. I just came from confession and I'm very happy."

The conversation continued in such a supernatural tone, showing Lia how completely Montse had accepted God's will, that she was overwhelmed. Montse told Lia of her conversation the previous night with her parents, and of her realization of how much they were suffering. She mentioned that she knew her mother had expected her to say something, and said, "Nothing occurred to me. I just thought that I had to be strong. I kissed my crucifix and said 'serviam [I will serve].'"

From then on, Montse spoke of her death with a great naturalness, even though she often found it hard to believe because the pain in her leg had diminished. She wrote to the founder of Opus Dei, asking him to pray that she would know how to be strong and to offer her sufferings for the work. She wrote, "I'm not afraid of pain because I think that if I'm faithful to God each day in what He asks of me, he will help me when the hard part comes."

Montse continued as she had been before. The only noticeable thing was a bit of a limp, which she made jokes about to her friends. She remained cheerful, and tried to act normal at all times. She continued her outings with her friends, and took part in a benefit presentation of a play in which she had the role of an old lady. Her mother became worried that Montse had forgotten that she was going to die soon, and one day asked her if she felt she would be cured. Montse answered with a simple "no." She never spoke of her disease, made light of her suffering, and developed a knack for changing the topic of conversation if her condition were mentioned.

In September, the disease worsened, and Montse began to experience a great deal of pain. She had often expressed the desire to go to Rome and see the pope and meet the founder of Opus Dei. Her parents wanted to satisfy this wish, so on November 11, 1958, her parents saw her off on a plane from the Barcelona airport. On her week's trip, she stayed at a residence directed by the women's branch of Opus Dei called Villa delle Palma. The day after her arrival, she met Monsignor Escrivá and after their visit he thoughtfully suggested that they have their pictures made to send home to her family. Her visit to Saint Peter's impressed her deeply, and she particularly enjoyed meeting girls from a number of nations at the Villa.

On her arrival home, Montse greeted her

From a publication featuring Montse's story.

family joyously and shared with them all the delights of her trip. Her little brother was entranced with her thoughtfulness in bringing him a number of specimens for his bottletop collection that she had remembered to pick up at all of the places she had visited.

After her return, the cancer progressed rapidly. She went to Llar daily, in spite of the great effort the short trip cost her. From her notebook, where she kept the record of her examination of conscience, one can notice the constant progress of her interior life and the demands she made on herself. During this last phase of her life, she lived so close to God that externally you couldn't notice that she was in pain. She remained cheerful and accepted her death peacefully. Little by little the disease followed its normal course: sleepless nights, and increasing, nearly unbearable pain. By the middle of February, her leg was so swollen that the skin began to crack. The treatments were painful, but instead of complaining, Montse always had an affectionate word for those who treated her.

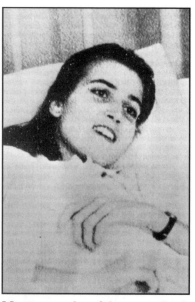

Montse was cheerful, even as death drew near.

With great fortitude, Montse offered her pain to God for the intentions of the pope and for the founder of Opus Dei. Her courage impressed all who visited her. Around her one seemed to breathe serenity and peace. Toward the end, she was unable to eat; a piece of ice was a treat for her. One day she told her father, "We're the happiest family in Barcelona. When I die, I don't want anyone to be sad. There has to be joy." To console her family and friends, she frequently said, "I assure you that from Heaven I'll help you a lot. I'll never leave you." The end came rapidly.

She received the Blessing of the Sick. Early on the morning of Holy Thursday, Lia, the directress at Llar, was sitting with her. Montse whispered a request for her to pray, since she herself couldn't talk anymore. About ten o'clock, she tried to sit up to see the picture of Our Lady that she had in front of her bed. She whispered her last words, "How much I love you. When are you coming to take me?" At noon, those who were with her prayed the Angelus, and then began a rosary. They had just finished the first mystery when she died. Montse's death, as did her life, occurred without spectacle or noise. It was the crowning of a generous life that became more heroic and dedicated during a long trial of great suffering. The pastor of the Church of Our Lady of the Pillar commented, "In a case like this, instead of being sad and offering sympathy, you have to intone the Alleluia."

Montserrat's reputation for sanctity began to spread immediately after her death. The diocesan informative process was begun, and completed, within ten years of her death. The decree approving her writings was issued in 1974, and in May 1992, the Congregation for Causes of Saints issued the decree approving the validity of the process of her cause.

Father Peter Chang Wen Chao, C.I.C.M. (Scheut)

1894-1948

Chinese Martyr

Chapter

25

From the time of Christ, in all parts of the world, there have been those so faithful to God that they are willing to suffer anything rather than give Him up. With heroic fidelity, these Christian martyrs stand as beacons for all of mankind.

In a letter to the superior general of the Missionhurst Fathers of Scheut (Belgium) at the end of his novitiate, a young Chinese priest, Peter Chang Wen Chao, had explicitly expressed his readiness, if this would please the Lord, "to drink the chalice of suffering with Him." Twenty years later, that chalice was offered to him, undiluted. Father Peter Chang drained it to the bottom.

Peter Chang Wen Chao was born in the little village of Hsiamiaoerhkow in eastern Inner Mongolia (China) on July 3, 1894. He came from a deeply Christian family, and at the age of twelve he attended the high school of the nearby central mission station of Sungshutsuitze. Later, he transferred to the seminary where, in addition to the humanities, he also studied philosophy and theology.

Under the guidance of Father Florent de Preter, this seminary was considered one of the top three in the country. Here the students studied Latin, mathematics, and sciences in a program modeled after the European pattern. In addition, the students studied the Chinese language for twelve or more hours each week. The lengthy curriculum resulted in seminarians who were usually ordained at about the age of thirty.

Father Peter Chang was of average intelligence, and was not one of the seminary's outstanding students. He had a particular aptitude for Chinese and did very well in the study of his mother tongue. From 1922 to 1926 he studied theology at the new regional major seminary of Tat'ung. At this time, all the mission congregations in China were being urged to accept native candidates.

Gradually, Peter had felt drawn to the religious life as so aptly witnessed by these Belgian missionary priests of the Immaculate Heart of Mary C.I.C.M. (Scheut). His views were expressed in a detailed letter he wrote in exquisite Latin to the General Superior of the order, Father Rutten. Peter wrote that he was not simply attracted to the apostolic mission works of the order. What attracted him was the religious life with its call for personal sanctity. Through the vows of poverty, chastity, and obedience, Peter aimed to strive more consciously for perfection.

The young Peter Chang Wen Chao, C.I.C.M. (Scheut).

Peter discussed his hopes with the director of the seminary, who encouraged him. The director promised to write the General Council in Scheut in support of his application. While he waited for the answer to his application for acceptance as a member of the order, Peter was ordained and appointed for pastoral work. Father Chang was ordained on May 16, 1926, two months before his thirtieth birthday. He was assigned as the assistant priest at the village of Liukiatze.

In the encyclical *Rerum Ecclesiae*, published in early 1926, Pope Pius XI expressed his hope that suitable candidates from mission countries be granted admission to local congregations. In light of this encyclical, the order decided to establish a novitiate in China.

In addition to Peter Chang, some other Chinese candidates had requested admission. In 1927, Father Peter, along with another Chinese priest, Joseph Ch'ang Shou I, was admitted to the novitiate established at the order's house of studies in T'ientsin. Father Richard Quintens, procurator, was to serve as Novice Master to the two young priests. For a year, fathers Chang and Shou followed a program similar to that in Europe. The two young priests were allowed to pronounced their vows on December 27, 1928. In his report to the General Council, Father Quintens described Peter as "a man with a practical bent; he makes a good impression and is well-mannered. Average intelligence, but sound common sense. . . . Naturally reserved. . . . Very pious priest, obedient, punctual, modest, dignified, full of conviction, and energetic. Health rather weak." In this and in later reports, Peter's accommodating character and his great charity are pointed out.

Father Peter Chang Wen Chao, C.I.C.M. (Scheut)

Peter was sent to the newly established Vicariate of Tsining as a teacher at the minor seminary, which was temporarily entrusted to the Belgian Missionhurst priests. A year later, he returned to eastern Inner Mongolia. In 1930 he served as assistant priest at Laohukow, and then for three years he was parish priest at Hinglung. Here, with pious dedication and practical hard work, he succeeded in making this new station into a model mission.

The regional seminary of Tat'ung included in its curriculum a thorough study of classical Chinese. Lay instructors had proven ineffective and expensive. The directing bishops of the governing board of the seminary unanimously proposed that Peter Chang be assigned to teach this subject. Peter was sent to a university in Peking to take an intensive course in Chinese literature, and began his teaching position at the seminary in August 1934.

A colleague of his there remembers him as a dedicated and diligent professor. Although Peter gave the impression of a Chinese scholar in perfect control, he did not much care for this assignment. Most of the seminarians did not have a good background for this subject and they were not attracted to the classical literary language. They did, however, like and appreciate their professor. In a true spirit of obedience, Father Peter carried on until 1943. In addition, he was also appointed as a professor of homiletics and of "good manners."

When the Japanese put the C.I.C.M. confreres in internment camps in 1943, Peter was sent by his superiors to Shanghai to take care of procuration transactions. Under difficult circumstances, he carried out this task ably for two years until, at the end of 1945, he was allowed to return to his region of origin.

At home again, Father Peter encountered only unrest and misery because of the civil war and the Communist occupation. For the next year, he served as the parish priest at Tach'engtze, where he had a difficult time protecting the mission from troops fighting against each other. In January 1947, he was put in charge of the episcopal residence in the city of Lingyuan.

The Missionhurst annals record the account of Peter Chang's martyrdom: "In June 1947, the city was captured by the Reds. The pastor bravely carried on his pastoral work. Up to the last day, he taught the catechumens. On December 3, feast of Saint Francis Xavier, all the missionaries were summoned before the people's court. Father Chang had repeatedly encouraged his confreres with the words: *"Moriamur fortiter* [Let us die bravely]."

The people of the town had all been called together to observe the procedures of the court. Father Chang was called before the judges. He professed his Catholic faith boldly and explained the role of the priest. This was not pleasing to the judges at all. Time after time he was whipped and jeered at. Finally, he was told to stop speaking. Later on, together with five confreres and another Chinese priest, he was led to Meiiingtze, a village in the neighborhood. There they were locked up in jail. The night of January

7, Father Chang was once again submitted to a long hearing. This time he was tortured. Close to daybreak, his broken body was dragged back to his cell; his legs were smashed. The end came soon; he died near noon.

Peter Chang had proved the strength of his faith with heroic fidelity.

Blessed Peter ToRot

1912-1945

Martyr for Marriage

<table>
<tr><td>

Chapter

26

</td><td>

"Do not cry. Go home and pray for me," Peter ToRot told his elderly mother on the day of his death. She was visiting him in the Japanese prison. The police had informed him that the Japanese doctor would come to give him medicine. "I suspect that this is a trick. I am really not ill at all and I cannot think what all this means."

</td></tr>
</table>

He asked his wife to bring his best clothes — his shirt, his *laplap* (loin cloth), and his cross. Death was inevitable. The efforts by the Methodist chief of Navunaram and the Catholic chief of Rakunai to have Peter released had failed. Peter told them, "Do not worry about me. I am a catechist and I am only doing my duty. If I die, I die for my faith." To another, he said of his imprisonment, "I am here because of those who broke their marriage vows and because of those who do not want the growth of God's kingdom."

When the doctor arrived, the Japanese sent the other prisoners outside. Despite their precautions, Arap ToBinabak, one of the prisoners, could see the brightly lit room where Peter had been summoned. The doctor gave Peter an injection, then something to drink, and finally stuffed his ears and nose with cotton wool. Then the doctor and two police officers made him lie down. Peter was stricken with convulsions and looked as though he was trying to vomit. The "doctor" covered his mouth and kept it closed. While the doctor held him, the convulsions continued for a time. At last, the sturdy lay-catechist breathed his last and lay still.

Arap ToBinabak silently spread the word of Peter's death to his companions. Several of the prisoners, taking advantage of the night-time absence of the Japanese, wanted to see his body. Later, they were able to verify his death.

The next morning, a Saturday in July 1945, fellow prisoners found the carefully arranged body. The Japanese, summoned by loudspeaker, registered great surprise when they saw Peter's corpse. Later, they told an old family friend, Anton Tata, that Peter died from a secondary infection. Word was sent to his family, who were allowed to take his corpse for burial, which took place in silence without a religious ceremony.

The immense crowd that attended Peter's burial, in spite of the presence of the Japanese police, immediately acclaimed Peter a martyr. In the Tolai language, Peter was called a *"martir ure ra Lotu,"* a martyr for the Faith.

Peter ToRot was born in 1912 in Rakunai, New Britain, an island off the northeast coast of Papua New Guinea. He was the third of six children of Angelo ToPuia, the village "big man," or chief.

English Methodist missionaries had arrived in New Britain in 1875 along with teachers from Samoa. Sacred Heart missionaries arrived later and spread along the coastline of the Island. They found a primitive people with pagan beliefs, some of whom practiced cannibalism.

Blessed Peter ToRot, a martyr for marriage.

In 1898, Angelo ToPuia came to the coast from his village in the hills and requested the Catholic missionaries to come and teach his people. After instruction, he was received into the Church. Angelo was the *lulual*, or chief, of the village for more than forty years.

Angelo ToPuia was an exceptional individual. Although his ancestors were pagans, he accepted his new religion with great heart. He attempted to bring peace in the area, overcoming the *wantok*, or clan system. He assisted the poor and often took orphans into his own home. He supervised the building of an impressive church and swayed many of his Tolai tribe to accept the gospel. His wife, Maria IaTumul, was a kind and gentle person who backed her husband in this Christian lifestyle.

Peter was raised in this loving and Christian home, learning a charity that went beyond tribal custom and which embraced all who crossed his path. As a child, he got into his share of mischief and trouble, but was honest in admitting his misdemeanors. He was encouraged by his parents in his prayers and devotions. Peter was a good student, an athlete, and a natural leader. Daily, Peter sat and discussed his schoolwork with his parents. He was particularly adept at learning sections from the Bible.

One of the major features of the evangelization of New Guinea was the extensive use of lay-catechists. A school for training catechists was set up at Taliligap and the Sacred Heart Brothers were active in recruiting and teaching the catechists.

The role of the catechist in the village was well-outlined. They were to run the school, instruct people for baptism, gather them and conduct prayer services if the priest was absent, look after the sick and those in need. A demanding program, and the results have proved that it was a fruitful apostolate for evangelization.

Beginning in adolescence, Peter had a strong inclination to piety and obedience. His love for Christ in the Eucharist led him to make frequent visits to the Blessed Sacrament and receive daily Communion. He had a calm and generous nature. Peter also had an intense prayer life. The parish priest, Father Emilio Jakobi, felt that the boy should become a priest. Angelo ToPuia, however, felt that this would be premature and that none of his people were ready for the priesthood. He did agree, however, that Peter should become a catechist.

Peter enrolled at Saint Paul's Mission School in 1930 at the age of eighteen. He obtained the catechist's diploma in 1933 after a little more than two years' study. He was described as being "modest, and there was not the slightest vanity in him, neither with regard to his background nor capability. He let the older catechists guide him in his work and accepted their advice, but eventually eclipsed them all and soon became their recognized leader, although he was younger."

In 1933, Peter was assigned to the mission in his own village. He began to gather large and small groups for instruction and prayer and became acquainted with people's real-life situations. All those who had him as their catechist recall his straightforward and effective teaching. He referred constantly to the Bible and always carried it with him, quoting it directly as the occasion required. He was particularly sensitive in discovering the inner problems in people's lives. Kind and gentle, ToRot was loved because people sensed that he lived up to his teaching. For Peter, his work as a catechist was not merely a job; it was the total dedication of his life to God. He was particularly devoted to those who had fallen away from the practice of the Faith. He explained simply to them how much God loved them and was eager to forgive them. Many returned to the Church.

On November 11, 1936 — the only certain date we know in Peter's life — he married the young Catholic Paula La Varpit, who was from a neighboring village. Their marriage was celebrated in church, but many of the traditional local customs were also joyously included. Fifty shell necklaces to "buy the bride" were presented, and native food and music were included. Three children were eventually born from the union: Andrea, who died after the war; Rufina La Mama, who is still alive and who testified at Peter's beatification process; and a third child, a girl, who was born shortly after Peter's death in 1945 and who died soon thereafter.

As a husband, father, and catechist, Peter carried out his duties with joy and zeal. Before starting work in the morning and before going to bed in the evening, the couple faithfully prayed together. Those who knew them vividly recalled his tenderness to his wife and children.

The decisive turning point in Peter ToRot's life and mission occurred when the Japanese occupied the island during World War II. When they arrived in March 1942, they drove out the small Australian garrison within twenty-four hours and made Rabaul their headquarters for the South Pacific.

At first, the Japanese showed no opposition to any religion practiced by the people. Shortly after their arrival, however, the activities of the expatriate missionaries began to be restricted and later they were confined under guard. This meant that the life of the Church in the villages depended exclusively on the people themselves. When Father Laufer, M.S.C., was sent away, he shook hands with Peter and said, "ToRot, I am leaving all my work here in your hands. Look after these people well. Help them, so that they don't forget about God."

Other catechists did their job with varying amounts of fervor, but Peter ToRot was outstanding as the organizer of his village for prayer, baptisms, communions, weddings, and burials. When the church was destroyed, he built a bush church just outside of Rakunai, and he faithfully carried out his duties from his home, because the mission was closed. He kept records of baptisms and weddings and attempted to help all those in trouble, supporting the other catechists who were confused about the changes brought by the Japanese. At first, he got on well with the Japanese Naval Authorities, who ran things in the early days of the war, and he even learned a little of the Japanese language.

After the Battle of the Coral Sea, the Japanese began to tighten up their lenient policy on religion. They had not succeeded in winning the loyalty of the local people, and the Military Police took over the administration of local affairs. Suspicious and intolerant, they imagined that the local people were praying to their Christian God for the defeat of the Japanese forces and they decided to stop Christian worship. "Too much Christo," they said.

Christian worship, including all types of religious gatherings both public and private, was forbidden. In an attempt to force the local chiefs into collaboration, they decided that the Tolais should return to their previous practice of polygamy, a severe blow after almost half-a-century of missionary work. Peter firmly opposed this and disagreed publicly with his own brother, Joseph.

Few other of the Catholic or Methodist leaders were prepared to stand up to this decree, but Peter ToRot did not hesitate. At one of his last Sunday prayer gatherings he said, "They want to take our prayers away from us, but never fear, I shall see that my ministry continues."

In Rakunai, he organized things so that the people met in smaller, less conspicuous groups, and hid the parish records. He taught his people, "True, this is a bad time for us and we are all afraid. But God our Father is with us; He is looking after us. We must pray and ask him to stay with us always." When his wife, Paula, suggested more prudence, he replied, "You are not going to stop me from doing my work. It is God's work."

At the same time he took steps to guard his people, he took a firm and public stand against the return to polygamy policy, condemning his own brother Joseph Tatamai, and a native policeman who worked for the Japanese and who had his eye on a Catholic lady of Rakunai. This stand against the decision of the Japanese Military Police brought him once again to their notice.

Inevitably, Peter was caught. A couple came from another village to get married. Chatting happily, they told a native policeman about the ceremony. The policeman reported to the Japanese, and Peter ToRot was arrested with his brothers and put in a compound that served as a jail and a medical treatment room. Peter was charged with holding religious assemblies and with interfering with the Japanese plan to promote polygamy. Although his brothers were released, Peter was held and even his village chief could not force the authorities to give him a release date. He was never given a trial or a chance to defend himself. Daily, Peter's mother, his wife, and his children were allowed to visit him in prison and to bring him food. He knew, however, that it was a contest of wills between himself and the Japanese, and he did not expect to be released, because he knew he would not give in. He asked his wife to bring his catechist clothes so that when asked to meet God he would be properly dressed.

After the Japanese "found" Peter's dead body, they saluted the spirit that had left and allowed his people to take it for burial. This was about a month before the Japanese surrender in Japan, which eventually ended the war. The closest Peter's death can be dated is a Friday in July 1945. Public records were not kept at this time, and most of the church records were destroyed during the Japanese occupation.

Peter's burial was accomplished without any religious ceremony in the presence of a large crowd of people. His grave was marked. This heroic native catechist was held in such high esteem by his fellow villagers that his grave became a place of pilgrimage almost immediately.

Peter ToRot was an ordinary village boy of New Guinea who never traveled further than fifty kilometers from his place of birth. Although he was well-educated for his place and time, the sturdy lay-catechist was dead by the age of thirty-three. Throughout life, he showed an appreciation of his Catholic faith that was exceptional. When his people were threatened by the Japanese he continued his care and served them well, facing his death for the Faith calmly and serenely.

Through the years, the people remembered Peter ToRot's example. They came to pray at his grave. The reputation of his martyrdom did not fade, but spread throughout New Britain and other parts of the country. In 1983, a special committee of laypeople was set up in Rabaul with the aim of promoting his canonization under an initiative approved by the archbishop of Rabaul and supported by the National Bishop's Conference of Papua New Guinea and the Solomon Islands. A postulator was appointed and the first canonical proceedings were accomplished in 1985. A historical expert was appointed in 1987 and effectively carried out his work. In an exceptionally short time, the Congregation for the Canonization of Saints accepted the arguments that Peter ToRot was put to death because of his faith, "*in odium fidei.*"

Of Peter ToRot's beatification on January 17, 1995, during the pope's visit to Papua New Guinea, Father J. Michael Miller wrote, "As the second millennium enters its twilight, Pope John Paul II has asked the Church to safeguard the memory of this century's martyrs in God's 'great cause.' Just as the Church of the first millennium was nourished by their blood, this heritage of sanctity that marks our own day must not be forgotten. In its simplicity, the life and death of Peter ToRot show how a devout, humble and dedicated life is a sign of God's power at work in those who love him. Defending the truth of marriage, ToRot offered his life as a 'living sacrifice of praise.' His beatification is a fresh inspiration to married couples throughout the world, strengthening their resolve to trust that God will reward their fidelity to Him."

Blessed Pier Giorgio Frassati

1901-1925

Saintly Student

Happiness and enthusiasm were the hallmarks of the life of a young Italian student, Pier Giorgio Frassati, who died of polio at the young age of twenty-four. Divine Love marked him, and this love was returned by Pier Giorgio as charity to his fellow man.

"You ask me if I am happy and how can I not be? As long as faith gives me strength I am happy. Any Catholic can't but be happy. Sadness should be banned from Catholic souls. Pain is not sadness, which is a disease worse than any other. This disease is nearly always caused by atheism, but the end we are created for shows us the way which may be full of thorns but is not sad. It is happy even through pain."

Pier Giorgio Frassati had everything the modern world seems to value: good looks, a great personality, education, athletic ability, and social status. Although his kindness and charity were known or suspected by many in his circle of university and ecclesiastical friends, his own family, with the exception of his sister, was astounded on the day of his death when a veritable flood of the city's poor and downtrodden came to pay their last respects to the young man who had brought them so much comfort with the light of faith.

Beneath the exterior of the pragmatic activist was a vibrant mystic. His rich spiritual life was nourished by the Eucharist and the rosary. "Jesus comes to me every morning in Holy Communion and I reciprocate in the only way I can by visiting the poor." Speaking of the rosary, he showed it to a friend with the words, "I always carry my will in my pocket."

His active charity was completely Christ-centered: "The faith given to me in baptism suggests to me surely: of yourself you will do nothing, but if you have God as the center of all your action, then you will reach the goal."

In the turbulent days in Italy after World War I, amid the pervading spirit of anticlericalism, Pier Giorgio was a political activist who worked for social justice. This activism was firmly rooted in his faith. He held that Christianity, a religion of love, absolutely could not agree with fascism, a doctrine that exalted force and violence.

Pier Giorgio Michelangelo Frassati was born in Turin on April 6, 1901. He appeared to be having breathing problems, so he was baptized the same day. The formal baptism ceremonies were completed on September 5 in the Church of Saint Sebastian at Pollone, where the family had a country home. The following year, his sister and lifetime confident Luciana was born.

Alfredo Frassati, Pier's father, was the founder and director of the liberal newspaper *La Stampa*. He became influential in Italian politics, first as a senator and later as ambassador to Germany, a post he resigned when Mussolini came to power. His mother, Adelaide Ametis, was a painter who had a high-strung, negative, and nervous temperament.

In the lives of many saints, their ultimate personality has been imprinted by their foundation in a loving, Christian home. This was not the case for Pier Giorgio. The Frassati children grew up in a strictly controlled and isolated environment. As his sister Luciana later wrote, "Our father's agnosticism hurt me much less than the Ametis household's 'piety.' We never heard a word against the Church from him, whereas our mother's hypercritical temperament might have created an impression of her being anticlerical. In her own family nothing was looked at from a really Catholic point of view. Our mother and her sister, who would not have missed Sunday Mass or days of obligation for anything, were never seen by us to visit the Blessed Sacrament or to go to benediction. They never went to Communion or were seen to kneel and say a prayer."

Throughout his life, Pier Giorgio felt that his first duty was not to desert the post in which he felt God had put him: the small trench in which he defended his parents' so-called conjugal unity. Although he carried out his duty to the peak of his ability and with much sacrifice, his parents' marriage crumbled and his father had asked for a legal separation shortly before Pier Giorgio's death.

Time and again, he submitted his will to his parents' wishes. In renouncing hopes of marrying a young woman of whom he real-

Pier Giorgio Frassati was a Dominican tertiary and a model student.

ized his mother would never approve, he simply said, "Why create one family to tear apart another?" Pier Giorgio studied for an engineering degree in order to enter the field of mining and thus put himself at the service of those whom he considered to be the most unhappy of workers. His father, without ever saying a word to his son, planned a career for Pier Giorgio at the newspaper. He asked a journalist friend to pass on the verdict to the already sacrificed victim. With tears in his eyes, Pier Giorgio asked, "Do you think this will please Papa?" On receiving a nod in the affirmative, he replied, "Well, tell him I accept."

Having immersed his whole life in Jesus Christ, Pier Giorgio attributed a creative value to renunciation and suffering. "Human sorrows affect us but if they are seen in the light of religion, and thus of resignation, they are not harmful, but healthy, because they purify the soul of the small and inevitable stains with which we mortals with our most imperfect nature so often mark it."

His family could not understand him, or his need for being joyful. His mother's overbearing and hypercritical nature and his father's seeming indifference led to his being the victim of a progressive misunderstanding by his family that lasted until his death. The swift progress of his final illness occurred at the same time his grandmother was dying in the same house. On the eve of his grandmother's death, three days before his own, his mother reproached him, saying, "It seems impossible that whenever you are needed you are never there." She did not know that Pier Giorgio had fallen down three times to go and pray with the family in his grandmother's room, and that he had only been able to get up again by clinging to the corridor wall and had spent the whole night on the billiard table. As usual, he put up with his mother's nervousness in silence.

Pier Giorgio's inherent thoughtfulness and generosity were noted even in his early childhood. Having learned what an orphan was, he was distressed by the thought. One evening, he suddenly appeared in his nightshirt while his parents were entertaining and tearfully asked, "Was Jesus an orphan?" His mother put the tearful child back to bed with the remark that "Jesus had two fathers, one in heaven and one on earth." When he was four, a poor woman came to the door with a barefooted child in her arms. Quickly Pier Giorgio stripped off his own shoes and socks and handed them over, before anyone in the house could question his actions. Another time a beggar came to the door and his father sent the man away cursorily, without giving him anything. Alfredo had noted what his son had not; the man reeked of alcohol. Pier Giorgio rushed to his mother in tears, and the only way she could calm him down was to tell him to run after the man and bring him back and the family would give him some food.

Pier Giorgio made his First Communion at the age of ten, and was confirmed four years later. At this time, his spiritual director suggested that he

Pier had a robust and outgoing personality, and enjoyed having fun with fellow students.

should receive Communion frequently, as had been encouraged by Pope Pius X a few years earlier. Although his mother protested at first, fearing that frequent reception of the sacrament would lessen his respect for the Eucharist, Pier Giorgio was soon attending Mass and receiving Communion almost daily.

The Frassati children began their education at home with a Salesian tutor, and later attended a state school and finally one run by the Jesuits. At the Social Institute, he joined several organizations which encouraged prayer and devotion. In November 1918, he enrolled in Turin's Royal Polytechnic, planning a degree which would lead to a career in mining engineering. This choice reflected his concern for the welfare of the workers; he felt miners to be among the most unhappy of workers and planned a Christian apostolate among them. With his family's wealth and position, he could have chosen a life of ease; instead, he pursued a goal that reflected his spirit of detachment from comfort and wealth.

The main outlet for Pier Giorgio's social work was the Society of Saint Vincent de Paul, which he joined in 1918. His work with the "conference" was inspired by the words of Saint Paul on love in 1 Corinthians 13, and he encouraged his fellow students in this charity. The work brought him face-to-face with all manner of human suffering: broken homes; illegitimate children; the destitute; the sick; the bereaved; the unemployed. He was not scandalized, and as a friend later wrote about him, "He knew how to walk amid this lurid world's mud without getting dirty." Even in his charity, however, a deep sense of humility reigned. He said of his work with the Saint Vincent de Paul Conference, "The members who visit these families are, I would say, unworthy instruments of divine providence. As we grow close to the poor bit by bit, we gain their confidence and can advise them in the most terrible moments of this earthly pilgrimage. We can give them the comforting words of faith and we often succeed, not by our own merit, in putting on the right road people who have strayed without meaning to." When asked how he could overcome repulsion when his first welcome to the home of the poor was usually a nauseating stench, Pier Giorgio replied, "Don't ever forget that even though the house is sordid, you are approaching Christ. Remember what the Lord said: 'The good you do to the poor is good done to me.' Around the sick, the poor, the unfortunate, I see a particular light, a light that we do not have."

In the midst of his group of young Christian students, Pier Giorgio often noticed things that the others did not. Once, as the group entered a club, he hung back, noticing that the porter seemed sad. The man's grandson had died, and Pier Giorgio offered him consolation and prayers. A year later, the thoughtful young student remembered to tell the same man, "Today is the anniversary of your grandson's death," and assured him of his continual prayers.

In 1922, Pier Giorgio took the scapular of the Third Dominican Order, whose spirituality drew Pier because of its expression of his own twin desires for contemplation and action. The name he picked was Fra Gerolamo, in honor of Savonarola. He had a fervent admiration of this Dominican friar, who died as a saint at the stake. In becoming a tertiary, Pier Giorgio wanted to take Savonarola as a model, and often said, "May I imitate him in the struggle and in virtue."

Although his family was wealthy, Pier Giorgio did not feel that any part of it was his. Throughout his life, he remained frugal and did not spend much on himself; the money he distributed to the poor came in the form of gifts, loans, and his own sacrifices. More than once he walked home, saving the bus fare for charity. When his father offered to buy him a car on graduation, he told him he preferred the money instead, which he planned to use for the poor. In Germany, when his father was ambassador, Pier Giorgio saved the leftovers from the embassy table to distribute to his protegees, even going as far as to take the flowers to put on the coffins of the poor. "But I am poor like all the poor," he told a bricklayer at the family's country home, who mentioned his surprise at seeing Pier Giorgio studying continually considering the family's wealth.

In spite of his goodness and charity, Pier Giorgio was never typecast as an overly-pious, bland personality. Instead, he was known as a prankster and for his robust and outgoing temperament. He was nicknamed "Robespierre" by a friend, and a group of his friends became

Pier led an active life, including mountain-climbing and skiing trips.

known as the "Riff Raff" club. Mountain-climbing excursions and skiing trips were his passion. He said that on top of the mountains he felt close to God.

In the political turmoil that was Italy at the time, Pier Giorgio was known as a political activist. He was a student of the encyclical *Rerum Novarum* and kept the needs of social justice continually in mind. With Father Filippo Robotti, O.P., he went to promote Christian ideals in the Facist-influenced outskirts of Turin. Good nerves and firm fists were needed, because the hecklers often passed from words to action. His friends warned him to be careful of Fascist factions. Knowing how cowardice opens the way to violence and injustice, he replied, "One ought to go and one goes. It is not those who suffer violence that should fear but those who practice it. When God is with us, we need not be afraid."

A formal portrait of Blessed Pier Giorgio Frassati.

By 1922, Fascism was coming to power. Taking part in a procession then meant risking insults and blows, but Pier Giorgio continued in the lines winding after the holy images in the streets of Turin. A militant Catholic, he regarded it as an obligation to be present at all religious demonstrations. He became familiar with prisons where, in witness to his faith, he was often "remanded" following encounters between the royal guards and the Fucini. When detained, he calmly intoned his rosary. Once, while he was eating lunch with his mother in their flat, a group of Fascists broke in, intent on vandalizing the home of the director of *La Stampa*. On hearing the maid's scream, Pier Giorgio rushed out and began beating the brigands off, in spite of his mother's fears that they were armed. To his embarrassment, his heroism in running them off was reported in the paper and made much of by his family.

In his charity, Pier Giorgio had a special love for the sick. He ignored his own health in his attendance at the side of many of the sick poor, from one of which he apparently contracted poliomyelitis in the summer of 1925. By July 1, he was ill with terrible pains in his back, a high fever, and vomiting. His grandmother was dying in the same house at the time, and Pier Giorgio recited the prayers for the dying for her when he, himself, was dying. His last days were sheer physical torment, but he was so humble and self-denying that even his sister barely noticed.

His final walk was to the nearby parish church to call a priest to bless his dying grandmother. His mother was so upset by her mother's illness and the coming family separation that Pier Giorgio kept his agony to himself so as not to disturb her. Heroically, he made a joke and smiled in the presence of his cousin Mario, who had begun to suspect that Pier Giorgio's illness was more than a bad case of the flu. His grandmother died on the evening of Wednesday, July 1. When the family, including his beloved sister, left for the funeral, Pier Giorgio was already paralyzed below the waist, but no one in the house knew it. His mother stayed home at the last moment because of "tiredness" and to keep Pier Giorgio company. The heroic young Christian was misunderstood by his mother to the last, and when his friend Marco Beltramo came to visit, she spoke sharply: "Pier Giorgio could choose a better moment to be ill." An unexpected telephone call hastened the funeral in Pollone and called the family back to Turin. Adelaide met them at the door with the words, "Pier Giorgio is ill, very ill!"

The day before his death, with one arm still spared from paralysis, he pulled a packet of medicine from his jacket pocket and wrote a note of instructions regarding the poor person who needed it. His last night the sister who kept watch helped him make his last sign of the cross. He was given Extreme Unction at four in the morning, and a short time later he quietly slipped from this earth.

By Sunday morning, the doors began to open to let in a silent throng of people, unknown to his family, as was his life. With faces blank or wet with tears, they went in to him, touching him like a relic. The crowd continued to pour in until the moment when Pier Giorgio crossed the threshold for the last time, through two lines of kneeling people. His beloved poor, faithful and despairing, accompanied him for the final journey. His funeral was the first witness that his process of canonization had begun.

At the beatification of this vivacious and much-loved university student in 1990, Pope John Paul II said, "By his example he proclaims that a life lived in Christ's Spirit, the spirit of the Beatitudes, is 'blessed. . . .' He testifies that holiness is possible for everyone, and that only the revolution of charity can enkindle the hope of a better future in the hearts of people."

Blessed Pierina Morosini

1931-1957

Martyr for Purity

Chapter 28

On April 4, 1957, the young factory worker Pierina Morosini was walking the long, forested way toward her home after a tiring work day. Suddenly, she was accosted by a man. Although she fought against her rapist, her attempts at escape were in vain. The man threw her into a hedge. She reached for a rock to defend herself, but he grabbed the rock and struck her again and again. Dazed and bloody, the young woman staggered and fell. Again the cruel rock rained blows; her skull was broken; she was raped.

Shortly after the attack, Pierina was found by her brother, who was coming from home to meet her and finish the long walk home with her. The dying girl moved her hand, but did not speak or open her eyes. Gently her brother wrapped her broken head in his scarf and raced for help.

Pierina was taken to the hospital. Mercifully, the badly wounded young woman had slipped into a coma. Without recovering, she died two days later. One doctor said, "Now we have a new Maria Goretti." The Diocese of Bergamo had lost a Christian worker and gained a saint.

Pierina Eugenia Morosini was born January 7, 1931, and baptized the next day at the parish church of Fiobbio, in the hills near Albino, Bergamo. She was the oldest of nine children, and the only daughter. Her father, Rocco, was a night guard who became an invalid. Her mother, Sara, cared for other children to make money.

At fifteen, Pierina became a shift worker in a cotton-textile factory in Albino, to help support the family. She was respected by supervisors as well as the other workers. One of them recalls:

> Pierina was well educated, really good, and very conscientious. She had a great passion for work and a calm competency which she

maintained while working. She was one of those who worked almost without tiring because she used her head as well as her hands and feet and knew how to produce a lot.

Pierina rose at 4:00 a.m. in order to be able to attend Mass in Albino before arriving for work at six. During their half-hour break for breakfast, Pierina ate her sparse meal hurriedly, so she would have a few minutes to go to the chapel at the nearby church of the Madonna del Pianto for a few moments of prayer. When she was changed to second shift, 2:00 p.m. to 10:00 p.m., she continued getting up early to attend Mass. Work and prayer were the hallmarks of Pierina's life. When friends advised her to rest, she'd respond, "I'm not tired. Work is prayer." Sometimes she would add, "I can't be a day without receiving Jesus." Pierina felt that time was more precious than gold, so the only rest she allowed herself was a monthly retreat for silence, meditation, and adoration.

Pierina (far right) with a group of friends.

Pierina's father recalls that once Pierina asked him, "If I wanted to be a sister, would you let me go, Papa?" He replied, "Pierina, look at the family, you see our situation. You earn a living for everyone. Think, think of Mama. What would she do without you? You can do good at home, if you want, but if it is your vocation, I can't forbid you." The innocent girl replied, "No, no Papa, I'll stay at home." She never mentioned it again.

Pierina's spirituality was Christocentric. A priest later said of her that Holy Communion was the center of her life. She herself said, "When I receive Him in the morning, I am no longer afraid. I feel stronger."

In one of her notebooks, Pierina wrote, "My vocation is to let myself be led like a child, one day at a time."

Her friends at work said she was a pretty girl who dressed like a "sister" with long sleeves and black stockings which she made herself and wore even in the summer. She usually wore clogs on her feet. During the winter, she would walk along the path in her stocking feet so as not to slip on the ice. She prayed the rosary on the walk to work.

A healthy girl, Pierina had dark hair and blue eyes. She had a sweet temperament and was a calming influence to all around her. No one ever remembers seeing her upset. She listened to everyone, but did not talk a lot.

A friend later testified that once on break she told Pierina all her problems, even though Pierina was younger. She didn't say anything, but that Christmas Pierina sent the girl a card with beautiful words of comfort. This friend preserved the card, which was later entered as part of the beatification process.

In school, Pierina had made excellent grades. She wanted to be a teacher, possibly a religious missionary. Her parents needed her to help support the family. Therefore, for Pierina the family would be her convent, the factory would be her school, and her mission would be the parish. On the advice of her spiritual director, she made private vows of chastity, poverty, and obedience, and wrote a short, twelve-point rule of life for herself. At seventeen, she joined the apostolate of reparation, offering in a spirit of faith the small difficulties she encountered each day.

At home, Pierina was her mother's best helper. After elementary school, she took a course in sewing. An excellent seamstress, she made all the clothes for the family. A born teacher, she taught catechism classes to the younger children. Even after a hard day at work, she found time for others. She helped with the chores in the house and participated in Catholic Action. At sixteen, she was named the parish director of the youngest age group of Catholic Action. She also dedicated herself to volunteer work on behalf of the missionaries and the diocesan seminary. She was devoted to the Sacred Heart and never missed the First Friday devotions. She became a Franciscan tertiary.

When someone once asked Pierina why she dressed so plainly, she replied, "Because the world doesn't interest me. I go dressed like this because I like to; the world doesn't interest me a bit." Pierina's mother said that Pierina prayed even while she worked at home. "She told me a story about a tailor who recited the ejaculation 'Jesus, Mary, I love you, save souls!' with each stitch and she [wanted to imitate] him."

Pierina accepted everything joyfully from God's hands. In April 1946, she was hurt at work. Her leg became infected and she had to go to the hospital for nearly a month. She never complained and when visitors came to cheer her up, they discovered that it was Pierina who encouraged them instead of the other way 'round.

In April 1947, sixteen-year-old Pierina had the opportunity for a trip to Rome with the young women of Catholic Action to attend the beatification of Maria Goretti. Pierina had read the life of this heroic young martyr and one of her treasures was the book on Maria Goretti that Pierina's aunt Theresa had given her. Pierina had a small picture of Maria which she framed and hung in her room. Although the trip would be expensive, her mother man-

A formal portrait of Blessed Pierina Morosini.

aged to borrow the needed money, and Pierina was given a new dress and sandals for the trip.

On her return from Rome, she visited her aunt, a nun, and told her "the beauty of Maria Goretti transformed her life." A quote from Saint Teresa of Ávila, "Virginity is a profound silence of everything earthly," was later discovered written and signed by Pierina. Shortly before her death, Pierina prophetically told her brother Andrew, "I'd rather be killed than commit a sin."

On the train coming home from Rome with her friends, the girls were all looking at the souvenirs they had bought: rosaries, rings, holy cards. When Pierina showed what she had bought, she had only a package of holy cards of Maria Goretti to give to her catechism children at Fiobbio. A friend asked her, "What did you buy for yourself?" Pierina replied, "Me? I have my souvenir here in my heart."

About a month before her death, Pierina wanted to go to a nearby town to visit her brother, who was in military service. She planned to go on Holy Saturday. Her mother forbade the trip because she would have to travel at night. The obedient daughter immediately forgot her plan and sent the money she had saved for the trip to her brother for spending money.

Today, two markers, as silent and compelling as Pierina herself, stand in the forest where Pierina was attacked and where her body was later found. A white marble cross marks the location of the attack; a small monument containing the photograph of the blessed memorializes the spot where her body was discovered. The monument replaced a wooden cross surrounded by palms, put up by her father and brothers.

At the conclusion of her diocesan process for beatification, Bishop Giulio Oggioni of Bergamo said Pierina was like "the tip of an immense iceberg of the hidden and heroic sanctity in many families." In a homily in 1983, he said, "Pierina Morosini became a martyr on the street and of the street.

Because of her intense and holy relationship with the street, Pierina is a model especially for our time. It's obvious to everyone today that people, especially the young, spend much more time than in the past on the street. The means of communication, needs of work, business, entertainments, the desire for speed has made our streets one of the most frequented and dangerous places — physically and spiritually. The street is the emerging place of our civilization. Therefore, the Christian must learn to live as a Christian also on the streets."

Just as the mother of Maria Goretti was able to attend her martyr-daughter's beatification, so, too, the mother of this new martyr of purity heard the beautiful words spoken by Pope John Paul II on October 4, 1987, at her own daughter's beatification:

"Rejoice with me and with all the Church, brothers and sisters of the Diocese of Bergamo. . . . The roots of her spirituality are in your midst. Growing up in an atmosphere of highly developed spiritual life incarnated in the family, Blessed Pierini followed the poor and humble Christ in the daily care of her many brothers. Having discovered that she could be a saint without entering a convent, she was open with love to parochial life, to Catholic Action, the apostolate of her vocation. Personal prayer, daily participation in Holy Mass, . . . led her to understand the will of God and the expectations of her brothers to make the decision to consecrate herself privately, in the world, to the Lord. For ten years she lived the difficulties and joys of a laborer in the textile mill of the area, always making the trip to work on foot. Her colleagues testify to her fidelity to the world, her friendliness united to reserve, the esteem she enjoyed as a woman and as a believer. On the trip home, thirty years ago, her martyrdom was accomplished, the extreme consequence of her Christianity. Her footsteps have not stopped, however, but continue to signal a shining path for anyone attracted to the Gospel challenge."

Pierina on her trip to Rome to attend the canonization of Maria Goretti.

Blessed Rafka de Himlaya

1832-1914

Blind Mystic of Lebanon

Chapter 29

Today, when so many attempt to escape human suffering, the life of the blind, paraplegic Blessed Rafka serves as a trumpet which blasts forth a message of the value of Christian acceptance of suffering. Those who feel that only the full use of our senses and facilities can make life worthwhile, as well as those who are proponents of suicide to escape painful or terminal illness, can learn from her that there is value in all human life.

For seventeen years, this humble Lebanese Maronite nun suffered; her pain was continuous, yet her sisters never heard her complain. Instead, she told them that she thanked God for her sufferings "because I know that the sickness I have is for the good of my soul and His glory," and that suffering "accepted with patience and thanksgiving purifies the soul as the fire purifies gold."

We are not required to imitate certain exceptional vocations like that of the mystic Rafka; however, to teach mankind the value of suffering and the glory of the cross, history is marked with holy men and women who have been generous enough to offer themselves to God as victims of Love. Sister Rafka was one of those chosen souls.

Like Rafka, we are all called to holiness. Christ said, "Whoever wishes to come after me must deny himself, take up his cross, and follow me" (Matthew 16:24). We are called to be courageous and heroic in our daily lives. Sin and suffering are part of the normal human lot. This cross to which the Lord refers is, for us, the acceptance of our daily problems and frustrations which, in unity with Him, serve as a means of sanctification. If our lives include more than the average human suffering, Christ himself can become our Simon of Cyrene, helping us to carry our cross; Blessed Rafka can serve as our model for Christian suffering.

There are no known photos of Blesses Rafka. Here are two representations of her.

"But rejoice to the extent that you share in the sufferings of Christ, so that when his glory is revealed you may also rejoice exultantly" (1 Peter 4:13).

Boutrossieh Petronilla Al Rayes was born June 29, 1832, in Himlaya, a small village near Bickfaya, Lebanon. She was named in honor of Saint Peter, because she was born on his feast day. The daughter of a poor village couple, Petronilla was very close to her mother, Rafka, who taught her a tender devotion to the saints, especially the Blessed Mother of God. From the time she was only a tiny child, her mother took Petronilla to church with her; at home, the family was a loving and close one. The family were members of the Maronite rite, a branch of the Aramaic Church of Antioch. Her mother died when Petronilla was only seven, and her father remarried. Her new stepmother had a son a few years older than Petronilla, and soon two new daughters joined the family.

At the age of ten, Petronilla began working as a maid for a wealthy family from Lebanon living in Damascus, in order to help her family with expenses. She stayed with the couple for four years, and they cared for her and educated her as if she were a daughter of the house. When she left their service, they provided her with a dowry for her future life.

A beautiful and gracious girl, Petronilla had begun to feel the call to religious life, and spent much of her free time in prayer at the parish church. Her father hoped to prepare her for a suitable marriage, and her stepmother wanted her to marry her own son.

Petronilla became convinced that her vocation was to the religious life and talked the matter over with her confessor, Father Joseph Gemayel, who had founded a new order of nuns — the Congregation of the Maries — the first Maronite congregation with an active apostolate. The main mission of the congregation was education. Although Petronilla felt drawn to a contemplative lifestyle, Father Joseph encouraged her to join the Maries because she was educated and would be an asset to the community.

One day, Petronilla overheard her stepmother and her aunt arguing angrily about her future. She sat down on the road and prayed, asking God for the solution to this difficult situation. She received an inspiration and jumped up and headed for the convent of Our Lady of Deliverance in Bickfaya. On the way she met three of her friends and told them she was going to join the sisters. She invited them to join her and two of them, seeing the joy and determination in her face, decided to go with her.

Walking along, the other two speculated about religious life and talked; the silent Petronilla was thinking of her Divine Bridegroom and wondering if she were going to be able to devote her life to Him as she planned. As soon as they entered the church, Petronilla felt a wonderful peace flow over her, and standing in front of the picture of the Blessed Mother she heard an interior voice telling her that she would become a nun.

The Mother Superior had been advised by Father Joseph of Petronilla's intentions, and welcomed her without any of the usual questions. She kindly told the other girls to return home and think more about their decision. If they chose, they could return later and she would accept them.

When Petronilla's parents learned of their daughter's defection, they went to the convent to demand her return. The Mistress of Postulants was sent to fetch her, and told her that her father and mother had arrived to take her home.

"I would prefer that my mother take me out of this world before I go back home," the determined postulant answered.

Not realizing that the woman in the parlor was not Petronilla's real mother, the puzzled Mistress asked the superior to talk to the girl. Petronilla explained that ever since she had decided to join the convent, she felt her mother in heaven had guided her and that she would rather die than leave. The superior was able to communicate this desire to the girl's parents so well that they dropped their objection.

Petronilla was professed in 1855, taking the name of Sister Agnes. She was sent to Ghazir and for seven years was a teacher in several of the nearby villages. In 1860, when the Christians were being massacred, Sister Agnes went with some of the Jesuits to Deir El Kamar.

One day a little boy, terrified because he was being chased by soldiers, ran to Sister Agnes for protection. Quickly, she hid him under her cloak, saving him from near certain death. The Jesuits dressed a number of young boys in girl's clothing and hid them in the school in order to save them. For a time, the sisters fled to Beirut to avoid the massacre of the Maronites and Christians by the Druses who were incited by the Turks. They later returned to Ghazir. In 1864, Sister Agnes and another sister opened a school in Ma'ad, where she remained for another seven years. The people of the village there soon grew to love her and to admire her purity and holiness.

In 1871, the Jesuits decided to merge the Congregation of the Maries with a new order. The resulting disturbance caused the loss of several vocations. Although she seemed quietly accepting of the changes, the foment in the congregation had disturbed Sister Agnes, who sought solace and direction from God by praying in the Church of Saint George. Here she begged to know God's will for her future. She fell asleep and suddenly she felt a hand tapping her on the shoulder. A voice whispered, "You will be a nun." She awoke to find herself alone in the church; on thinking of the incident the idea came that perhaps she was meant to join a contemplative order. That night, she dreamed that three men appeared to her: a monk with a white beard and a cane, a soldier, and an old man. The monk drew close to her and touched her with his cane, telling her to join the Lebanese Order.

A drawing of Blessed Rafka as a nun.

The next morning she discussed the dream with her friend Anthony Issa, who identified the monk as Saint Anthony of the Desert and the soldier as Saint George, the patron of the local church. He could not guess the identity of the old man.

Her application to join the Baladita Order (the Lebanese Maronite Order of Saint Anthony) was immediately accepted and she entered the novitiate at the Convent of Saint Simeon of the Horn on July 12, 1871. When she first entered the church connected to the convent, she noticed a picture of Saint Simeon and immediately recognized him as the old man of her dream.

After her canonical year of novitiate, she was professed at the age of forty on August 25, 1872. She took the name of her beloved mother, Rafka.

One day in October 1885, Rafka was praying alone in church when she was inspired to protest to God, "Why, O my God, why have you distanced yourself from me and have abandoned me? You have never visited me with sickness! Have you perhaps abandoned me?" When Rafka later related her prayer to her superior, she told her, "At the moment of sleeping (the night after her prayer), I felt a most violent pain spreading above my eyes to the point that I reached the state you see me in, blind and paralyzed, and as I myself had asked for sickness I could not allow myself to complain or murmur."

For the next twenty-nine years, the remainder of her earthly life, Blessed Rafka endured severe pain and suffering. She was first blinded in one eye. A botched operation, performed with no anesthesia, led to the loss of her right eyeball; it was only with difficulty that the hemorrhaging in the socket was finally stopped after several days. Then the disease spread to her left eye. She spent ten years in blindness, never complaining. Her patience edified her sisters and when the other sisters saw her they thought of the blood flowing down into Our Lord's eyes. They would hear Rafka whisper, "O Christ, I unite my sufferings to yours, my pains with your pains as I look at your head crowned with thorns."

During this time, Rafka attempted to share in the work of the community as much as possible and did not ever take advantage of her condition. A number of times when the superior attempted to exempt her from her duty of washing dishes or weaving, Rafka gently reminded her that the rule made no exemptions for anyone who could work.

In 1897, a group of nuns moved to the new convent of Saint Joseph Ad-Daher. Mother Ursula, the superior of the new foundation, asked to have Sister Rafka included because she wanted to have her example for the sisters as they met with the hardships that always attend the establishment of a new foundation.

Here Rafka spent the last seventeen years of her life in her greatest sufferings, as well as her greatest spiritual joys. Her example and assistance proved invaluable in the establishment of the new convent; the novices especially were impressed with the blind nun's spirit of prayer, humility, and charity. Sensitive and kind, if Rafka became aware that one of the sisters was sad or depressed, she would be the first to go and talk to her, consoling her and praying for her. If the superior imposed a punishment on one of the nuns, Rafka would ask pardon for the nun and kneel with her, her arms outstretched in the form of a cross. She would remain until the superior allowed the guilty one to get up. Constantly she taught by her example the value of suffering and obedience.

One day in 1907, Rafka began to experience a new kind of pain; her body was numb and she was completely paralyzed. She became weak and began to lose weight; her right hip became dislocated, the right leg was extended, and the knee became disjointed. Soon she was unable to stand and was confined to bed.

The superior came one day to study Rafka's condition and as she lifted the bones on Rafka's right side, she noticed that they could be freely turned in all directions and did not bend normally at all any more. The invalid simply smiled and with her usual quiet humor asked the superior if she wanted to put some screws in her bones to put them back in place and change what the Lord had done.

Later the tibia of the right leg became dislocated and pierced the skin; soon her left hip also pierced the skin and her leg locked in an awkward position. Her spine was displaced and she could only sleep on her right side, which was uncomfortable as her shoulder didn't touch the bed. Completely immobile, her lower jaw touched her benumbed knees; she was covered with a number of sores and abscesses. Only her hands remained in their natural position and Sister Rafka thanked God continually for this favor because she could still weave socks for the sisters. For the last seven years of her life, Rafka suffered as a blind paralytic; by her quiet, calm, smiling patience she can be compared to the greatest of the saints. In a medical report published in 1981 during the canonical process, three specialists in ophthalmology, neurology, and orthopedics diagnosed the most likely cause of her condition as a tuberculosis with ocular localization and multiple bony excrescences.

During her illness, a number of special favors were granted to Rafka that have no natural explanation. One year on the Feast of Corpus Christi, Mother Ursula asked Rafka how she was feeling. With her customary lack of complaint, she replied that she was fine. She mentioned, however, that she wished she could attend Mass on the great feast day. Mother Ursula was surprised at the request, knowing that even when the sisters gently lifted her while they changed the sheets Rafka's pain became worse. At Rafka's request, two of the sisters attempted to sit the paralyzed nun up in her bed, but she could not move. The others then left for church. Shortly after the Mass had begun, the nuns were astonished to see Rafka enter the church, dragging herself with great effort. Mother Ursula and some others moved to help her but she motioned them not to touch her. They placed a pillow on the floor in the middle of the church for her to lie on. After Mass, Mother Ursula asked some of the nuns to carry the invalid back to her room, but she begged to be allowed to remain in the church for a while to pray. Some hours later, she was carried back to her bed by two of the sisters.

When the superior asked her how she was able to go to the church, Rafka replied, "I don't know. I asked my Lord to help me and I suddenly felt my feet touching the ground. So, I got out of bed and dragged myself to church." That was the only time she left her bed during the years of her paralysis.

A few years before Rafka died, Mother Ursula asked her if she ever regretted the loss of her sight and if she sometimes wished she could see the new convent. Sister Rafka answered simply, "I would like to see just for an hour, Mother, only to be able to see you." For Rafka, her superior took the place of Christ on earth; that is why she so loved the vow of obedience. Surprised at the response, Mother Ursula questioned her if she would be content with a single hour, and the humble sister replied that she would. At that, the superior turned to leave the room when Rafka exclaimed, "Mother, I can see you!"

Startled, the superior turned to see a glow on Rafka's face that should have convinced her that Rafka was not teasing. However, in order to make certain the phenomenon was real, she asked Rafka to describe the objects on her dresser. Rafka correctly identified two books. Fearing that Rafka might have guessed the titles of the only two books usually read to her, Mother called three sisters into the room. There was a lovely multicolored spread on her bed, and in the presence of these witnesses, Sister Rafka pointed out each of the colors.

As Sister Rafka had requested, her sight lasted only for an hour, after which she fell into a deep sleep. Mother Ursula waited by the bed for a time and then decided to wake the sleeping nun to see if her vision had been restored. After several attempts to wake her, the superior realized that Rafka was not actually sleeping but was in some type of trance. Suddenly Rafka moved her head and awoke.

The superior questioned her as to what had been happening and whether or not she could still see anything. With no regret in her tone of voice, Sister Rafka explained that she could no longer see, and that she had been in the company of some people who entered a huge, beautiful room adorned with flowers. "The ceiling was shining brightly and there was a light that I could see from time to time. I especially noticed many fountains, very artistically built, with water flowing through them. There were many people around, all trying to get into the place and I found myself being carried along with them. I was immensely happy during all of this time."

"Why did you come back?" asked the superior.

"You called me, Mother," the obedient nun replied simply, "so I came back."

Rafka died quietly in the presence of her community

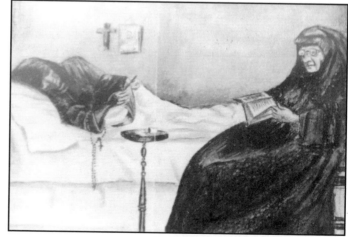

Blessed Rafka on her sickbed with her rosary.

on May 23, 1914, at the age of eighty-two. She was buried in the cemetery of the convent.

A few days after her burial, the brother of the superior came for a visit and spent the night in a room adjacent to the convent. The window faced the cemetery. During the night, he was awakened by a light coming from outside which illuminated his room. Thinking it was dawn approaching, he did not pay much attention at first. Then, realizing it was not sunlight, he got up to see where the light was coming from. As he looked out the window, the light suddenly disappeared, but he understood that the light had been coming from the tomb of the humble Rafka. A number of other villagers later testified to seeing the light emanating from the nun's tomb. The light has appeared many times since Rafka's death, usually whenever a cure has occurred there, allegedly through the use of the dirt around her grave. She who lived and died in the obscurity and silence of a convent is now shining by the benefits God is granting through her to mankind.

Human nature shies away from suffering, death, and corruption because of the unpleasant feelings of repugnance they generate. Suffering, however, is the lot of every human, and our destiny depends on how we integrate suffering into our daily lives. Blessed Rafka welcomed suffering with joy, accepting it as a gift, and her heroic patience led her surely to sanctity.

During the jubilee of the Year of the Redemption, 1984, Pope John Paul II wrote an Apostolic Letter, *Salvifici doloris*, on the Christian meaning of human suffering. The life of Blessed Rafka is an exceptional example of the discovery, by a simple and fragile creature, of the salvific value of suffering shared with Christ.

Santos Franco Sanchez

1942-1954

Small But Large in Faith

Chapter

30

"Help me because I am so small. . . . Mother, how I love you." The little boy, wracked with pain, spoke softly. His mother crossed to the bed and asked if he were speaking to her. Santos clarified: "I am talking to my Blessed Mother who is right here."

"God's will be done," whispered the little boy. At the age of only eleven years, Santos Franco Sanchez had learned and lived a simple faith so well that today he is being considered for the honors of the altar. At the height of his intense suffering from the deadly meningitis which killed him, this young child spoke to his family, gathered at his bedside. "Soon I am going to heaven; I have very little time left. I will not forget you. I love you very much. Don't cry, because I am happy. What do sufferings matter? Heaven! How beautiful, God and the Blessed Mother are there."

"What will you do in heaven?" his sister asked.

Santos replied, "Be with the Lord and the Blessed Mother."

Again his sister questioned him, "What do you think is better, heaven or to be healed?"

Immediately the child responded, "No, I don't ask to be healed. Do you know what heaven is? Heaven! It's like a crystal palace, pearls and jewels; it's like the sun. And there is God, the Blessed Virgin, the angels. If you knew what heaven is!"

Santos Franco Sanchez was born July 6, 1942, in Hinojosa del Duque (Córdoba), Spain. He was the sixth child of Manuel and Maria del Carmen Franco, an exemplary Christian couple. Manuel ran a small shoe factory and Carmen spent her days carrying out the multitude of chores demanded by her large and bustling family. Ten of their thirteen children survived infancy. Both parents were Carmelite tertiaries and active members of Catholic Action. Carmen inculcated in each of her children a deep love for Jesus in the Blessed Sacrament, encouraging them to make a visit daily before going out to play. She also taught her children a tender love for the Blessed Mother, explaining to them that she had consecrated each of them to the Virgin of Carmel while they were still in her womb.

Santos was a normal child who grew up playing and enjoying himself with his family and friends. In the evenings, the children played noisy games in front of the family home. A neighbor, who often watched the children at play through her window, remembers that Santos was the peacemaker of the group. Additionally, he invariably took the side of the weaker companions in any dispute. At home, he was also known as a buffer between his brothers and sisters. His goodness and charity were obvious even at a young age, but he was subject to all the little limitations of a child his age.

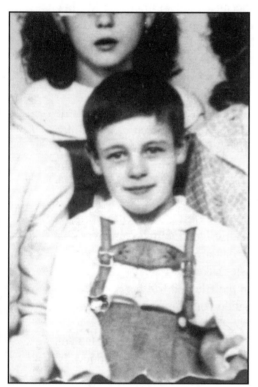

Santos as a young boy.

Santos was an obedient child but sometimes, when asked to do certain tasks, he would "defend his rights" and tell his parents that this or that task was usually meant for girls, of which the family had plenty. Then he would go ahead and do his parents' wishes, and he knew how to say "I'm sorry" when needed. His younger sister Carmela recalls his rebellious spirit when he was once sent for bread because another sister didn't feel like going. She remembers, too, his contrite apology when he lost the money for an errand because he stopped to play with his friends.

His sisters remember Santos as a playful, sometimes mischievous child, who was tranquil, usually smiling and agreeable, although not quiet. Although he played many pranks and could get into quite a bit of mischief like any normal child, he was also sincere, good, and humble. His next oldest sister, Rafi, now a Carmelite nun, recalls that he was observant and asked questions about many things. Although they were only a year-and-a-half different in age, she says that he didn't share in games with her, preferring to play alone as if he had a secret, intimate pact with God. She says, however, that he was very affectionate and played well with the younger children. Carmela remembers making mischief of one kind or another with Santos many times as a child. Once they climbed up a dangerous ladder to play on the roof of the shed that held firewood. Carmela hurt her toe, and Santos consoled her by promising to confess that it was all his fault. Somehow their mother never suspected what had happened. They also made many childish "journeys" to the countryside to gather clay for making figurines or other treasures of nature. In May, they gathered flowers and Santos organized a little procession along the patio. The younger children and their friends sang and decorated the Holy Cross in honor of the Virgin's month.

Santos was an external student at the Carmelite "minor seminary" at Hinojosa. Here the friars made a strong impression on him and he often said he wanted to be a *Marianus* (minor seminarian) and to be a Carmelite when he grew up. Father Augustine Cobos, a young Carmelite priest, was Santos's teacher for two years and often visited the child during his illness. Father Cobos says of Santos:

He was a boy to whom you paid attention for his candor, his humility, his obedience and for many other qualities or virtues which are not frequently found in youngsters his age. He was intelligent and studious, but this did not make him feel superior to others. On the contrary, when he gave the answer to something that the others had not known, you could see him blush as if ashamed of himself. He was a very devout youngster. I frequently met him in our church in Hinojosa, making a visit to the Lord or participating in the rosary in honor of the Blessed Virgin. He went to confession to me on many occasions with so much devotion that if I hadn't known his devout parents, I would have been astounded. When he fell ill and I found out about it, as the one responsible for the elementary section of our school, I went to see him. This made him happy. The first time I tried to encourage him; I told him that he would soon be better and that he would be able to return to school again. But afterwards, seeing the conformity with which he had accepted the will of God, when I returned to see him, I came home edified by his manner of speaking. He was offering his suffering for sinners and for vocations, because his desire — as he had revealed to me on several occasions — was to become a Carmelite Marianus. On the day he died, I remember that we spoke about it in community, since we were united to the Franco Sanchez family by bonds of friendship. At the beginning of class on Monday, we prayed to the Lord for his soul and I said to his school companions: surely he is in Heaven. God wished to purify him by means of his painful sickness, which he accepted with authentic faith and love, because he loved the Lord very much.

At the end of November 1953, when Santos was eleven years old, he suffered a severe earache. He came home from school very sad, holding his hand to his ear, saying that it hurt him very much. The next morning, he didn't want to go to school because it hurt so much. The older children teased him that he was just afraid of mathematics class. A discharge of pus caused his worried mother to take him to the local doctor, who told her that it was nothing to worry about. Although the discharge stopped, the child began to experience a constant and painful headache, so severe that he had to stop attending school. Again the worried parents took him to the doctor, and again the diagnosis was a simple cold. Holding his aching head, Santos told his mother, "My head hurts a lot, but the doctor says I don't have anything. Don't worry about it, Mom. Let what God wants be done."

In December, the headaches became worse and Santos developed a fever. Intent on accepting his sickness as part of God's will for him, Santos did not become irritated or impatient, but had to admit to the pain of the severe headache. The family took him to a young eye, ear, and nose specialist. This doctor concluded that the headache had nothing to do with his previous earache since the ear had stopped festering. He prescribed a tranquilizer, thinking it was a nervous disorder. Instead of getting better, Santos began to have dizzy spells. He told his family, "This doctor doesn't believe me either. He says that really my head does not ache. The Lord knows that it does ache, but I want His will to be done. Don't be concerned for me; I'm offering up everything to the Lord."

As Christmas approached, the pain, fever, and dizziness increased to the point that Santos had to remain in bed. The local doctor visited him, but continued to believe that it was only an ear infection that would soon pass with the help of ear cleaning and tranquilizers for the pain. The young specialist would not make a house call, convinced the child was neurotic. The loving parents could not bear to see their child in constant pain and

Santos (second from right) with some of his brothers and sisters.

determined to take him to an experienced specialist in Córdoba, but because of the holidays the visit was put off. Santos did not want to spoil the holidays for the rest of the family, so he told them he was feeling better and even tried to joke with his younger brothers and sisters. In spite of the pain, he tried to keep a smiling face, but sometimes it got the better of him. He told his mother, "Tell the children not to yell so much; I can't put up with the noise. But don't tell Dad; he will suffer too much. I want God's will to be fulfilled. I offer up everything to Him for sinners, for the missions, and for everything God wishes."

Right after Christmas, one morning they found Santos silent and immobile. Maria del Carmen ran to the young specialist, who again refused to make a house call, telling her that Santos was neurotic and that her anxiety only provoked his illness. Manuel then took things in hand and went to find an old friend of his who was a retired doctor. He returned with Manuel immediately and his diagnosis was rapid and sure. "The boy is suffering from an attack of meningitis. Take him to Córdoba immediately for urgent attention."

In Córdoba, an ear specialist gave them the sad news. It was too late to hope for a cure. The infection had spread to Santos's brain and nothing could be done except to alleviate some of the pressure, and thus some of the pain. A priest friend, Don Juan Jurado, accompanied Santos and his mother to the hospital. He suggested that their suffering be offered up for the Church and for the missions. The young patient calmly replied, "Father, from the first moment that I began to experience pain, I haven't stopped offering everything to the Lord for all those intentions — and also for sinners." The priest, both touched and startled, blurted out, "You are an angel! God loves you very much."

The specialist operated, making an incision behind Santos's ear to drain off some of the infected pus. For forty-eight hours, Santos remained at the hospital. All of the staff who came in contact with the boy were amazed at the serenity of the young patient. At last the hospital authorities released him for home care, giving the family no hope of recovery.

At home, the devout parents called the priest to come and anoint their son, bringing him Communion in the form of Viaticum. Surrounded by his family, Santos attentively followed the last rites celebrated for him. Very weak, he softly begged his mother to stay with him to help him. Then, with a maturity far beyond his years, he quietly prayed, "My God, take me to Heaven. I'm too small to suffer so much. However, Your will be done. Everything just as you will it. I offer it to you for sinners, for the missions."

Throughout the month of January, Santos suffered violent convulsions every day or two, writhing in pain. After the convulsions passed, he became as still as a corpse, and his family sometimes took his pulse to see if he was still alive. On one occasion, he opened his eyes and said, "No, not yet. I still have more to suffer. God only knows when I'll go to Heaven. I offer everything to Him." Sometimes he was heard to murmur that he was offering his sufferings for children. At other times, he seemed to be speaking to Jesus and to Mary as if he could see them present with him. One day toward the end of January, Santos began crying. Asked if he were in pain, he replied, "Jesus carried the cross on his back; they are gong to crucify Him. He is covered with blood. He can do no more. He falls. My Jesus, sins. . . . I too will go with you. I offer you my sufferings for sinners. If people would only know, they would not sin any more." Another time, he described the Child Jesus coming to him, surrounded by a host of angels. He told his mother that he had been given a crown of red and white flowers.

His schoolmates came to visit him in groups. They remember the boy

with the bandaged head lying still with wide-open eyes and clutching his crucifix, which he held on top of his covers. He smiled at them as they stood in his doorway. The doctor, an avowed atheist, came daily, early in the morning. Sometimes he stayed, reflecting on the spirit of this child who was suffering and dying in such a manner. He said, "This child has something special about him; if I didn't see him myself, I wouldn't believe it." Santos told him, "Doctor, do you know why I can suffer so much? Because God is with me." Santos also told the doctor about the Blessed Virgin's visits to him, and spoke of his guardian angel

Santos as a student at the Carmelite minor seminary.

protecting him and giving him strength. Years later, that same doctor met Santos's sister Blas in Córdoba and told her,"That child was a saint." The doctor converted to Christianity before his death.

On one of his last days, Santos's oldest sister (now a Carmelite nun) was sitting with him while their parents went to get something to eat. Normally the little patient lay still on his bed with his lips moving, although little could be heard. Suddenly he sat up in bed holding his crucifix out and shouting, "Get out of here, get out of here, ugly evil one. Look at the cross of Christ crucified. Get out of here, ugly one." Then he fell back into his usual quiet and immobile condition. His shocked sister remained seated and his parents, hearing the noise, came running in to see what had happened. Clearly and joyfully, Santos told them, "It was the devil but he was scared away by the cross. He can do nothing against it."

Santos remained in a stationary condition until February 6 when he seemed to take a sudden turn for the better. He even admitted to his startled parents that he was hungry and thirsty, although he was unable to swallow even a little water. He tried, unsuccessfully, to move in his bed. At noon, when the Angelus bell sounded, he was heard praying, "Take me, take me up to Heaven, my Mother." Along with his sister, he prayed a favorite prayer to Our Lady. Then, he whispered for the final time his often-repeated "God's will be done." In the presence of his parents and his sister, he gave a large sigh and his soul left his body.

The funeral procession for Santos seemed like a triumph. There were children big and small, the youth of Catholic Action with their flags, members of the Nocturnal Adoration group, the Carmelite Fathers and the Marianos, and his doctor. Most of the town seems to have turned out. In the center was Santos's small coffin. All seemed to know of his goodness and of his pain offered with love to Jesus for all.

At a tender age, Santos Franco Sanchez was called by God to become a holocaust of pain. With the maturity of a giant in faith, he responded, "Thy will be done."

Saint Teresa of Jesus Fernandez

1900-1920

The Fourth Teresa

Chapter

31

"I am the happiest person on earth. I desire nothing more because my entire being has been seized by God who is Love."

Saint Teresa of Jesus of the Andes was a young contemplative nun whose entire spirituality was marked with joy. The first canonized saint of Chile is also the fourth saint of the Carmelite order to bear the name *Teresa*.

"To offer ourselves to the Father, to fulfill His adorable will; this is the path of holiness as I understand it."

By living an intense life of conscious prayerful communion with God, Saint Teresa of the Andes became increasingly aware of God's goodness and perfection. She constantly offered herself as a spiritual victim for the good of the Church and the world, especially for the sanctification of priests.

This young Chilean girl discerned her path of personal sanctity, set her feet sturdily on the way, and walked swiftly and surely to holiness. She died in 1920 at the age of nineteen, after only a year in religious life. Less than a lifetime later, we are already permitted to hold her life as an example of heroic fidelity to the will of God and a beacon of Christian joy.

Little known outside her own country, Teresa of the Andes set forth a simple way to holiness that everyone can follow. Just as the "little way" of Saint Thérèse of Lisieux rapidly spread from Europe throughout the world, today the perfume of this new flower of the Americas is beginning to spread her message from our own corner of the world.

As is the case with many mystical souls, externally Teresa gave little indication of the depths of her interior life. Although some mentioned that her bluish eyes seemed to see farther than others, in most respects she seemed like a normal, if exceptionally good, girl of her time and culture.

Like Saint Thérèse of Lisieux and Blessed Elizabeth of the Trinity, two of the Carmelite saints on whose writings she based her own spirituality,

Young Juanita on her First Communion Day.

Teresa of the Andes simply appeared to be an ordinary and faithful nun. After her death, her diary and her letters revealed the clear picture of a favored soul.

Saint Teresa of the Andes was born in Santiago, Chile, on July 13, 1900. The fourth of six children of a wealthy mining family, she was baptized with the impressive name of Juana Enriqueta Josephina of the Sacred Hearts Fernandez Solar. Her family and friends simply called her Juanita.

Juanita's family was warm, loving, and staunchly Catholic. She was especially devoted to her maternal grandfather, who taught her at an early age to ride horses at his enormous hacienda at Chacabuco. This became her favorite sport. Even as a young child, Juanita was inclined to religious piety and often asked her mother questions about religion. She developed a close relationship with Our Lady. ". . . From the time I was seven years old, there took root in my soul the greatest devotion to Mary, . . . I confided to Mary everything that was happening to me, and she spoke to me. I heard her voice within me, quite clearly and distinctly. She advised me and told me all that I had to do to please Our Lord. I thought that was a perfectly normal thing, and it never occurred to me to relate to others what [she] was telling me."

The child, already receiving divine favors, accepted them with naturalness. In her innocence, she thought others experienced things in the same way. After a long and intensive preparation, she made her First Communion at the age of eleven. "[This] was a day without clouds for me . . . a year of happiness and of the purest memories I shall have in my whole life. I asked Him a thousand times that He would take me, and I heard His sweet voice for the first time. . . . I went to Communion every day and spoke with Jesus for long periods of time. From the day of my First Communion Our Lord spoke to me after Communion. He told me things I never expected Him to tell me, and even when I questioned Him, He told me things that were going to happen, and they did happen. I still continued to believe such things were happening to everybody who went to Communion. Once I told my mother of this matter. She told me to speak with Father Colom, but I felt too ashamed to do so. . . ."

Juanita's early experience with the Eucharistic Lord marked her internally with a profound desire for Him. She wrote, "From that day forward the earth held no attraction for me."

Through the fortunate order of one of her spiritual directors, Juanita began keeping an intimate diary when she was fifteen. Although she intended to destroy it when she entered Carmel, her mother begged to be allowed to keep it as a remembrance of her. After her death, the family gave the diary to her convent. A faithful record of the development of her spiritual life was thus preserved. She had her own style: simple, logical, and elegant. It is astonishing that, at such a young age, she was able to understand her own vocation, assimilate the message of the gospel, and transmit clearly these and other profound religious ideas in a way that anyone can understand them. Her writings showed a rare maturity and balance.

While the internal life of Juanita's soul began to blossom, she bloomed externally into an attractive young woman. As a teenager, she is described as being tall, strong, and well-proportioned with an oval face, fair skin, and a swarthy complexion. She had blue eyes circled with dense dark lashes and heavy eyebrows. When she smiled, her eyes sparkled and her dimples showed; she was a well-groomed and beautiful young lady. Juanita was a good student and earned high marks in all her classes. She played the piano and other musical instruments and was very athletic. She dominated in tennis, swimming, and horseback riding.

She wrote of herself that she had to work hard to control her vanity and pride and to force herself to obey. "From my earliest years they used to say that I was the prettiest of my brothers and sisters and I did not pay any attention to this; but they kept repeating these words to me when I grew up, unknown to my mother, for she did not approve of this. Only God knows what it cost me to conquer this pride and vanity that was so strongly entrenched in my heart as I grew up! It was difficult for me to obey. Especially when they commanded me to do anything, I would take my good sweet time in doing it."

Juanita was a normal teenager. Although she felt the call to Carmel and a life of dedicated virginity at an early age, courtship was an entertaining diversion and she often felt an attraction for the married state. More than once she had a crush on one of the young men, and

Juanita as a young lady of eighteen years.

she liked the idea of dating. She wrote that she knew marriage would not have separated her from Christ, but that it was not the path marked out for her and she felt that no human being could have alleviated the thirst for eternal love that was devouring her.

During the school year, Juanita found time to sew for the needy, visit the poor, act as a catechist, and collaborate with the priests in their missionary activities. During vacation and holiday breaks, she worked with the priests on their missions in the countryside. She often went with them on horseback to consecrate homes to the Sacred Heart. She used her own funds for her charitable projects, once even pawning her watch.

After finishing school in 1918, she returned home for a few months before entering the Carmelite Monastery at Los Andes in May 1919. She received the habit at her clothing ceremony in October, taking the name Teresa of Jesus.

Living fully the life of Carmel, she became completely possessed by God's love, immersed in the contemplation of divine realities and the object of many mystical experiences, without, however, seeming anything other than a good and faithful nun, even to those she lived with. Her letters to family and friends were often jewels of good counsel and always expressed joy. "We have no desire other than to glorify God by fulfilling at every moment His divine will. Let's always live with great joy. God is infinite joy."

Sister Teresa loved the Crucified One. In Him, she contemplated not only His supreme suffering, but also His supreme love for mankind. "Everywhere I go, He is with me, within my poor heart. He is the little home where I dwell . . . He is my heaven on earth."

From the time she was a child, Teresa had a presentiment that she would die early in life. At the beginning of Lent, 1920, she told her confessor that she felt she would die within a month, and asked to do extra penance for the sins of mankind. He didn't attach any special importance to this request, simply telling her to put herself completely in God's hands.

Sister Teresa obeyed her confessor's order and redoubled her service to others. Although she must have realized that she was sick, she ignored the symptoms and asked for no relief from the rigors of the Lenten customs. She spent hours in prayer before the Eucharist.

On Good Friday, her novice mistress noticed that Sister Teresa's face was flushed and discovered that she had a high fever. Although the doctor was called immediately, and remedies were tried, nothing helped. The young novice was suffering from a virulent form of typhus. She received the sacraments of the sick on April 6 and fell into a delirium. Shortly after midnight on April 7, when she came back to her senses, she was allowed to make her religious profession because she was obviously in danger of death. Sister Teresa died quietly on the evening of Monday, April 12, 1920, and was buried two days later.

Uncharacteristically for the death of a cloistered nun, the Santiago newspaper published a number of eulogies of Sister Teresa's virtues. Letters began to arrive at the Carmel, and many favors were reported. Her cause for beatification was opened and she was beatified in Santiago in 1987.

In 1988, a group of Santiago teenagers were celebrating the end of school when a young girl, Marcella Riveros, apparently drowned. After she was rushed to the hospital, it was determined that she was asphyxiated and water had entered her lungs, which should have caused grave damage from the deoxygenation of her blood. Some of the mothers who accompanied the group to the emergency room began praying, asking Blessed Teresa to save the teen. After forty-five minutes, Marcella revived and was later declared perfectly healthy, both physically and neurologically. The cure, recognized as scientifically unexplainable, paved the way for Blessed Teresa's canonization.

Saint Teresa of Los Andes was canonized March 21, 1992, by Pope John Paul II. He held up the life of this nineteen-year-old to the faithful, especially the young, as a model to be admired and imitated with this message: "God is infinite joy. Only in Him will you be completely happy."

Sister Teresa in her Carmelite habit.

Venerable Thecla Merlo
1894-1964
Apostle of the Good News

Modern media — the press, motion pictures, radio, television, and other technical inventions — were recognized as effective tools for preaching and catechizing by Vatican Council II in the document *Inter Mirifica*. "They can reach and influence not only individuals, but the very masses and the whole of society. The Church recognizes that these media can be of great service to mankind, since they greatly contribute to men's entertainment and instruction as well as to the spread and support of the Kingdom of God."

Thecla Merlo radiated a passion for the Word. With broad vision, she anticipated the Second Vatican Council's decree on the "Means of Social Communication," and dedicated her life to spreading the gospel through modern media. With a rare combination of gifts, in cooperation with Father James Alberione, she launched a new form of Christian witness. Young and inexperienced, but wholly consecrated to Christ and extremely sensitive to the needs of modern man, Thecla Merlo entered the bold undertaking of an apostolate of the media of social communication. A contemplative in action, she lived her life completely dedicated to seeing God in everything, serving Him, and communicating Him.

An original "flying nun," as superior of her congregation she traveled all over the world. Aware that native sisters would know better than anyone else how to reach the people of their own country, she prayed and worked for native vocations. Once she sighed, "Oh, if I only could print sisters as we print books."

Teresa Merlo was born February 20, 1894, in Castagnito d'Alba, Piedmont, Northern Italy. She was the second of four children and the only daughter of Hector and Vincenza Merlo, a respected farmer and his wife.

As a child, Teresa was happy, lively, exact, orderly, clean, and devout. She was intelligent and learned quickly. Her health, however, was delicate. Often anemic, Teresa was never physically strong.

Teresa received her training in religious precepts and principles from

The young Teresa in her habit.

her devoutly Catholic parents. From the time of her First Communion at the age of eight, Teresa began to share an intimate and joyous relationship with Jesus in the Eucharist.

Teresa attended the first three grades at the elementary school at Castagnito. Because of her delicate health, her parents then sent her to a private teacher. She was a serious and determined student who learned quickly. Teresa attended the Providence Retreat conducted by the Sisters of Saint Anne to learn sewing, embroidery, and lace-making, and later took more classes in sewing in Turin, where she lived with friends of her parents. She became an expert in needlecraft.

In 1912, Teresa began teaching sewing and embroidery to young girls at a small workshop in her family home. She included the recitation of the rosary and spiritual reading in the program of the day for her school. For Teresa, it seemed logical to combine prayer with work.

At the age of twenty, Teresa made up her mind to consecrate herself to God. She applied for entrance to the Sisters of Cottolengo, but they hesitated to accept her because she was anemic and weak. She began trying to improve her health in order to be accepted.

Teresa's brother Costanzo had entered the seminary, where he encountered the dynamic young priest Father James Alberione. In June 1915, as Costanzo was saying goodbye for the summer to Father Alberione, the priest told him, "Since she is a good seamstress, I need your sister, to teach sewing to young girls. Ask your mother to let her come."

At first, their mother refused to even consider letting Teresa go to help Father Alberione, claiming that her daughter's health was too poor. Finally, however, she yielded and accompanied Teresa to see Father Alberione.

At their first meeting, Father Alberione asked Teresa to help him form a female apostolate of the press. She said "yes." Teresa had discovered that saying "yes" is the secret to answering the call of God. Later, a sister asked her how she loved God. Teresa answered, "I love Him simply by doing His will, moment by moment."

Teresa began her mission by doing the very ordinary work of sewing shirts for the soldiers in the First World War. On June 15, 1915, she and two other young women moved into quarters left vacant by a typography school. On June 29, 1916, Father Alberione received Teresa's temporary private vows.

One day, Father Alberione was speaking of the newspaper as being the great teacher of the masses. He repeated the well-known expression of Kettler, "If Saint Paul were to return to the world, he would be a journalist." Teresa began to think of Saint Paul as a father and powerful protector for herself and the new congregation, and she developed a deep devotion to the saint.

The *Ladies' Workshop*, as the sewing shop of the three young women was called, was transformed into a small store for religious articles. Later, it was called the *New Book Center*. The three young women were now sewing together the parts of the catechism booklets printed by Father Alberione's typography shop. The days passed in a round of work, study, and the teaching of catechism.

In 1918, Father made arrangements to revive the diocesan newspaper at Susa, and asked Teresa and her companions to compose, print, and diffuse it. In spite of the fact that they did not know all of the technical skills needed, the girls agreed to go. They arrived in Susa in 1918, and only fifteen days after their arrival, they published the first issue of the paper, which had not been published for three years because of the war.

At Susa, the young congregation gained their first experience in the apostolate of writing, printing, and diffusing literature. They also opened a book center. On July 22, 1922, Teresa, together with eight other young women, took perpetual private vows. These professions marked the institution of the Pious Society of the Daughters of Saint Paul. Teresa Merlo adopted the religious name *Thecla*, after Saint Paul's first female companion. Father Alberione appointed her mother superior of the congregation.

Outwardly, Mother

Mother Thecla Merlo was the original "flying nun."

Thecla's life was in every respect like that of the other sisters. She was outstanding not by reason of her position, but for the utter simplicity with which she held it. Following the example of their patron, the community spread the word of God by the most practical and modern means: the press, radio, motion pictures, and other media. Under Mother Thecla's leadership, the Daughters of Saint Paul spread worldwide. At the time of its papal approval in 1953, the Daughters of Saint Paul labored in twenty-four countries.

When the community considered opening a house in Bolivia, the sisters hesitated because of the high illiteracy rate of the country. In her practical manner, Mother Thecla overcame the objection by proposing, "If the majority of people don't know how to read, then we will do good through pictures and records. There, too, it is necessary to open a center of apostolate. There, too, it is necessary to make the Lord known. In Bolivia, too, we must diffuse the Gospel in some way!"

Mother Thecla

Mother Thecla's spirit was imbued with a natural humility and a love of poverty. Once as she prepared to visit a bishop, one of the sisters chided her for her appearance and told her that she should wear a better veil. Mother Thecla replied, "I was waiting for someone to tell me that because I thought I was just being vain."

Her charity and sensitivity were obvious in all her dealings with other people. During World War II a Benedictine monastery was destroyed, and a priest asked Mother Thecla if she could take in some of the homeless nuns. She told him to send all of the nuns to her so that they would not be forced to separate. When one of the sisters mentioned that she

felt they were imposing on the Pauline's hospitality, Mother Thecla reassured her by saying, "Do not fear. Our house is God's, not ours, and so it is yours too. No one will ever tell you to go away." The old, the poor, the sick, soldiers during the war, all turned to her when in need. When the sisters asked her how she could give so much, she chidingly reminded them of God's providence to those who trust in Him.

One project suggested to Mother Thecla by Father Alberione which captured her heart was the building of a hospital for sick religious. Queen of Apostles Hospital For Religious was opened in 1949 at Albano Laziale near Rome. Here, sick and suffering religious could offer up their pain and illness to God. Mother Thecla had always seemed a member of the family here. She frequently visited the sick, both the members of her own congregation and those of other congregations. In 1957, she came to the hospital not as a visitor, but as a patient. Doctors had discovered that she had breast cancer, and she needed a radical mastectomy. The surgery was both timely and effective. The doctor recalls that Mother remained her usual matter-of-fact self, rejecting sympathy and telling him, "You will do what you must."

Mother Thecla constantly had the members of the entire Pauline family in her thoughts and prayers. During the spiritual exercises for the feast of the Holy Trinity in 1961, she offered her life for the sanctification of her spiritual daughters. She told the Daughters, "It is hard to become saints, but we don't want to give up the idea just for that. Let us work steadily, with faith, and in the best way we know how. God sees. God is a good cameraman, and at the Judgement He will project the film. See to it that you are good stars — shining stars."

First members of the young congregation.

In June 1963, Mother Thecla suffered a series of small strokes. Her health improved slowly over the summer months, but in November, another stroke seriously impaired her power of speech. While she was still able to speak, if someone asked her how she felt, she would simply smile and say, "As Jesus wants." Her smile was constant, and she became a living prayer, alternately praying the rosary and kissing her crucifix.

Mother Thecla died quietly on February 5, 1964, just two weeks before her seventieth birthday. In October 1967, less than four years after her death, the informative process of the cause for beatification of this modern apostle was opened in the Vicariate in Rome. On January 22, 1992, Pope John Paul II signed the decree which recognized the heroic character of Mother Thecla's virtues and conferred on her the title of Venerable.

Selected Bibliography

Agasso, Domenico. *Thecla Merlo, Messenger of the Good News*. Boston: Saint Paul Books and Media, 1994.

Aguilo, Francisco, M.D., ed. *Carlos M. Rodriguez: A Puerto Rican Saint?* San Juan: Circulo CMR, 1995.

Ball, Ann. *Blessed Miguel Pro, S.J., Mexican Martyr*. Rockford, Ill.: TAN Books, 1996.

"Beata Pierina Morosini." Clackson. *Bergamo*, March, 1988.

"Be United to Christ in Prayer." *L'Osservatorio Romano*, No. 4, January 25, 1995.

Bolt, Anthony, M.S.C. "Peter ToRot, Catechist and Martyr." *Annals Australia*, November/December, 1994.

Bulletin of Mère Marie Léonie. Le Centre Marie Léonie Paradis, Nos. 40-43, 1980.

Centenary, Daughters of Mary Help of Christians. Daughters of Mary Help of Christians, 1972.

Coles, Robert. "Meeting Dorothy Day." *Catholic Digest*, October, 1993.

Cruz, Joan Carroll. *Secular Saints*. Rockford, Ill.: TAN Books, 1989.

Curupira, A Brazilian Indian Who Married the King. Petropolis: Dominican Nuns, l983.

D'Amando, F. *Carla Ronci*. Rome: Passionist Fathers, l982.

Day, Dorothy. *The Long Loneliness*. San Francisco: Harper and Row, 1981.

De Bernardi, Vittorio. *Pierina Morosini, Operaia e Martire*. Seminary of John XXIII, 1983.

DeCarolis, Annette. *Saint Gaspar del Bufalo, Apostle of the Precious Blood*. Toronto: Informco, 1984.

Decker, Randall E. "Gaspar del Bufalo." *Extension Magazine*, February, 1955.

de Lourdes, Mother M. Bernadette, O. Carm. *Woman of Faith, Mother M. Angeline Teresa, O. Carm*. New York: Carmelite Sisters for the Aged and Infirm, 1984.

De Stefano, Lucio, M.S.C. "Peter ToRot, First Saint for PNG?" *Annals of Our Lady*, 1987.

Dodds, Bill. "Chaplains remember: I was just doing my job." *Our Sunday Visitor*: November 11, 1990.

Dominican Nuns. *Curupira: A Brasilian Indian Who Married the King*. Petropolis: Dominican Nuns, 1983.

Dowe, Lt. Ray. "The Ordeal of Chaplain Kapaun." *The Saturday Evening Post*, January 16, 1954.

Dragon, Antonio, S.J. *Au Mexique Rouge*. Montreal: *L'Action Paroissiale*, 1936.

Eguibar, Mercedes. *Montserrat Grases: Christian Heroism in Ordinary Life*. New York: Scepter, 1975 and 1980.

Espinoza, P. Jose Armando, M.G. *Martires Mexicanos*. Libreria Parroquial de Claveria, 1992.

Fanning, James, M.H.M. *Clementine Anuarite*. Karen-Nairobi, Kenya: St. Paul Publications, 1986.

Father Forgive Them: An Account of the Death of Three Carmelite Nuns. Patterson, N.J.: St. Anthony New York Guild Press, 1949.

First Centenary of Don Bosco's Missions. Rome: SDB Publishers, 1977.

Fleming, Sister Mary Celine, S.A. *Woman of Unity*. Garrison, N.Y.: Franciscan Sisters of the Atonement, 1956.

Foley, Barbara. *Zélie Martin: Mother of St. Thérèse*. Boston: Daughters of St. Paul, 1960.

Forest, Jim. "What I Learned About Justice from Dorothy Day." *Salt of the Earth*: July-August, 1995.

Franco Sanchez, Sister M. Guadalupe. *El Pequeño Santos, Gigante en la Fe*. Hinojosa del Duque, Spain: Monjas Carmelitas, Carmelo de Santa Ana, 1993.

Frassati, Luciana. *Man of the Beatitudes*. Slough, England: St. Paul Publications, 1990.

Gabriel, Sister M., O. Carm. *Seed Scattered and Sown*. Germantown, N.Y.: Carmelite Sisters for the Aged and Infirm, undated.

Galleria de Martires Mexicanos, Narraciones Veridicas. San Antonio: Imprenta Universal, undated.

Gardiner, Paul, S.J. *An Extraordinary Australian, Mary MacKillop*. Alexandria, Australia: E.J. Dwyer, 1994.

Gardiner, Paul, S.J. "Love Was Soul of Mary MacKillop's Virtues." *L'Osservatore Romano*, January 25, 1995.

Gendron, Sister Thérèse, p.s.s.f. *Leonie Paradis, Foundress of the Little Sisters of the Holy Family*. Sherbrook, Quebec: Editions SADIFA-C2L, 1984.

Gneuhs, Geoffrey. "Why Dorothy Day Loved the Church." *Catholic Digest*, April, 1995.

Goti, Graziella. *La Ragazza dalla Sciarpa Rossa*. S. Gabriele: Editrice ECO, 1984.

"Green Light for Beatification." *The Texas Catholic Herald*, August 13, 1993.

Griffin, Michael D., O.C.D. *A New Hymn to God*. Washington, D.C.: Teresian Charism Press, 1993.

Grzebieniak, Mary F. "Maronite Catholics, Inheritors of a Proud Tradition." *Our Sunday Visitor*, November 25, 1990.

Hachem, P. Basile. *A Message from Lebanon*. Rome: Postulazione Generale Dell'Ordine Libanese Maronita, 1985.

Havers, Guillermo and Sanchez, Ramiro V. *25 Martires Mexicanos*. Mexico City: Libreria Parroquial de Claveria, 1992.

"Holy Father Beatifies Australian Religious." *L'Osservatore Romano,* January 25, 1995.

Houston Catholic Worker, The. Various issues, including: May/April, 1987; November, 1988; October 1990; December 1990; November, 1991.

Husslein, Joseph, S.J., ed. *Heroines of Christ*. Milwaukee: Bruce, 1949.

Joseph Moscati: Lay-Man, Man of Science, Saint. Naples: Causa Moscati, 1975.

Kalberer, Augustine, O.S.B. *Lives of the Saints: Daily Readings*. Chicago: Franciscan Herald Press, 1975.

Kelly, Francis Clement. *Blood-Drenched Altars*. Rockford, Ill.: TAN Books, 1987.

Laupus, Dr. Carmelita. "Life of Dr. Joseph Moscati." Paper given at the National Conference of Catholic Physicians Guild, November, 1989.

La Voce Misteriosa. Bologna: La Grafica Emiliana, 1953.

"Let Your Light Shine Before Men." *L'Osservatorio Romano*, No. 4, January 25, 1995.

Liptak, Reverend David Q. *More Saints for Our Time*. New Jersey: Arena Letters, 1983.

MacAdam, Eily. *Maria of Mexico*. Dublin: The Anthonian Press, 1940.

Macias, Jose, S.J. *La Martir de Coyoacan*. Mexico City: Editorial Tradicion, 1986.

Magnabosco, A. *The Wild Forest My Terror, My Glory*. Rome: Institute FMA, 1989.

Mahfouz, Pere Joseph, O.L.M. *Rafqa de Himlaya, Moniale Libanaise*

Maronite. Rome: Postulation Generale de l'Ordre Libanais Maronite, 1980.

Mead, Jude, C.P. *The Servant of God Mother M. Angeline Teresa, O. Carm, Daughter of Carmel — Mother to the Aged*. Petersham, Mass.: St. Bede's Publications, 1990.

Miller, J. Michael, C.S.B. "Catechist, Husband, Father, Martyr." *Our Sunday Visitor*, January 29, 1995.

Miller, William D. "All is Grace: The Spirituality of Dorothy Day." *Our Sunday Visitor*, June 21, 1987.

Nadeau, Eugene, o.m.i. *Your Ways Make Known to Me*. Sherbrooke, Quebec: Ediciones Mont-Sainte-Famille, 1975.

Norman, Mrs. George. *God's Jester*. New York: Benzinger, 1930.

O'Brien, Felicity. *Saints in the Making*. Dublin: Veritas Publications, 1988.

O'Brien, Lesley. *Mary MacKillop Unveiled*. Victoria, Australia: Collins Dove, 1994.

Papasogli, Giorgio. *Giuseppe Moscati, Vita di un Medico Santo*. Rome: Postulazione Generale della Compagnia di Gesu, 1975.

Parsons, Wilfred, S.J. *Mexican Martyrdom*. Rockford, Ill.: TAN Books, 1987.

Pedrosa, Ceferino Puebla, O.P., ed. *Witnesses of the Faith in the Orient*. Hong Kong: Provincial Secretariat of Missions, Dominican Province of Our Lady of the Rosary, 1989.

Pena, Silvia Novo. "Pope John Paul II to Canonize 117 Vietnamese Martyrs June 22." *Texas Catholic Herald*, June 10, 1988.

"Peter Knew Value of Suffering." *L'Osservatorio Romano*, No. 4, January 25, 1995.

"Peter ToRot, a Friend of Jesus." Rome: Cause, undated.

Pierina Morosini, Una Ragazza Bella ed Eroica. Milan: Mimep-Docete, 1987.

"Pierina Morosini un Modello Particalarmente Adatto al Nostro Tempo." Lettere, Bergamo, 1983.

Pio X, Fernando da Riese. *For the Love of Life: Gianna Beretta Molla, doctor and mother*. Milan: Molla cause, 1981.

"Pope Disappointed by Snub from Buddhists." Houston: *Texas Catholic Herald*, January 27, 1995.

Purroy, P. Marino. *Teresa de Los Andes: Su Vida, Su Ideal*. Los Andes: MM. Carmelitas, 1983.

Raskin, Albert, C.I.C.M. *Peter Chang Wen Chao, CICM*. Rome: CICM Archives, 1982.

Rayness, P.H. "Peter Maurin: A Catholic Worker in Tramp's Clothing." *Our Sunday Visitor*, October 19, 1986.

—— "Working for Peace, justice in the real world." *Our Sunday Visitor*, July 31, 1988.

Renson, Raymond. *The Cause of Our Martyrs*. Rome: CICM Archives, 1995.

Roascio, Father Guy. "The Three Carmelite Martyrs of Guadalajara." *Messaggero del S. Bambino Gesu di Praga*. Padri Carmelitani Scalzi, 1987.

Simeone, Renato, M.S.C. "Despite Threats, the Catechist Peter ToRot Led Prayer Services, Taught Catechism, and Baptized." *L'Osservatorio Romano,* No. 4, January 25, 1995.

Simonnet, Christian. *Théophane Vénard, A Martyr of Vietnam*. San Francisco: Ignatius Press, undated.

"Soto Cenere Umilissima Ardentissima Brace." *Alere,* May, 1983, No. 5.

"Sui sentieri di Pierina e di Papa Giovanni." *Lettere,* May-June, 1988.

Teolis, Reverend Anthony, C.PP.S. *The Saint Gaspar Story*. Carthagena, Ohio: Messenger Press, 1986.

"The Medical Missionary." *Society of Catholic Medical Missionaries,* various issues: 1930 — October and December; 1933 — January, February, March, April, May, August, September, October; 1939 — May, September, October; 1941 — May; 1942 — May; 1944 — May.

"The Salesian Bulletin," July- August, 1981.

"Three Martyrs Beatified in St. Peter's Basilica." *L'Osservatore Romano*, October 5, 1987, p. 20.

Tonne, Father Arthur. *The Story of Chaplain Kapaun*. Emporia, Kan.: Didde Publishers, 1954.

Trotter, Reverend Maurice. *A Garden in the Kingdom of Love*. Boston: Little Sisters of the Holy Family, 1967.

Valabek, Redemptus. "Carmel's Youth Candidate: Santos Franco Sanchez." *Carmel in the World*, Vol. XXXIII: 3, 1994.

Valabek, Redemptus. "The Scapular Devotion Has Its Martyr: Isidore Bakanja, Member of the Scapular Confraternity." *Carmel in the World*, Vol. XXVI: 2, 1987.

Valabek, Redemptus. "Mother to the Aged and Infirm — Mother M. Angeline Teresa, Foundress of the Carmelite Sisters of the Aged and Infirm." Rome: *Carmel in the World*, Vol. XXIX:3, 1990.

Valabek, Redemptus Maria, O.Carm. *Isidore Bakanja, Africa's Scapular Martyr*. World Apostolate of Fatima: Washington, N.J., 1990.

Valabek, Redemptus, O.Carm. *Profiles in Holiness*. Rome: Edizioni Carmelitane, 1996.

Walsh, Very Reverend James A., M.AP. *A Modern Martyr*. Maryknoll, N.Y.: Catholic Foreign Mission Society of America, 1928.

Woman of Faith. Boston: Daughters of Saint Paul, 1965.

Wust, Louis and Marjorie. *Louis Martin: An Ideal Father*. Boston: Daughters of St. Paul, 1957.

Zélie Martin: Mother of St. Thérèse. Boston: Daughters of St. Paul, 1969.

Zappulli, Cesare. *The Power of Goodness*. Boston: St. Paul Editions, 1980.

Zayekl, Bishop Francis M. *Rafka, The Blind Mystic of Lebanon*. Still River, Mass.: St. Bede's Publications, 1980.

Zwick, Mark and Louise. "Dorothy Day and the Catholic Worker Movement." *Communio International Catholic Review*. Vol. XXIV, No. 3, Fall 1997.

Thank You

A special thanks to all of the following and to all who have supported and encouraged me in the work of telling the stories of God's friends, the saints. Much appreciation to those who have provided photos for each chapter. If I have inadvertently failed to mention one whose name should be listed here, I pray that Our Lord will provide them my thanks. And for Bea, who always helps with photos, books, and life, an extra thanks.

Sister Mary Agnes, O.P. (R.I.P.), translator, Menlo Park, California
Francisco Aguilo, M.D., San Juan, Puerto Rico
Reverend P. Fillippo D. Amando, C.P., Rome, Italy
Reverend Enzo Annibali, C.P., Rome, Italy
Sister Adele Arsenault, P.S.S.F.; Sherbrooke, Quebec, Canada
Reverend Bradley K. Arturi, Opus Dei, New Rochelle, New York
Reverend Oscar Sanchez Barba, Postulator for the Mexican causes, Rome, Italy
Charles Berry, Dayton, Ohio
Reverend Louis Diaz Borrundo, Mexico City, Mexico
Reverend Dominic Britschu, Secretary General of the Salesians, Rome, Italy
Enrique Cardenas, S.J. (R.I.P.)
Carmelite Nuns of Lisieux
Sister M. Catherine, Daughters of Saint Paul, Boston, Massachusetts
Sister Anthony Clare, S.A., Graymoor, Garrison, New York
Celia Clay, Houston, Texas
Celeste Cottingham, Houston, Texas
Reverend Robert M. Cox, Dallas, Texas
Reverend Timothy E. Deeter, Director, The Frassati Society, Orangefield, Texas
Mother M. Bernadette de Lourdes, O. Carm., Germantown, New York
Dominican Nuns, Monastery of Cristo Rei, São Roque, Brazil
Sister M. J. Emanuel de Rosario, O.P., São Roque, Brazil
Sister de Montfort, O.S.B., Wichita, Kansas
P. Lucio De Stefano, M.S.C., Postulator, Missionari del Sacro Cuore, Rome, Italy
Sister Ignatius Marie Desmond, Archivist, Medical Mission Sisters, Philadelphia, Pennsylvania
Brother Robert Dias, S.D.B., Rome, Italy
Direttoro, Opera San Gregorio Barbarigo, Bergamo, Italy
Discalced Carmelite Nuns, Guadalajara, Spain

Faces of Holiness

Sister Patricia Edward, F.S.P. , Daughters of Saint Paul, Boston, Massachusetts
Very Reverend Mario Esposito, O.Carm., Middletown, New York
Mary Catherine Fernandes, Claretian Publications, Chicago, Illinois
Brian Finnerty, Opus Dei, New Rochelle, New York
Sister Mary Celine Fleming, S.A., Graymoor, Garrison, New York
Reverend Richard Flores, St. Rita's Church, Ft. Worth, Texas
P. Giovanni Forguera, O.F.M., Rome, Italy
Reverend James Gaunt, C.S.B., Manuel, Texas
Rossana Gani, Lima, Peru
Robert New York Gavin, Garden Grove, California
Sister Thérèse Gendron, P.S.S.F., Secretary, Le Centre Marie Léonie Paradis, Sherbrooke, Quebec, Canada
Father Michael Griffin, O.C.D., Washington, D.C.
Sister Mary Annunciata Griffitts, S.A., Graymoor, Garrison, New York
Sister M. Gabriel, O.Carm., Germantown, New York
Sister M. Guadalupe, O.Carm., Las Palmas de Gran Canaria
Instituto Figlie di Maria Ausiliatrice, Rome, Italy
Reverend Basile Hachem, Procuratore Generale Dell'Ordine Libanese Maronita, Rome, Italy
Sister Mary Jeremiah, O.P., Lufkin, Texas
Eamon Kennedy, Wagga Wagga, Australia
Gregory Knowles, Manchester, England
Clare Koch, R.S.J., Mary MacKillop Secretariat, North Sydney, Australia
Reverend Pasquale Liberatore, S.D.B., Rome, Italy
Reverend Gary M. Luiz, C.Pp.S., historian, Province of the Pacific, Newark, California
Sister Silvana Magnani, Casa Generalizia Suore Minime Dell'Addolorata, Bologna, Italy
Sister Mary Leonora Major, Archivist, Medical Mission Sisters, London, England
Reverend Jude Mead, C.P. (R.I.P.)
J. Michael Miller, C.S.B., Houston, Texas
Father Angelo Mitri, O.M.I., Rome, Italy
Father Paul Molinari, S.J., Postulator, Rome, Italy
Stephanie Morris, Eastern Division Archivist, Medical Mission Sisters, Philadelphia, Pennsylvania
Karin Murthough, Houston, Texas
Mrs. William Offutt, Butte, Montana
Reverend Z. Pazheparampil, S.J., Christ the King Seminary, Nyeri, Kenya
Silvia Novo Pena, Texas Southern University, Houston, Texas
Dung Phan, Houstan, Texas
Col. Cletus Pottebaum, Wichita, Kansas
Henri Proust, Director, Pelergrinage Sainte Thérèse de Lisieux, Lisieux, France

Albert Raskin, C.I.C.M., Rome, Italy
Reverend Edward T. Rehkopf, S.J., Houston, Texas
Raymond Renson, C.I.C.M., Archivist, Rome, Italy
Phillip Runkel, Marquette University Archives, Milwaukee, Wisconsin
Reverend Fernando Suarez, S.J., Vice Postulator of the Cause of Blessed Miguel Pro, S.J., Mexico City, Mexico
Reverend Kevin Shanley, O.Carm., Joliet, Illinois
Reverend Simeone della S. Famiglia, O.C.D. Postulazione Generale Carmelitani Scalzi, Rome, Italy
Reverend Miguel Solarsano, St. Pius V Church, Pasadena, Texas
Brother David Tejada, F.S.C., (R.I.P.)
Msgr. Arthur J. Tonne, Marion, Kansas
Sister Mary of the Trinity, O.P., Lufkin, Texas
Reverend Atanasio M. Linh Uy, C.M.C., Carthage, Missouri
Redemptus Maria Valabek, O.Carm., former Postulator for Carmelite Causes, Rome, Italy
Reverend Timothy V. Vaverek, Vice Chancellor, Diocese of Saint Maron, Brooklyn, New York
Reverend Innocenzo Venchi, O.P., Postulator General of the Dominicans, Rome, Italy
Dianne Walde, Salt Magazine, Chicago, Illinois
Bea Whitfil, Houston, Texas
Paul Zigo, St. Paschal Books, Erie, Pennsylvania
Reverend Giovanni Zubiani, C.P., Curia Generalizia dei Passionisti, Rome, Italy
Mark and Louise Zwick, *Houston Catholic Worker*, Houston, Texas
M. Reverend Postulatore, Curia Diocesana di Rimini, Italy

Index of Saints

Listed by last name

General Index

Our Sunday Visitor...
Your Source for Discovering the Riches of the Catholic Faith

Our Sunday Visitor has an extensive line of materials for young children, teens, and adults. Our books, Bibles, booklets, CD-ROMs, audios, and videos are available in bookstores worldwide.

To receive a FREE full-line catalog or for more information, call **Our Sunday Visitor** at **1-800-348-2440**. Or write, **Our Sunday Visitor /** 200 Noll Plaza / Huntington, IN 46750.

Please send me: __ A catalog
Please send me materials on:

__ Apologetics and catechetics   __ Reference works
__ Prayer books   __ Heritage and the saints
__ The family   __ The parish

Name_____

Address_____Apt._____

City_____State ____Zip_____

Telephone ( ) _____

A73BBABP

Please send a friend: __ A catalog
Please send a friend materials on:

__ Apologetics and catechetics   __ Reference works
__ Prayer books   __ Heritage and the saints
__ The family   __ The parish

Name_____

Address_____Apt._____

City_____State ____Zip_____

Telephone ( ) _____

A73BBABP

 **Our Sunday Visitor**
200 Noll Plaza
Huntington, IN 46750
1-800-348-2440
OSVSALES@AOL.COM

Your Source for Discovering the Riches of the Catholic Faith